OUR NAZI

CHICAGO VISIONS AND REVISIONS

Edited by Matthew Briones, Melanie Newport, Carlo Rotella,
Bill Savage, and Robert Stepto

OUR NAZI

An American Suburb's Encounter with Evil

MICHAEL SOFFER

The University of Chicago Press

CHICAGO AND LONDON

The University of Chicago Press, Chicago 60637
The University of Chicago Press, Ltd., London
© 2024 by The University of Chicago
All rights reserved. No part of this book may be used or reproduced in any
manner whatsoever without written permission, except in the case of brief
quotations in critical articles and reviews. For more information, contact
the University of Chicago Press, 1427 E. 60th St., Chicago, IL 60637.
Published 2024
Printed in the United States of America

33 32 31 30 29 28 27 26 25 24   1 2 3 4 5

ISBN-13: 978-0-226-83554-9 (cloth)
ISBN-13: 978-0-226-83555-6 (e-book)
DOI: https://doi.org/10.7208/chicago/9780226835556.001.0001

Library of Congress Cataloging-in-Publication Data
Names: Soffer, Michael, author.
Title: Our Nazi : an American suburb's encounter with evil / Michael
    Soffer.
Other titles: American suburb's encounter with evil | Chicago visions +
    revisions.
Description: Chicago : The University of Chicago Press, 2024. | Series:
    Chicago visions and revisions | Includes bibliographical references
    and index.
Identifiers: LCCN 2024002487 | ISBN 9780226835549 (cloth) |
    ISBN 9780226835556 (ebook)
Subjects: LCSH: Kulle, Reinhold, 1921-2006. | Oak Park and River
    Forest Township High School. | Ex-Nazis—Germany. | School
    custodians—Illinois—Oak Park. | Nazi hunters—United States.
    | Fugitives from justice—Germany. | Fugitives from justice—
    Germany—Public opinion. | Public opinion—Illinois—Oak Park. |
    Communities—Illinois—Oak Park—History—20th century. | Ex-
    Nazis—Illinois—Chicago. | Oak Park (Ill.)—History—20th century.
Classification: LCC F549.O13 S64 2024 | DDC 977.3/1—dc23/eng/
    20240215
LC record available at https://lccn.loc.gov/2024002487

♾ This paper meets the requirements of ANSI/NISO Z39.48-1992
(Permanence of Paper).

For
Rachelli,
Amiel,
and Talia

In memory of
Sara Berkowicz z"l

CONTENTS

PREFACE
"A NAZI WORKED HERE?"

"Wait, Mr. Soffer. Hold on. A Nazi worked here?"

I leaned forward in the gray, cushioned dining room chair we had brought upstairs to make the bedroom-turned-virtual-classroom more comfortable. I had been anxiously awaiting the 2020 school year, my fourteenth as a history teacher at Oak Park and River Forest High School (OPRF). The previous fall, the district had unanimously approved the Holocaust studies elective course I had developed in response to a slew of antisemitic hate crimes on the high school's campus. Such a class is a rarity in a public school, but after the attack at the Tree of Life Synagogue in Pittsburgh and reports about Americans' waning Holocaust awareness, it felt especially important. Now, nearing the end of the course's inaugural semester, we were considering issues of justice in the aftermath of the Holocaust.

"Today you're going to pretend it is 1983 and you are OPRF school board members," I said, sharing an article from the *Chicago Sun-Times* on my screen. "You have to decide what to do about your head custodian."

"Oh no, that's not good," a young woman said over a smattering of gasps.

I took a breath. "In late 1982, Reinhold Kulle was accused of having been a Nazi, a member of the SS, a guard at the Gross-Rosen slave labor camp. In Google Classroom, you'll find a slew of documents to help in your deliberations: some about Gross-Rosen and his time there, some about OPRF and his time here. Before you get started, are there any questions?"

A barrage followed.

"Why did it take so long to find him?"

"Were there other Nazis in the area?"

"How does a Nazi even get a job in a school?"

"Did he ever get in trouble at work?"

"Did he admit it or apologize?"

"Did he kill anyone?"

Before I could answer, another student jumped in.

"This is Oak Park. We are nationally famous for integration and diversity. This guy was a literal Nazi. I can't imagine it took more than a few minutes to fire him."

I stared back at the monitor, saying nothing.

"Right? Mr. Soffer? Right?"

1
"MURDERERS AMONG US"

On December 4, 1982, Dr. Jack Swanson walked into his second-floor office at Oak Park and River Forest High School. This three-room suite next to the board room had been his for the last eight years, after he had beaten out sixty other administrators vying to run the storied suburban high school just west of Chicago. It had been a hectic semester. Today, though, the normally bustling building was quiet, the school's 3,400 students enjoying the unseasonably warm Saturday morning at home.[1] Swanson exuded calm and professionalism. Deeply religious, he was in some ways a throwback to Oak Park's more genteel past, when the village was informally known as "Saints' Rest." When he first took the reins of the community's flagship institution, Swanson had streamlined the school's administrative structure, and had told the local papers that he wanted to ensure that Oak Park was a "viable community" for people from diverse backgrounds.[2] Oak Parkers had always felt there was something special about their community. The town had raised Ernest Hemingway and was home to a dozen of Frank Lloyd Wright's iconic Prairie Style structures. Oak Parkers' pride was reflected even in the high school's motto: "Those Things That Are Best." Though the civic pride remained, the village no longer resembled the conservative community that Hemingway once quipped had "wide lawns and narrow minds." Oak Park had become a national model for integration, garnering recognition as the National Civic League's "All-America City" at the end of Swanson's first year.[3]

Trim and dignified, the fifty-four-year-old high school superintendent readied for a quiet morning of paperwork. Outside his window, large Victorian homes sat across calm Scoville Avenue. Swanson settled into his chair, and opened the *Chicago Sun-Times*. A headline on the bottom right-hand corner of page 7 caught his eye: "Deportation Bid on Suburb Man."

He scanned the article, and a wave of shock rushed over him. It had to be a misprint, some kind of misunderstanding. Maybe it was a different man with the same name? No, the *Sun-Times* left no room for doubt.

Swanson fumbled for his phone, and dialed school board president Paul Gignilliat, unsure of what exactly he would say.

Gignilliat was relaxing at his home two blocks away when his phone pierced the morning quiet.

"*Have you noticed?*" Swanson bellowed. The next few seconds were a blur, the words almost impossible to believe. But Swanson wanted Gignilliat to hear the news from him directly: Reinhold Kulle, the high school's chief custodian, had been a Nazi.

Swanson ended the call abruptly—he had to call the rest of the school board—and Gignilliat was left almost immobilized by shock, pondering what might happen next.[4] His next call was to Leah Marcus, the board secretary and second-ranking member. He was unsure how the call would go. Marcus was the only Jewish school board member.

At her home in River Forest, Marcus poured a second cup of coffee, and leafed through the *Sun-Times*. The name jumped off the page. "Reinhold Kulle of 3504 Morton allegedly served as a member of the SS Death Head Division assigned to the Gross-Rosen camp in Silesia, which is now a part of Poland."[5] Her heart beat faster, an eerie silence belying the panic rising through her chest.

The phone startled her. Swanson tried to tell her what little he knew, but she stopped him. She was reading it, too. They would talk more soon, he said, before hanging up.

Marcus felt faint, and sick to her stomach. This would be so bad for the school. Kulle had always been so polite, quiet, and respectful. He had never said anything about this past. Her mind raced. She thought of his visits to her house. Kulle had to know She was Jewish. He had seen her lighting Shabbat candles, had stood under the mezuzah on her door frame. She tried to catch her breath, and slow her thoughts.[6]

Reinhold . . . a Nazi?

Five years earlier, Marcus had almost imagined this scenario. She had gone to Triton College, a community college just a few miles from her home, to hear a talk by Simon Wiesenthal, who had become the public face of "Nazi hunting." Marcus and her teenage son had joined 370 others in a large lecture hall to hear the talk, billed as "Murderers among Us" after Wiesenthal's 1967 book of the same name.[7]

Something had happened outside. Faint sounds of yelling and screaming trickled into the lecture hall, and a Triton police officer dashed outside. After a few minutes, calm returned and Wiesenthal took the stage. Later, Marcus heard that a group of neo-Nazis had been protesting and that a fight had broken out. "Sick men," she thought.[8]

Wiesenthal had spoken of the work to bring Hitler's henchmen to justice, and demanded those efforts be taken seriously. The issue had become less theoretical over the past few years. It was one thing when it was Adolf Eichmann or Herberts Cukurs caught in Latin America; Nazi ratlines to Argentina and other regimes sympathetic to the Nazis were shocking, though not surprising. But now Nazis were popping up in America, too: a housewife in Queens who had been a guard at the Majdanek camp in Poland, a Long Island man who had collaborated with the Nazis in Latvia, and a handful of others.

"When you know and recognize a danger," Wiesenthal had explained, "you can find steps to prevent it. When you ignore it, later you become a victim of that danger." The Holocaust, he had stressed, must be understood in universal terms; Jewish pain alone would never elicit public concern. Marcus had been captivated.

Wiesenthal had ended his lecture with a stark warning: Only a small percentage of the Holocaust's perpetrators had been brought to trial. A former Nazi could be found—and eventually would be found—as a public employee in a community close by. How would they respond when it happened? Marcus had shuddered. It was a horrifying idea.[9]

Just a few miles south, Reinhold Kulle was working the night shift at the local high school. Wiesenthal had briefly been a prisoner at Gross-Rosen, and now, thirty years later and thousands of miles from that Silesian slave labor camp, the prisoner and the guard were again near each other.[10]

"We need to bring these men to trial as witnesses for history," Wiesenthal had concluded.

On the way out of the lecture hall, Marcus had turned to her son. "You may never again come so close as you did tonight to the Holocaust." He had barely heard her, because he was distracted by the TV cameramen interviewing bloodied boys in Nazi brownshirts not much older than him.[11]

2
REINHOLD

As German soldiers marched down the Avenue des Champs-Élysées in occupied Paris, nineteen-year-old Reinhold Alois Kulle reported to the SS training center at Radolfzell. A long road led to the wide three-story barracks. Kulle passed the armed guards manning twin sentry posts in front of the building, large black flags with the white ᛋᛋ symbols of the Schutzstaffel (SS) on either side. Centered high above the entryway, the imperial Nazi eagle stood watch. Above the building, a large red flag with a black swastika flapped in the wind. Kulle knew the training would be intense, but in just over a month he would join the elite ranks of the SS, the Nazis' elite paramilitary organization.[1]

A generation earlier, Reinhold's father Alois had also left home to serve the Reich, and had been wounded as Germany desperately tried to stave off defeat in the last weeks of World War I.[2] Following Germany's loss, Alois and his wife Anna had settled in the outskirts of Breslau, and he had worked as a longshoreman on the Oder River. They had welcomed their first child, Reinhold, on March 5, 1921. But Alois's injuries had taken their toll, and he had died when the boy was just three years old.[3]

As the Kulles mourned Alois's death, a sense of betrayal loomed over the country. The postwar economy was in ruins, with almost unbelievable hyperinflation. The Breslau region was a tinderbox of instability and a hotbed of right-wing extremism, and Jews quickly bore the brunt of the frustrations.[4] Antisemitism had long been entrenched in the area, which housed one of Germany's most important Jewish communities. Thousands of Breslauers had signed an 1880 petition calling for the removal of Jews from teaching and government jobs, and throngs had overcrowded one of Breslau's largest halls in 1892 to hear a rabble-rousing address titled "Why Anti-Semitism Must Succeed." The Great War only exacerbated Breslau's anti-Jewish racism, as Jews became common scapegoats for Germany's loss. Leaders of the German youth movements spread false rumors that Jews had shirked their military duties, and a series of antisemitic political parties gained power in the region. Breslau became one of the largest support bases for the growing Nazi Party, and the already bleak conditions for Jews deteriorated further.[5]

Four years after Alois's death, Anna remarried. Young Reinhold now had a stepfather and a stepbrother. Soon, Anna bore another son as well.[6] In 1933, just weeks before Reinhold's twelfth birthday, Adolf Hitler was appointed chancellor. Banners with swastikas adorned every major building in Breslau, and streets and buildings were renamed after Nazi leaders. In late March, the Nazis opened their first concentration camp at Dachau. Other camps, including a short-lived one in Breslau, were built to house supposed enemies of the Reich. Over the next few months, Jewish shops were boycotted, Jewish books burned, and synagogues were destroyed. As Breslauers embraced the Nazis, Jews fearfully emigrated from the region en masse.[7]

Soon, the curriculum at all schools in the Reich was Nazified. Jewish children faced open hostility from their classmates and teachers, and more and more Nazi flags began to adorn classroom walls. Kulle and other German school children said *"Heil Hitler"* fifty times every day.[8] Nazi ideology was even apparent in arithmetic questions, where students were asked to divide the number of Jews by the number of total inhabitants of Germany to determine the "percentage of aliens" present. In Kulle's last few years of schooling, new subjects like "race science" were being added to the curriculum. German schoolchildren learned how to classify racial groups and were taught that Aryans were superior; teachers contrasted successful Germans like Goethe and Beethoven with antisemitic caricatures of Jews. Students' time in physical education classes, which largely consisted of premilitary training, increased significantly.[9]

In 1935, Kulle's stepfather moved the family to Alt Ellguth, a hamlet in the Silesian lowlands, to try his hand at farming. He pulled Kulle out of school to work on the farm. The boy's only remaining education was at a farming school during the next two winters, though his stepbrother was allowed to learn a trade. Kulle was frustrated by the seemingly unfair treatment.[10] German probate law limited his opportunities as well: a stepchild had no legal right to inheritance.[11]

Germans of Kulle's age were growing up in a time of prolonged hunger, worldwide depression, and waves of political violence in the streets, and they had few places to turn. Their parents were often unsympathetic, and the nation's youth movements were stagnant. The growing Nazi Party channeled their frustrations, playing up intergenerational conflict with chants like "Make way, you old ones!" Members of the Nazi Party were visibly younger than those of other parties, and gave young supporters special privileges. Many young Germans came to see Hitler as the symbolic replacement of the father or older brother the Great War had taken. With the promise of a restored Reich and ample scapegoats for Germany's struggles, the Nazi movement appealed to the disaffected and alienated, and young men of Kulle's generation were eager to don uniforms to fight for the national cause.[12]

In 1936, Kulle did just that, joining the Hitler Youth. He hoped one day to enlist in the cavalry.[13] In the afternoons and on weekends, Hitler Youth groups met to study maps and engage in war games with actual fighting. Most boys in the Reich were familiar with guns. They began using small-caliber rifles by their early adolescence, competing in shooting matches that sharpened their appetite for real-life combat. Like their schooling, the Hitler Youth stressed physical fitness, blind obedience, and Nazi ideology. The state, the Nazis stressed, was more important than the family. That was a powerful message for someone like Kulle, frustrated with life at home.[14]

Kulle and other Hitler Youth were told that Germany was preparing for an "unavoidable war."[15] Germany's supposed enemies were not just external, but internal too. Thousands of prisoners were interned at the Dachau, Sachsenhausen, and Buchenwald concentration camps, and their respective subcamps. In Silesia and across the Reich, the Nazis were seizing Jewish property and enforcing boycotts of Jewish stores.[16]

In March 1938, the Wehrmacht (German Army) marched into Austria unopposed. Throngs of cheering Austrians took to the streets, waving Nazi flags and heiling Nazi salutes to welcome the Anschluss, the reunification of Germany and Austria. New concentration camps were added at Flossenbürg, near the Czech border, and at Mauthausen in Austria. Waves of arrests accompanied the physical violence, largely directed at Jews, that had become commonplace across the Reich.[17] Repressive policies and antisemitic riots imperiled the Jewish community in Oels, the closest city to the Kulles' farm, and chants of "Hang the Jews" were common.[18]

In September, British and French officials urged Czechoslovakia to cede the Sudetenland, a culturally Germanic region that Hitler promised would be his last territorial claim in Europe. Hoping the cession would appease him and prevent war, the great powers met in Munich on September 30, 1938, to formalize an agreement. "Nazi demands met," the *New York Times* reported.[19]

Just over a month later, Nazi leadership signaled for a pogrom against Jews across the Reich. On November 9, 1938, Silesia and the rest of Germany erupted in vicious and brutal attacks that came to be known as *Kristallnacht*, the "night of broken glass." Rampaging through the night, Nazi paramilitary groups vandalized Jewish stores and burned the synagogue in Oels.[20] Hitler Youth regiments eagerly joined in the terror, and gangs of German teens attacked Jews anywhere they could be found. Newspapers in the region reported the events with pride. "Demonstrations throughout Silesia," one described them. "How Breslau Got Even with the Jews," another explained. A passerby said he felt as if he "was in the Middle Ages."[21]

In March, the Nazis seized Czechoslovakia. Poland was next,

carved up by Germany and the Soviet Union under a secret agreement. SS men followed the Wehrmacht into Poland, committing heinous atrocities against Jews and members of the Polish intelligentsia.[22] The SS plundered Jewish shops, blew up synagogues, and lined up civilians before firing squads in waves of mass executions. Their barbarity was no secret. One disgusted Wehrmacht general wrote a long memorandum cataloging the SS's crimes. Members of the Hitler Youth, like Kulle, learned of the SS atrocities when older friends returned home, bragging of their bloody exploits in the east.[23]

With few prospects at home, Kulle applied to join the cavalry. At the physical examination, however, he was rejected for being too heavy. Some of his older friends encouraged him to join them in the Waffen-SS, the military branch of the Nazi paramilitary unit. The SS was an "elite group," they told him, and there were rumors that SS men might receive government jobs, or even farms, when the war ended. Other boys in the Hitler Youth were wary of joining the SS, alarmed at the prospect of committing atrocities. Kulle, though, was undeterred.[24]

Kulle enlisted on June 20, 1940, and left for Radolfzell. He was a handsome young man, with dark hair, blue eyes, and an athletic—if slightly heavy—build. At Radolfzell he received weapons training, firing small machine guns and rifles in the recently constructed shooting ranges near Lake Constance. He learned how to read maps, use a compass, and fortify defensive positions in the ground.[25]

While Kulle trained, his future unit was in France, engaged in savage brutality, especially against those deemed racially inferior. After defeating a column of Moroccan troops near the village of L'Arbresle, the unit refused to take prisoners, murdering all thirty soldiers. Two days later, they took twenty-four white soldiers from France as prisoners, and euphemistically reported that another twenty-four Black soldiers "fell."[26]

Just weeks after France sued for an armistice, Kulle joined the SS-Totenkopfdivision (SS-TK) in occupied France. The Totenkopf, or Death's Head Division, was the creation of Theodor Eicke, an ardent Nazi ideologue and the commandant of Dachau. Eicke scrutinized each recruit, obsessed with maintaining the racial purity of his soldiers. He was disgusted with the batch, rejecting five hundred of the seven hundred recruits who joined the SS-TK between June and September. Reinhold Kulle was one of the few who met Eicke's standards.[27]

In November 1940 the SS-TK received instructions to prepare for Operation Barbarossa, the surprise invasion of the Soviet Union. Kulle and his comrades marched as many as sixty kilometers a day, practiced assaulting fortified positions, and simulated battle in villages and wooded areas. Military training paused just before Christmas, and switched to political indoctrination. The men studied "nationality and home," the history of German-speaking Europe, and Nazi theories of racial biology. If they needed clarification, they could consult *Schwert und Pflug* (Sword and Plow), a two-volume collection of Nazi ideology. The sword symbolized their role as elite protectors of racial purity; the plow symbolized the virtues of the hardworking German people. Kulle studied supposed Jewish plots against Germany, and discussed the need to eliminate the "Jewish threat." Military training resumed early in 1941, with such intensity that some soldiers lost their lives. Kulle, though, continued to excel.[28]

Just before daylight on June 3, 1941, the Nazis quietly slid train cars out of rail yards in Bordeaux. For four days and nights, SS-TK men boarded the trains one unit at a time, beginning their long trek to the Soviet border. Kulle was finally on his way to battle, soon to be attached to a motorcycle company in a reconnaissance unit. The trains deposited the men at Marienwerder, forty miles southeast of Danzig. Over the next two weeks, more than three million German soldiers amassed at the border.[29]

In the hours before dawn on June 22, 1941, Kulle and the other men prepared themselves for combat. Kulle wore his greenish-gray *feldgrau* uniform, with a wide, closed collar and dark lapels buttoned to his shoulders. A cap with the ominous *Totenkopf* skull sat atop his head. A second *Totenkopf* skull, indicating that Kulle was in the SS-TK, appeared on his right collar. Even among the elite SS, his unit merited distinction.[30]

Eicke lectured his men that the coming war had to be fought as an ideological conflict against "Judeo-Bolshevism." The men were under strict orders to kill any Soviet political commissars they encountered. There was to be no mercy; the fate of Germany hung in the balance. Eicke harangued the men over and over about the brutal nature of this war. They were to be fanatical and merciless.

Just before 3 a.m., unit commanders read Hitler's proclamation of war to the SS-TK men. A few minutes later, Kulle and his comrades invaded the Soviet Union.

Atop his motorcycle, Kulle was at the front of the attack. He rode close to enemy lines, scouting Russian soldiers' positions as the unit marched toward Leningrad.[31]

The Wehrmacht's Army Group North charged through Soviet-occupied Lithuania, advancing quickly into Latvia and Estonia. One day, Kulle spotted Russian horses and artillery in a large forest, somewhat hidden from view. He and his unit surrounded the equipment, and saw a Russian soldier. They captured him, and then saw others, and still more others. They captured the whole column, and continued marching east.[32]

As the Nazis conquered Soviet territory, millions of Jews fell under Hitler's control. Nazi *Einsatzgruppen* (mobile killing units) carried out mass murders in ravines and forests with the help of local collaborators, who joined out of violent antisemitism, local political rivalries, and naked opportunism. Despite the Nazi advances, fully 10 percent of the Totenkopf men were killed, wounded, or missing in the first few weeks of the invasion. By October the snow began, and by November temperatures dropped well below zero Fahrenheit. For the next few months, Kulle and the rest of the SS-Totenkopfdivision were entrenched in a series of bunkers southeast of Lake Ilmen. The weather continued to worsen, and even the elite members of the SS-TK were so poorly provisioned that Kulle and his comrades were left to rifle through abandoned homes for extra clothing.[33]

On January 7, 1942, in a blizzard with the temperature forty degrees below zero, the Russians counterattacked. Bullets and screams filled the cold air. Amid the chaotic fighting, Kulle entered a wooden house. There was a flash of light and a loud explosion; shards of glass sprayed up, splintering his face. His chin hurt, too—due to a shell fragment from a Russian tank grenade. A week later, in another engagement, a bullet shot at his hip lodged in his belt. He pulled it out, lucky to be alive and relatively unharmed.[34]

Finally, in the middle of January, the SS-TK procured fur-lined parkas, long underwear, wool socks, boots, and gloves. But the extreme temperatures wreaked havoc on the Nazi equipment; their rifles often failed to fire, and the engines on their aircraft and locomotives refused to start. Between the cold and the unending series of violent encounters, Kulle's unit was depleted. Even Eicke was growing desperate. On February 23, as the Russian assaults escalated, snow poured down on Kulle and what was left of his battalion outside Demyansk. As they moved slowly through wooded and swampy terrain, bullets pierced the frigid air. One of them stopped Kulle in his tracks, penetrating his arm and his lung, and lodging above his groin. He fell in a heap on the frozen terrain.[35]

Kulle was rushed to a field hospital and doctors operated immediately, but the bullet was lodged deep, and removing it proved impossible. He clung to life for two weeks before he was strong enough to be loaded onto a Junker 52 aircraft and flown to a hospital in Nazi-occupied Pskov, Russia. The next day, a railcar brought him to the German border. Red Cross cars transferred him to Reserve Hospital II in Stettin, back inside the Reich.[36] Someone told him that the extreme cold had stopped him from bleeding to death. His recovery was slow, and he was long unable to walk. He spent three months recuperating in the hospital, dreaming of a return to the front.[37]

Finally, in the summer, he was released.[38] His abdomen was healing, but the scar would remain.[39] He was given sixteen days of leave and returned to Alt Ellguth, a wounded veteran like his father. After just two weeks at home, he had orders to join a convalescent company in Ellwangen, in central Germany.[40]

Still eager to fight, Kulle requested a return to combat, but his wounds were too severe and he was deemed unfit for combat duty.

Figure 1. Reinhold Kulle in his SS uniform, at Ellwangen, 1942. Kulle kept this photo for decades after the war, and presented it to the Office of Special Investigations during his deposition in 1982. Courtesy of US Department of Justice.

The Nazis had other plans for him.

At Ellwangen one day, Kulle's commanding officer handed him an envelope.

"You are going to Gross-Rosen," he said.[41]

It was not an uncommon assignment. The Death's Head Division had emerged from concentration camp guard units, and Nazi leadership believed that Totenkopf men—with their ironclad commitment to Nazi ideology—were uniquely suited for guard duty in the camps. Kulle did not protest the order or even ask to see the paperwork.[42]

The ride northeast back into Silesia took about a day before the train pulled into the redbrick train station at Rogoznica, some forty miles west of Breslau.

Kulle turned toward the slave labor camp, where he would spend the next two and a half years.[43]

3

UP THE CHIMNEY

Mieczysław Moldawa could feel the emptiness in his stomach. He had not had anything to eat or drink since he and 260 other prisoners were packed into a freight car at Dachau and sent east. The judge who sentenced him to Gross-Rosen had told him to be grateful, that he was showing mercy because Moldawa was only seventeen. Listening to BBC radio broadcasts was normally punishable by death.

After two hellishly long days, the train finally screeched to a stop in the dark of night. None of the prisoners had seen the small, tranquil village set amid green fields and gentle hills just over a kilometer away. Moldawa expected someone to let them out of the freight car, but the doors remained locked. The prisoners sat in the dark, confused and scared.

Early the next morning, the door swung open.[1]

"*Raus! Raus!*" Men in green uniforms yelled, whips and sticks at their sides.[2] German shepherds barked and snarled as the Nazis pummeled their new prisoners, ordering them to line up. Moldawa recognized the bars on the soldiers' lapels; these were SS-Totenkopf men, the same he had seen in Dachau.[3]

A terrified prisoner asked when they would be released. A guard approached, eager to deliver the ominous threat. There was only one exit, he sneered, pointing to the smoke billowing up from the camp's crematorium: "Up the chimney."[4]

Moldawa and the other prisoners were marched up a large hill. Slower, sick, and older prisoners dropped off, never to be seen again. The guards smiled menacingly, their faces almost matching the skulls on their uniforms. After two kilometers they passed the granite quarry, a deep crater with a steep cliff, before they finally reached the roll call yard, a half-acre expanse surrounded by two-story service buildings. The prisoners were counted, told to undress, and sprayed with Lysol. Then they were shaved, dull razors dragging and catching on their skin.[5]

Next came white uniforms with blue stripes and identifying patches. Moldawa's patch was an upside-down red triangle, for "political" prisoner, with the letter P, for Pole. The number 749 was affixed to both his chest and his leg. For the next four hours, SS men forced him and the other prisoners to perform army training exercises before being chased into their barracks and given a small serving of soup, their first food since leaving Dachau.[6]

* * *

Kulle walked from the train station, his black boots crunching the small stones along the kilometer-long path. A tall tower with an electrified fence overlooked the camp gate, searchlights on either side. Above him, an inscription arched atop the entrance: *"Arbeit Macht Frei."*[7]

Gross-Rosen had received its first transport of one hundred prisoners on August 2, 1940; barely twenty were still alive the following spring. Designated one of the most severe camps, it had undergone a phase of rapid growth beginning in May 1942, and had taken over the administration of dozens of subcamps.[8]

Farther east, the Nazis were establishing killing centers at Chelmno, Auschwitz-Birkenau, Belzec, Sobibor, and Treblinka, but the increasing need for labor to feed the war effort conflicted with their plans to exterminate Europe's Jews. A compromise was forged among Nazi leadership: they would murder the old, the young, the sick, and the weak, and any Jews who remained physically capable of exploitation would be sent to slave labor camps like Gross-Rosen. Then they, too, would be murdered.

In 1942 more than half of Gross-Rosen's prisoners died, but new transports constantly replenished the supply of slave laborers. By the time Kulle arrived toward the end of that summer, the prisoner population had grown to roughly six thousand.[9]

Figure 2. The entrance to the prisoners' section of Gross-Rosen.
Courtesy of Gross-Rosen Museum.

Kulle brought his orders to Arthur Rödl, the camp commandant, who told him to report to the First Company. Kulle would be stationed on the perimeter, tasked with preventing escapes and overseeing slave labor. On other days he served as the salute guard at the camp's entrance, ensuring that only proper personnel entered the camp. The Nazis were not keen on letting outsiders see what was happening here.[10]

* * *

At 5 a.m. a loud gong woke the prisoners, and orders of *"Aufstehen! Gup!"* echoed through the barracks.[11] Within two minutes, the prisoners were outside. Moldawa undressed to his waist, washing himself with cold water. Guards beat anyone who refused to remove their waistcoats. Moldawa was handed a half liter of thin "soup"—boiled water and turnips—in a tin bowl.[12] At noon he would have a slightly larger portion made from rutabaga; for dinner, a somewhat denser rutabaga or beet soup, and a small piece of bread with a tiny share of margarine. Within a month, he would lose forty pounds.[13]

Moldawa dunked his bowl in the stagnant water that had just rinsed the lice-ridden prisoners, and guards barked out the morning tasks. The *Blockführer* began the roll call as other guards pointed heavy machine guns at the prisoners. The chief commander came in, yelling at the prisoners to remove their hats. Moldawa removed his immediately. Shots whizzed past him, and bodies thudded onto the ground. Other prisoners had been too slow to react to the orders.[14]

Moldawa knew that despite the slave labor, the real mission of the Death's Head men was to eliminate the prisoners. The most brutal men seemed to always rise in the camp hierarchy, promoted by the Nazi regime for services rendered. The roll call square doubled as the site of hangings. On the gallows the SS placed a card, reading "*Hej, Ha! Ich bin schon wieder da!* [Hey, ha! I am here again!]." It was a constant reminder that the place where each day started could also be where their lives would end.[15]

By 6:30 a.m., guards sprinted the *Kommandos* (units of slave laborers) to their work sites. Moldawa dug into rock, creating foundation ditches for the camp's ongoing expansion. Prisoners who paused or fainted were beaten. At noon, a bell signaled a ten-minute meal break. Spoonless, Moldawa drank his soup, removing thicker portions with his fingers.[16]

He knew it could be even worse. No one sent to the quarry seemed to last longer than a month. Even the walk to get there was treacherous. Exposed to the northwest winds, prisoners fought frequent rains and blizzards on the steep slope. In the summers, dust and sand blew into their eyes.[17] SS guards, resentful of the long hours, tormented the prisoners, especially the Jewish ones, spilling out the cement sacks they carried and making them perform duck walks. Almost every morning, as the *Kommandos* passed a cliffside grove, some prisoners would leap to their deaths. SS guards shot at the falling bodies, rewarded with a day of furlough if their shot hit. The grove became known as "Suicide Corner."[18]

* * *

With his gun ready, Kulle stood guard as the three work units loaded and unloaded granite at the camp's railroad station. He and another SS

Figure 3. Gross-Rosen's quarry in its current state.
Courtesy of Gross-Rosen Museum.

guard marched the prisoners as they lugged impossibly heavy bricks of granite from the quarry to the station. Any prisoner not carrying bricks was ordered to run the entire way. When prisoners slowed or tired, they were killed.[19]

A few days after Kulle arrived at Gross-Rosen, he was one of six SS men to receive the East Medal for service in Russia.[20] He received the Iron Cross and Frozen Flesh medals as well.[21] In October, just two months later, more good news came. He was being promoted to *Rottenführer*. A second set of double silver stripes was added to his collar, and twelve men were placed under his command. The boy whose stepfather had thought him unworthy of a trade was now training the Nazis' most elite soldiers.[22]

* * *

After twelve grueling hours, the banging of rails signaled the end of the day's slave labor. Some of the men, starving and depleted, tottered listlessly back, too weak to stand, their cheekbones protruding, their eyes hollow. They lay on the ground, facing their homelands, pleading for someone to say goodbye to their families for them. The other prisoners called them *Muselmanner*—the "walking dead."[23] Totenkopf men beat them mercilessly, but the *Muselmanner* had already stopped responding to their environment. Moldawa watched in disgust, knowing there was nothing he could do. Death had come for the *Muselmanner* already, though their bodies had not yet fully acquiesced to their fate.[24]

Moldawa and the other prisoners carried the dead and the sick to the gate. The evening roll call awaited, and the SS needed the morning and evening numbers to match up. That some of those they counted were dead made no difference.

Once a prisoner became weak or sick, he had little chance of surviving. Epidemics swept through the camp, infecting most of the prisoners. Hundreds were put "on the syringe," murdered with phenol injections by SS men. Moldawa eyed the *Unterscharführers* (sergeants) nervously, knowing that several kept phenol on their person at all times. Other prisoners were sent to their deaths at Auschwitz.[25]

Gross-Rosen's crematorium, which could incinerate a body in six to eight minutes, was in continuous use. Piles of corpses mounted, and birds avoided the trees nearby. Even when camp officials ordered the burning of two bodies at a time, the crematorium struggled to keep up.[26]

* * *

At night, Kulle often manned the watchtowers. The next guard post was fifty meters away, ensuring full fire coverage of the outside zone. Other guards patrolled the grounds, police dogs at their sides. A barbed wire fence separated the watchtower from the custodial area; a forest separated the camp from the rest of his native Silesia. It was safer duty, but he missed the action on the front.[27]

On other nights, Kulle was assigned as a *Posten* on the perimeter. He walked for fifteen minutes to the left, his eyes fixed on the electrified fence, machine gun at the ready. Then he paced fifteen minutes back to the right.[28] His instructions were clear, written by Eicke years earlier.

A prisoner who attempts to escape *is to be shot without challenging.* The guard who shoots an escaping prisoner in the execution of his duty will not be punished.[29]

On his patrols, Kulle looked out past the camp. To the north was the small village of Rogoznica; to the south, Haslicht. One day, he saw a young woman walking on the road near the camp. She was looking back at him, and they locked eyes. Their families had known each other for decades. The walk between her house in Haslicht and Kulle's barracks was only a few kilometers, and they quickly fell in love.[30]

* * *

Moldawa looked up from his work duty. Off in the distance, a prisoner—too tired and weak to walk upright—crept toward the outer road, where a civilian was passing by. Moldawa could hear the guards discussing who would shoot the prisoner—which of them needed the three-day furlough the SS gave after a murder. By the time the prisoner reached the street, taking one and then two slow, bent-over steps into the outer road, the guards had come to a decision. One of them fired, and Moldawa watched as the prisoner collapsed to the ground: another body strewn about this hellscape.[31]

Another day, a group of prisoners crossed a green field on the way to their work post, and one of them, a twenty-five-year-old German, began doing cartwheels. None of the guards could take aim at the wildly moving target. Dozens of prisoners cheered as they watched him nearing the forest, but a guard finally had a shot. Moldawa was in awe; the prisoner had ended his life in a sort of fantasy.[32]

Eventually, the overused crematorium broke down. In 1943 the Reich Security Main Office sent some of its highest-ranking officers to Gross-Rosen to celebrate the installation of a new one. The SS staff greeted their superiors and celebrated the "miracle of technology" that their slave laborers had been forced to erect. It was a celebratory day.[33]

At Schuetzenfest, the folk festival that traditionally featured target shooting competitions, the new camp commandant, Johannes

Hassebroeck, had a special treat for the SS men. A transport of four hundred members of the Polish resistance had arrived that December. Instead of the wooden animals typically used as targets at Schuetzenfest, the SS men would get to shoot at the new prisoners.[34]

The construction of the new crematorium had been well timed.

* * *

More good news awaited Kulle. On September 1, 1943, he was promoted to *Unterscharführer*.[35] He had other forms to fill out, too. He was seeking approval to marry Gertrud Fichtner, the nineteen-year-old woman from Haslicht with whom he had fallen in love. The paperwork was detailed, meant to ensure that marriages involving SS men accorded to Nazi racial laws. In addition to being the Nazis' elite fighting force, the SS was to establish a racial aristocracy of pure Aryan blood. Kulle had to prove that both he and Gertrud were racially pure, and suitable genetic contributors for the continuation of Aryan supremacy.[36]

The first of the required forms was the Race and Settlement Questionnaire, which asked for a life synopsis. In small and neat handwriting, Kulle wrote a terse biography, highlighting his time in the Hitler Youth and service on the Eastern Front.[37] Gertrud's forms focused on her family. Her father, Oskar, had joined the fledgling Nazi Party in 1931, nearly two years before Hitler's ascension to power; her mother had been a leader in the Frauenschaft, the women's wing of the Nazi Party, since its inception in 1933. Gertrud was a good, loyal Nazi too. She had grown up in the Bund Deutscher Mädel, the female corollary of the Hitler Youth, and had been serving the Reich's State Labor Service on the railway since May.[38]

Next, the couple submitted family trees to prove that neither of them had Jewish blood, and were examined by SS-approved doctors. A physician measured Kulle's nose profile, asked about his grandparents, checked his teeth and thyroid, and looked for any other indicators of Jewish roots or genetic failures. The doctors submitted forms certifying the couple's eugenic fitness. SS men understood that this process was vital to ensuring the racial purity of Germany, no different than the invasion of the East or the Final Solution to the Jewish Question.[39]

Both the mayor of Haslicht and the village's official administrator sponsored Gertrud as references.[40] Kulle's forms were signed by his commanding officer, *SS-Obersturmführer* Karl Brauer, and the couple soon received formal approval from Himmler's office. Kulle and Gertrud would marry that fall. They planned the celebration for August, and registered the marriage at the camp.[41]

* * *

As the snow melted in the spring of 1944, the Nazis surveyed the grounds next to Gross-Rosen. With the Red Army encroaching, they planned to make Gross-Rosen the "new Auschwitz," replacing the notorious camp to the east. A "train *Kommando*" began hauling materials; Moldawa and other slave laborers cleared trees for the construction.[42]

That summer, Hungarian Jewish women were sent to Gross-Rosen and to the women's subcamps connected to factories. Transports poured in throughout the second half of 1944, and Gross-Rosen grew beyond overcrowded. Though it had been built to hold a maximum of thirteen thousand prisoners, there were now more than forty thousand inmates. Moldawa's bunk, which a year earlier he had begun to share with another prisoner, would now be shared with a third. The sewage system was overwhelmed, and fecal matter flowed into the stream that supplied the prisoners' drinking water.[43] Even the new crematorium could no longer keep up.[44]

In October, Soviet bombs rained down on Breslau. In November, teams at Auschwitz dismantled the camp's Crematorium II. The motor went to Mauthausen, the pumps and gas turbine to Gross-Rosen, where prisoners were being forced to construct a two-room building with a preparation room and a gas chamber capable of murdering sixty persons. Moldawa was ordered to mark off where the gas pipes were to be laid, but a lack of bricks and other technical issues prevented the completion of the murder center.[45]

The Soviet advance provided the prisoners a glimmer of hope. At a roll call in December, a twenty-five-year-old Russian faced an SS guard, and defiantly yelled, "We will show you!" The rest of the prisoners were forced to watch SS guards hang him.[46]

That winter, Moldawa organized a Christmas pageant, which another prisoner had convinced the Nazis to allow. Carolers and folk dancers captivated the audience. Moldawa's crowning achievement was a satirical performance of *The Wedding*, a famed play about Poland's failed attempts at national freedom. He and other prisoners had revised the script, recasting it in the struggle against Nazi oppression. The performance crescendoed with a voice on stage bellowing, "From the East comes thunder and lightning, like the dawn." The audience was rapt, imagining the growing possibility of freedom.[47]

* * *

The continued Russian advance forced Nazi leadership to order Gross-Rosen's evacuation. Subcamps farther east were evacuated to the main camp on death marches in five-degree-Fahrenheit weather. SS men shot fallen prisoners in the back of the neck at close range, shattering their skulls and leaving them in frozen ditches along the road. Brauer, Kulle's commanding officer, was tasked with evacuating the Dyhernfurth subcamp. On January 23, 1945, he led a three-thousand-prisoner death march out of Dyhernfurth. His men shot any prisoner who stumbled on the freezing march, and burned documents and corpses in pits in a nearby forest. Wehrmacht officers expressed concern over the number of bodies left behind. The next day, Brauer and his men returned to Dyhernfurth. Children and those too sick to march were loaded onto a truck and driven to the Oder River, where they were killed and their bodies were thrown into the water.[48]

Though January 1945 spelled death for many of the prisoners, it brought new life to the Kulle family. On January 30, Reinhold and Gertrud Kulle welcomed a baby girl. They named her Ulricke, meaning "of rich, powerful heritage."[49] Just as the SS had prepared him to attack Soviets and oversee slave labor, it prepared him for fatherhood. *Das*

Schwarze Korps, the official newspaper of the SS, stressed that domestic duties were not unmanly but helped fulfill men's racial duties to the Reich. To best secure the future of Germany, the SS taught, SS men needed to be ruthless toward the Nazis' enemies, but kind and loving to their Aryan children.[50]

A week after Ulricke's birth, the Red Army approached the Oder River, where Kulle's father had operated a ship years earlier. Transports from Auschwitz were still arriving each day, but there was no room in the main camp. Food supplies were completely exhausted, and preparations were underway to evacuate the main camp. Of the 1,391 prisoners on the first transport out of the main camp, only 285 were still alive when their train reached Dachau three days later.[51]

Kulle had received transfer orders himself. Brauer had been assigned to train new conscripts in Austria, and Kulle was one of the half-dozen guards selected to go with him. They would join the train leaving for Mauthausen, and walk together to their new post.[52]

* * *

On February 10, 1945, the prisoners gathered on the roll-call grounds. For eight hours they stood still, the snow building up around their feet. Moldawa watched in horror as the SS men marched the hospital's sicker prisoners behind the kitchen and shot them in the head at close range.[53]

Armed guards dragged Moldawa and the other prisoners to the train station, herding them onto open-air coal cars, exposed to the harsh Silesian winter. Four SS guards sat on a plank overlooking the two hundred tightly crammed prisoners, sometimes shooting into the cars. Some thirty prisoners were murdered during the trip in Moldawa's car alone. Kulle and Brauer sat together in a covered car occupied only by SS men.[54]

The Soviets reached Breslau, and German residents evacuated west. Roughly two-thirds of Silesia's inhabitants would leave by the war's end. The Reich was crumbling. A few days later, a powerful explosion echoed from the quarry at Gross-Rosen. The SS had demolished the crematorium, hoping to hide evidence of their crimes and the forty thousand victims they had murdered there. Only the chimney remained.[55]

At Mauthausen, after ensuring that the counts matched up, the SS removed and disposed of the dead bodies. Moldawa was transferred to Sachsenhausen, the concentration camp in Oranienburg, Germany, to which Gross-Rosen's staff had once reported.[56]

Kulle, Brauer, and a few other SS men walked to their new post.[57] Defeat was all but certain, but Kulle stayed, training new conscripts as they prepared to fight the incoming US Army, which had come from the West to end the Nazi reign of terror.

* * *

In the days following the German surrender, fear and confusion set in among the SS men. Rumors swirled that the Russians were sending German soldiers to Siberia. Kulle had no desire to find out if the whispers were true.

He removed his *feldgrau* uniform with the dark, triangular collars, and ditched the dark velvet cap with the Totenkopf skull and the imperial eagle. He fled to the American sector, hoping to avoid areas of the former Reich that had fallen into Russian hands. If he was caught, there would be no way to identify him as an SS man. The war had displaced so many men in Europe; he could pass as just another refugee. He trekked through the war-torn countryside for three weeks, avoiding capture or arrest.

When Kulle arrived in Nuremberg, a German police officer gave him a registration card to fill out, and told him to bring it to an American unit stationed there. Weeks earlier, Kulle had been in uniform, preparing troops to battle American soldiers like these. With his SS uniform still somewhere in Austria, there was no way for the Americans to know that the man in front of them had spent most of the war overseeing slave labor in the Silesian lowlands.[58]

4

VISA #6037

In 1957, the US Consulate in Frankfurt, Germany, was abuzz with activity. Catherine Geoghegan, one of the consulate's veteran officers, ushered a new visa applicant and his family into her office. A physician had just examined them, drawing their blood and listening to their hearts. This interview was the final step in the months-long visa process. It was exciting and nerve-wracking for the applicants, but routine by now for Geoghegan. She placed the applicants under oath, and offered them a seat.[1]

Geoghegan looked at the soon-to-be American family in front of her. Reinhold and Gertrud Kulle made a handsome couple. He had kind eyes and a warm smile, and answered her questions patiently. Their daughter, Ulricke, was twelve; their eight-year-old son Rainer was the spitting image of his father.

Kulle had first contacted the consulate a few months earlier. It had sent him a detailed preliminary questionnaire to fill out, along with an information sheet, translated into German, that explained the application process and listed the classes of individuals who were ineligible for American visas.[2]

Geoghegan looked over the paperwork and asked the family a series of questions through a German-language interpreter, one of the consulate's local staff members.[3] Kulle had served in the German Army, which was not surprising; nearly every German man had been conscripted by the end of the war. But on the preliminary questionnaire, he indicated that he had not been in any organizations, such as

Form FS-256a
(Revised August 1935)

Approved Bureau Budget
No. 47-R108.4

FOREIGN SERVICE OF THE UNITED STATES OF AMERICA

APPLICATION FOR IMMIGRANT VISA
AND ALIEN REGISTRATION

I- 1665353

I, the undersigned, being duly sworn, state the following facts regarding myself, and hereby make application for an IMMIGRANT VISA and ALIEN REGISTRATION under the Immigration and Nationality Act to the American _____ Consul at s..Ganara1......

at _____ Frankfurt/M,-Gy _____:

1. Family name	Given name	Initial	2. Place and date of birth	Age
KULLE	Reinhold	Alois	Jungfernsee, Silesia, Gy.now Poland, 36.	

3. Other names by which I have been known	4. Last permanent residence
	5 Mar 1931 9 Burgstr., REICHENBACH/Lehr,Gy

5. Address in the United States	6. Name and address of person to whom destined, if any
1307 South Elgin Ave., Forest Park, Ill	Fritz FICHTNER' addr. as in #5

7. Name and address of nearest relative in home country	8. Travel documents presented
Mother: Marie Anna Budras, Essen-WEST, Meppenerstr. 9	German PP. # 481/57

9. Hair	10. Eyes	11. Height	12. Weight	13. Nationality	16. Race	17. Sex	18. Marital status
brown	greygreen	5 ft. 7 in.	150 lbs.	German	German	M	Married [] Single []
			14. Complexion	16. Ethnic Classification		F	Widowed [] Divorced []
			fair	German			

19. Occupation	20. Distinguishing marks	21. Languages spoken, read, or written
Factory worker	none	German

22. Intended United States port of entry	23. Final destination	24. I have ($) (no) through ticket to destination	25. Purpose of going to the United States
New York	as in #5		to reside

26. Places of previous residence until 1936:Jungfernsee 1936-44:Alt Ellguth 1944-55:Haslicht, Gy 1945-50:Krempe, Gy 1950 to date: as in #4

27. _____

Figure 4. Kulle's visa application, 1957. Courtesy of Dr. Charles W. Sydnor Jr., Virginia Holocaust Museum.

the SS or the Communist Party, that would have barred him from entry, and no derogatory information had come back from the consulate's background check.[4] He had a job waiting for him with a rivet company in Chicago, and a place to stay, with one of his wife's relatives.[5] It was hard to imagine a better candidate. Geoghegan just had a few last questions that her bosses stressed she and other officials ask each candidate.

"Are you a member of the Communist Party?"

"Were you a member of the Nazi Party?"

"Were you a member of the Waffen-SS?"[6]

* * *

When the war ended and Lower Silesia was returned to Poland, the Kulles and other German families had fled westward, leaving their

28

past lives and most of their belongings behind. Farther east, countless Nazi collaborators had poured into displaced persons camps in Allied-occupied Europe, posing as innocent bystanders or even as victims. In the postwar chaos, it was often difficult to differentiate the perpetrators of Nazi atrocities from their victims. Jewish organizations called on Congress to improve the screening procedures, but little came of those efforts.[7] The presence of so many members of the SS and Gestapo being housed and fed in American displaced persons camps led one soldier to scoff, "You've probably got everything in this camp except Hitler."[8]

The Kulles had found their footing in Krempe, a northern German town just inland from the Elbe River. In 1949, on Kulle's twenty-eighth birthday, Gertrud had given birth to a son. They called him Rainer, an old Germanic name derived from the words for "good counsel" and "army." Shortly after Rainer's birth, the Kulles had moved to Lahr, a city thirty kilometers from the French border. Kulle had found work in a factory, but the family longed for more. They talked about America, about building a new life with more opportunities for the kids. But Kulle knew his time in the SS could pose a problem. He guarded his secret carefully, and bided his time.[9]

The Kulles were just one of the millions of European families who hoped to resettle in the United States, and a series of postwar changes to America's immigration laws made those American dreams more possible. In 1948, Congress passed the Displaced Persons Act (DPA), opening the country's doors to four hundred thousand refugees over the next four years. Though the act was couched in humanitarian rhetoric, the DPA was deeply rooted in Cold War exigencies. Congress understood that Western Europe could not possibly absorb the remaining million or so refugees from countries now under Soviet occupation. But the US government had little intention of absorbing the Jewish survivors lingering in displaced persons camps. During the debate over the DPA, members of Congress made little effort to hide their antisemitism. One senator complained that too many displaced persons were "related to residents of New York City"; another explained that the biggest holdup delaying the passage of the bill was finding a way to "keep out the Jews."[10]

That Congress wanted to keep Jews out was hardly surprising. America had largely closed its doors to Eastern European immigrants in 1924, believing they would dilute the country's gene pool. The American eugenicists whose writings underpinned that restrictive legislation worked closely with the German eugenicists who would emerge as leading theorists of Nazi "race science." Hitler had no shortage of apologists and supporters in America. Father Charles Coughlin spewed antisemitic vitriol to millions of listeners on his weekly radio show; a week and a half after Kristallnacht, he justified the Nazis' actions as the natural response to the threat Jews posed.[11] A few months later, fully apprised of the Nazis' terror, twenty-thousand Americans joined the German-American Bund's pro-Nazi rally at Madison Square Garden, during which President Franklin D. Roosevelt was called "Frank D. Rosenfeld," and his New Deal was called the "Jew Deal." With more than seventy chapters across the country, the Bund established pro-Nazi summer camps where German-American children wore Hitler Youth uniforms, raised the Nazi flag, and engaged in military-style drills.[12]

A cadre of far-right, antisemitic militia groups—some with large followings and significant caches of weaponry—operated openly, plotting violent insurrections to turn America fascist. The Christian Front, a Coughlin-inspired group based in Boston, called for America to "liquidate the Jews," and ended its meetings with Nazi salutes. The majority of Americans held low opinions of Jews, and more than three-quarters opposed allowing more Jews to enter the country.[13]

Even as tensions brewed between the United States and Nazi Germany, Charles Lindbergh and the America First Committee advocated against conflict with Germany. In September 1941, as Einsatzgruppen killing units massacred Lithuanian and Ukrainian Jewry, Lindbergh complained that Jews—not the Nazis—posed a serious threat to the United States. Dozens of prominent business leaders and politicians were members of the America First Committee. A not insignificant number of senators and congressmen who supported the committee would turn out to be part of a Nazi propaganda network paid by German agents to give pro-Nazi or antiwar speeches. President Truman later buried a report about the network because it named his friend, US Senator Burton K. Wheeler of Montana, an American First member. He instead fired the Justice Department investigator who had authored the report.[14]

Continuing these long-standing efforts to keep Jews out of America, the DPA prioritized ethnic Germans and Slavs, and proffered an extremely narrow definition of a "displaced person," carefully drawn up to exclude Jewish survivors. Truman called the bill "flagrantly discriminatory" but signed it anyway, hoping it would at least help stabilize Europe.[15]

The Displaced Persons Commission was quickly bombarded with letters advocating for the admission of non-Jewish refugees. Church groups expressed interest in bringing over Latvians and Estonians, noting that their predominantly Protestant makeup would make them "excellent citizens of the U.S.A."[16] One congressman asked the commission to only send Protestants to his district, noting that "any person who moves into a strange and a new country and community would prefer to be associated with people of the same religious belief."[17]

With just a short four-year window to process as many applicants as possible, the commission initially decided to "take the calculated risk" of foregoing serious background checks on applicants.[18] Jewish groups were concerned that the commission, along with the United Nations' International Refugee Organization (IRO), would enable Nazi perpetrators to escape justice. In November 1948, Simon Wiesenthal wrote to the IRO's chief eligibility officer about a recent antisemitic demonstration in Brazil involving Herberts Cukurs, a Latvian Nazi collaborator who had escaped to South America "with the help of I.R.O." Other collaborators, Wiesenthal wrote, had found their way into displaced persons camps; that the Allies were enabling Nazis' resettlement was an "outrageous injustice." The World Jewish Congress made sure the letter also found its way to the Displaced Persons commissioners.[19]

The concerns were valid. In one sample at the commission's Frankfurt headquarters, seven of the fifty-three applicants had been in either the Nazi Party or the SS.[20] The American Jewish Congress even noted that the commander of a Croatian concentration camp was one of fifty fascists awaiting completion at a processing center en route to the United States.[21]

Baltic émigré leaders, however, told the commissioners that Latvian, Lithuanian, and Estonian SS volunteers were simply resisting Communist occupation. CIA Director Roscoe H. Hillenkoetter agreed, writing in a confidential memo to the commissioners that many Eastern European groups "sided with the Germans during the war not on the basis of a pro-German or pro-Fascist orientation, but from a strong anti-Soviet basis." With the war over, he added instructively, those groups remained "strong anti-Soviet and, accordingly, find a common ground with new partners."[22]

Truman had appointed a Protestant, a Jew, and a Catholic to the three-member Displaced Persons Commission that coordinated the act's execution, but the commission was dominated by Edward Mark O'Connor, the Catholic appointee. A staunch anticommunist, O'Connor was sympathetic to those who had fought the Soviet Union, even if they had done so in an SS uniform. O'Connor redefined the Baltic Legions—Waffen-SS companies comprised of Latvians, Estonians, and Lithuanians that had decimated the Baltics' once thriving Jewish population—as distinct from the German SS and not hostile to the United States. Latvian and Lithuanian charities helped SS veterans gain entry into America, and provided food, money, and employment once they arrived. Later, O'Connor would become a leading activist in the Anti-Bolshevik Bloc of Nations, a neo-Nazi group whose membership included Nazi collaborators and prominent Holocaust deniers.[23] Unsurprisingly, with O'Connor at the helm, only 16 percent of the four hundred thousand refugees who entered under the DPA were Jewish.[24]

The DPA expired in 1952 and was followed by the McCarran-Walter Immigration and Nationality Act, which O'Connor championed. The new law prioritized immigrants from Northern and Western Europe, largely out of fear that Communists from Eastern Europe might infiltrate the country. The next year, the Refugee Relief Act was passed to aid those fleeing from the Soviet Union and other parts of Communist Europe.[25] The DPA had explicitly excluded former Nazis from entry, but neither the Immigration and Nationality Act nor the Refugee Relief Act continued such language. Instead, the Immigration Act excluded members of totalitarian organizations, and the Refugee Relief Act excluded any alien who personally "advocated or assisted in persecution." Jewish groups again protested that these policies would open America's gates "to those who are still active or sympathetic" to Nazism.[26]

Consular officials did their best to keep Hitler's men out of America, but their efforts often proved unsuccessful. The International Refugee Organization screened applicants, but former Nazi collaborators were coached to avoid detection, sometimes by IRO clerks themselves. The US Army's Counterintelligence Corps interviewed the applicants and their neighbors, but neighbors had frequently not known the applicants until after the war, and typically could not provide relevant information.[27]

Even background checks were often unhelpful. The repository of Nazi files at the Berlin Document Center (BDC) only contained records of Germans and Austrians. Eastern European collaborators could apply for visas, and no one would know any better. Other records were in Soviet archives, inaccessible to American officials. And even if the files were in the BDC or other Western archives, the legwork was labor-intensive and complicated.[28]

For a decade after the war, it was open season for Nazis who wanted to enter the United States. It is unclear how many immigrated, but estimates range upwards of ten thousand. Some were even brought over deliberately. Arthur Rudolph and Wernher von Braun were among the hundreds of Nazi scientists and engineers secreted over by the Army's Counterintelligence Corps as part of the originally covert Project Paperclip. The CIA employed others, like Tscherim Soobzokov, to carry out covert anti-Communist activities in a program that O'Connor helped coordinate.[29]

But many former Nazis obtained visas undramatically, claiming to have spent the war as anonymous soldiers in the German Army, as uninvolved students and farmers, or—most egregiously—as victims of the Nazis themselves. In 1941, the Romanian Iron Guard propagandist Valerian Trifa gave a speech that helped provoke a deadly pogrom against the Jews of Bucharest. When the Romanian dictator cracked down on the Iron Guard rebels, the Nazis stashed Trifa and other rebels as protected guests in a private corner of Dachau, under the guise of imprisonment. The men had their own rooms, a lounge area with a radio, and even a monthly stipend. After the war, Trifa kept up the ruse, showing US officials proof of his supposed incarceration, and in 1950 he entered the United States under the Displaced Persons Act. He moved to Michigan and became a prelate in the Romanian Orthodox Church.[30]

Former Nazis knew how to appear like every other potential immigrant. When Feodor Fedorenko applied under the DPA, he did not disclose that he had been an armed guard at the Treblinka killing center. After a brief stay in Philadelphia, he moved to Waterbury, Connecticut, and took a job at a metalworking factory.[31] Conrad Schellong's visa application did not mention his two years as an armed guard at Sachsenburg, or his three years at Dachau. This was certainly no mistake. When another form asked him to list every organization he had ever been a part of, Schellong neglected to include his membership with the SA, the SS-Totenkopfverbände, or a slew of other Nazi organizations, though he did remember to list his childhood soccer club.[32]

In 1948, a man calling himself Alois Anich entered the United States on a tourist visa. His real name was Andrija Artukovic, and he had served as interior minister of the Nazi puppet Independent State of Croatia. The fascist Ustaše movement he helped lead murdered close to four hundred thousand Serbs, Jews, and other "undesirables," and he was directly involved in the installation of Nazi racial laws and a concentration camp system. He moved to Surfside, California, and soon resumed using his real name.[33]

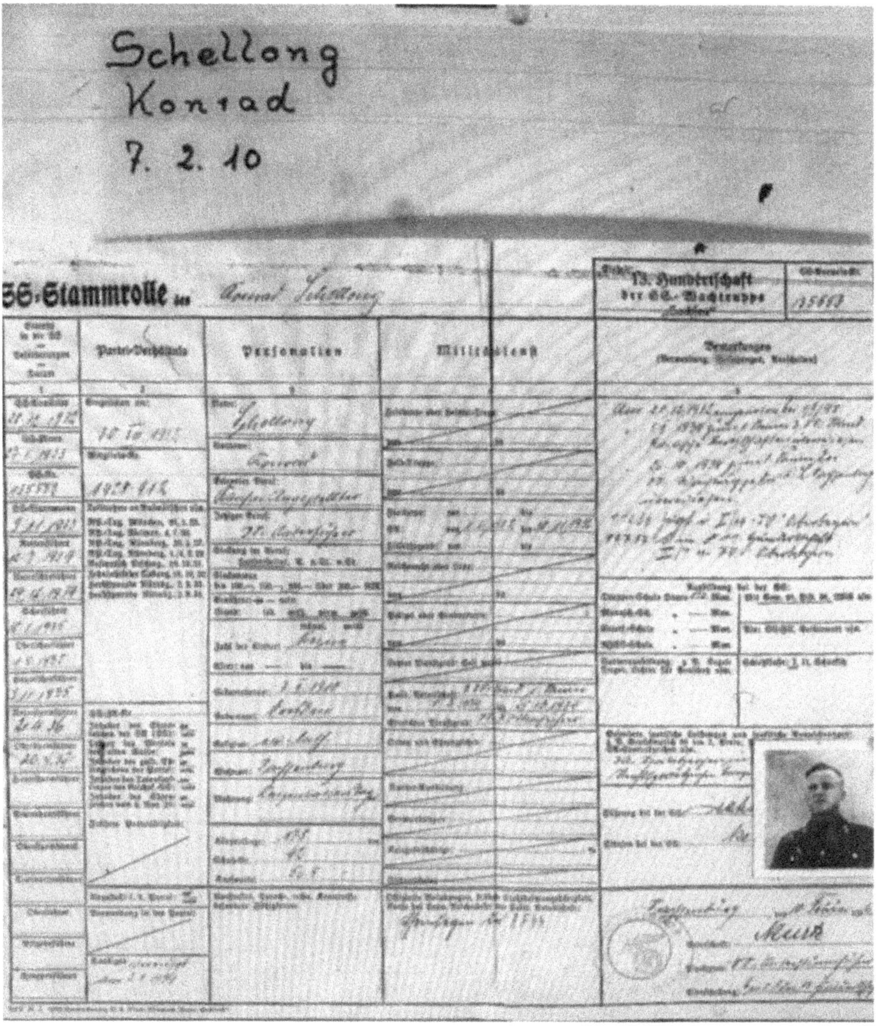
Schellong
Konrad
7. 2. 10
SS-Stammrolle des
13. Hundertschaft der SS-Wachtruppe

Figure 5. Part of Conrad Schellong's SS file. After the war, he moved to the Lakeview neighborhood of Chicago before settling in Portage Park on the city's Northwest Side. Courtesy of National Archives.

Surveying the situation, the *New York Times* could hardly contain its disgust. "It is easier for a former Nazi to enter the United States than for one of the Nazis' innocent victims," the paper fumed.[34]

In Geoghegan's office, Reinhold Kulle's warm smile covered the dark secret he had closely guarded for over a decade. He had kept it in

Krempe and in Lahr, and on the forms he had sent to the US Consulate. If Geoghegan somehow found out that he had been in the SS, everything would be over.

But she didn't.

On May 28, 1957, Geoghegan signed visa application #6037.[35] Reinhold Kulle was officially welcome in America.

5

CHICAGO

On October 26, 1957, the Kulles boarded the MS *Italia* at Cuxhaven, a port city situated where the Elbe River flows into the North Sea. The ship, originally built for the Swedish American Line in 1928, held more than 1,300 passengers. The Kulles arrived in New York two weeks later, and made their way west.[1]

With its patchwork of ethnic neighborhoods, Chicago was one of the most common landing spots for former Nazis. Liudas Kairys, a guard at the Treblinka killing center, was among the throngs of Lithuanian immigrants who settled on Chicago's Southwest Side. He arrived in 1949, claiming to be a displaced person, and took a job packaging candied popcorn at the Cracker Jack plant near Midway Airport. He married another Lithuanian immigrant, and they raised two American daughters in a redbrick apartment building around the corner from a small park. Kairys spent hours tending to his garden, and the family became involved in their church and in Lithuanian institutions in the neighborhood. Kairys edited a magazine about various Lithuanian topics, and was known for his growing collection of Lithuanian stamps and literature.[2] He was active in the PTA at his daughters' Catholic school, serving as its president for several years.[3]

A few miles south, Hans Lipschis was often up early to work on his house. A Lithuanian member of the SS at Auschwitz, Lipschis came to Chicago in 1956 and found work at a factory making guitars. He gained a reputation as a "beautiful gardener" and a "sweet man." His wife often clipped extra flowers for other women in the neighborhood, protesting that they had grown too many to keep them all for themselves.[4]

A year later, Conrad Schellong moved to the Lakeview neighborhood with his wife and three kids, living in several apartments within a few blocks of Wrigley Field. He worked as a welder, and as a janitor for the *Chicago Tribune*. Though his name briefly caught the CIA's attention, the investigation did not lead to deportation charges.[5] The Schellongs soon found a more permanent home among the 1920s bungalows in the Portage Park neighborhood on Chicago's Northwest Side. He took a job as a machinist, and after work the former concentration camp guard spent evenings talking and laughing with his neighbors on their shared back porch.[6]

There were others, too—Michael Schmidt in suburban Lincolnwood, Joseph Grabauskas on the Southwest Side, Bronislaw Hadja in Schiller Park, and Juozas Naujalis in Cicero—so many that investigators would later joke that America's Nazi-hunting organizations could have moved to Chicago and ignored the rest of the country. One war crimes investigator recalled standing in front of St. Anthony's Lithuanian Church in Cicero and realizing that he could throw rocks at the homes of half a dozen Nazi collaborators without straining his arm. Another investigator once parked on the Southwest Side and knocked on the doors of three different suspected Nazis without having to move his car.[7]

The throngs of new immigrants invigorated émigré communities. Dozens of Ukrainian churches and Lithuanian cultural institutions sprung up throughout the city, and the Chicago-based *Draugas* (Friend) became America's leading Lithuanian language newspaper. Home to the largest Lithuanian population outside Lithuania, Chicago housed the headquarters of many Lithuanian groups and organizations which helped settle the new immigrants. On Saturdays, Lithuanian churches held language schools to keep their mother tongue alive.[8]

As the growing émigré populations became acclimated to American life, the Ukrainian and Baltic communities remained closely connected to their fatherlands, the so-called Captive Nations now under

Soviet occupation. The charter of one leading Lithuanian community organization proclaimed that "a Lithuanian remains a Lithuanian everywhere and always," and newly formed émigré groups like the Assembly of Captive Nations and the Anti-Bolshevik Bloc of Nations held rallies in support of independence movements in their homelands.[9]

A generation or two earlier, Kairys and Lipschis might have faced a harsher welcome. But as Chicago's growing Black population moved into previously white neighborhoods, questions of racial integration were pushed to the fore, and differences between white groups blurred. Many residents of white neighborhoods saw the maintenance of their community's ethnic homogeneity as crucial to the maintenance of stability.[10]

For decades, Kairys, Lipschis, Schellong, and their counterparts blended into the fabric of their new neighborhoods. They worked, attended church, and reminisced about the old country. They were quiet but helpful, aloof but polite, modest but hardworking. Their doors were open if a neighbor needed help, and if their pasts came up in conversation, they were well practiced at not oversharing.

***

The Kulles first stayed with Fritz Fichtner, one of Gertrud's relatives, in Forest Park, a white working-class suburb a few miles west of Chicago.[11] Much of the land that became Forest Park had been purchased shortly before the Civil War by Ferdinand Haase, a German immigrant; and the village's first major businesses were Waldheim German Cemetery, the Frauenverein des Deutschen Altenheims (Women's Society of the German Old People's Home), and Karl Lau's sausage factory. Though it was becoming more ethnically diverse when the Kulles arrived, Forest Park still retained a large German cohort. German businesses were prominent, and a German band roamed the streets to celebrate the town's birthday.[12] Forest Park briefly made national headlines in early 1960 when, during a wave of antisemitic vandalism across the country, fifty gravestones in the Jewish section of Waldheim Cemetery were tipped, and swastikas were drawn on dozens more. A few weeks later, two other gravestones were knocked over; another month later, police found a foot-high swastika on a playground facing the cemetery. Next to the swastika, a sign in German announced, "All the good Jews are over there," above an arrow pointing to the Jewish graves.[13]

Though Kulle had originally arranged to work at the Chicago Rivet and Machine Company, he took a job at Suburban Cut Stone in nearby Hillside. The company sold industrial, commercial, and residential stone, along with other landscaping services. Kulle's previous experience with stone, in the granite quarries of Gross-Rosen, seemed a lifetime ago, and he knew to keep those stories to himself. To earn extra money, he worked on Saturdays as a janitor at Allen Radio, an electronics shop. Gertrud also worked for a few years, and then stayed home.[14]

The Kulle kids were among the many children of Nazis now learning in American public schools. In El Paso, Texas, and then in Huntsville, Alabama, the children of Nazi scientists brought to the United States in Project Paperclip studied English, recited the Pledge of Allegiance, and made dioramas of major events in American history. They ate hot dogs and wore cowboy suits.[15] The Paperclip kids received praise for their discipline and politeness, perhaps a remnant of the emphasis their German schools had placed on attention, industriousness, and order. Celebrated as successful symbols of the democratizing nature of American schools, these sons and daughters of Nazi slave masters did not take long to be perceived as less "foreign" than their Mexican-American classmates.[16] The Kulle kids were no different. Rainer picked up baseball, wrestling, and choir, and the family gradually acclimated to American life.[17]

In 1959 there was an opening on the custodial staff at Oak Park and River Forest High School, and Kulle applied for the job. He came well recommended; both his supervisor at Allen Radio and the superintendent of buildings and grounds at a school in neighboring Berwyn served as references.[18]

Before he could officially start the new job, Kulle had to fill out paperwork. He did so in English, though he was still learning the

Figure 6. Exterior of Oak Park and River Forest High School, 1963.
From *Tabula*, OPRF's yearbook.

language. In block letters, all capitalized, he wrote that he enjoyed gardening. During his physical, the medical examiner noted an "operational scar" on Kulle's abdomen and "2 wound scars" on his skin. Among the other papers in his personnel file was his marriage certificate, listing him as "SS-Unterscharführer Reinhold Kulle" and the registry office as "Groß-Rosen II." Stamped on the bottom of the page, the *Reichsadler* eagle looked off into the distance, a swastika below his perch. Kulle's birth certificate, filed as part of his marriage application, contained a *Reichsadler* stamp as well. If anyone at the high school was concerned, they kept it to themselves.[19]

Kulle's commute to OPRF was no more than seven or eight minutes. He would head north on Harlem Avenue, turning right when he saw the ornate green clocks of the Marshall Field's department store above Lake Street. He passed restaurants, bakeries, and the 1,400-seat Lake Theater before Frank Lloyd Wright's famed Unity Temple came into view out his passenger side window. Ernest Hemingway's childhood home was a block north, on Kenilworth Avenue. As Kulle neared Oak Park Avenue, he drove by the Scoville Institute—the Richardsonian Romanesque mansion that would soon be razed for a public library—and Scoville Park, the large public green in the center of town.[20] Before pulling up to the high school's campus, there was one last landmark—the school's stadium, built by some of Chicago's premier landscape architects. OPRF was said to be the birthplace of the "flea flicker," an innovation developed by the legendary football coach Robert Zuppke, who had once coached a clumsy Hemingway on the offensive line.[21] According to Oak Park lore, Zuppke brought OPRF's colors and fight song with him when he left to coach the University of Illinois, and those colors were then adapted by the city's new professional football team, the Chicago Bears.[22] In reality, the university had used both the colors and the fight song for a decade before Zuppke's arrival.[23]

Just miles from downtown Chicago and connected to the city by public transportation, the village became a popular suburban home for Chicago businessmen around the turn of the twentieth century, and its population grew quickly.

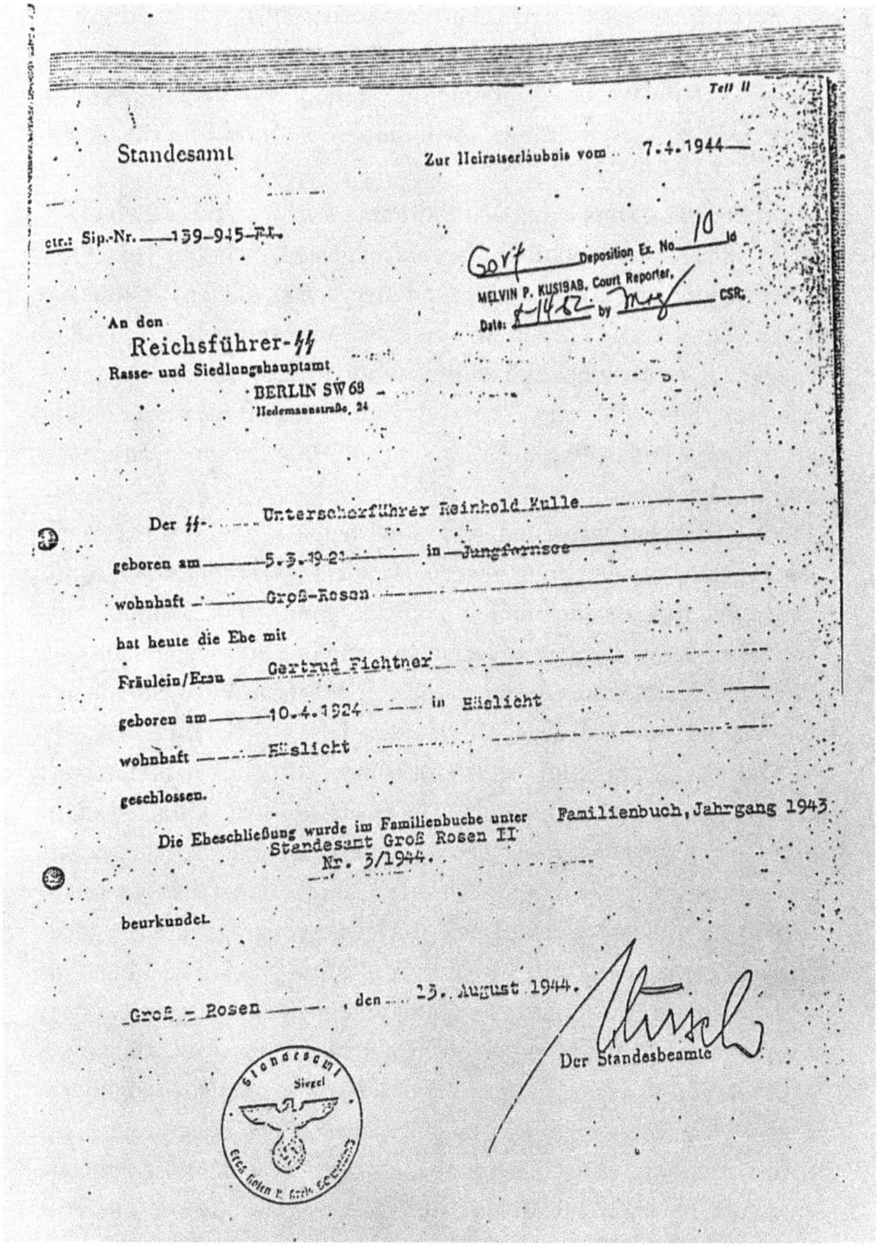

Standesamt   Zur Heiratserlaubnis vom   7.4.1944

ctr.: Sip.-Nr. ___159–945–R.I.

Gort   Deposition Ex. No. 10

MELVIN P. KUSISAB, Court Reporter,

Date: ___ by ___ CSR.

An den

Reichsführer-$$

Rasse- und Siedlungshauptamt

· BERLIN SW 68 ·
'Hedemannstraße, 24

Der $$- ___Unterscharführer Reinhold Kulle___

geboren am ___5.5.1921___ in ___Jungfernsee___

wohnhaft ___Groß-Rosen___

hat heute die Ehe mit

Fräulein/Frau ___Gertrud Fichtner___

geboren am ___10.4.1924___ in ___Hülicht___

wohnhaft ___Hülicht___

geschlossen.

Die Eheschließung wurde im Familienbuche unter   Familienbuch, Jahrgang 1943
Standesamt Groß Rosen II
Nr. 3/1944.

beurkundet.

Groß – Rosen ___ , den ___ 23. August 1944.

Der Standesbeamte

Figure 7. Kulle's marriage license, identifying his SS rank, listing Gross-Rosen, and featuring a *Reichsadler* eagle. A copy of this document is in his personnel file at the high school. Courtesy of Dr. Charles W. Sydnor Jr., Virginia Holocaust Museum.

From its earliest days, Oak Park had seen itself as a distinctly moral place. The village banned alcohol and prevented movies from being shown on Sundays. One prominent reverend joked that visitors knew they had reached Oak Park "when the saloons stop, and the church steeples begin."[24]

There was no mistaking that Oak Parkers were proud of their town. In the 1880s, many suburbs adjacent to Chicago, including Lake View Township, Hyde Park Township, and Austin, had voted to be annexed into the city. Oak Park not only rejected annexation but refused to change its street names and address numbering system to match and continue those of the city. "Let Oak Park Be Oak Park, one and indivisible, great and ineffaceable," one patriotic Oak Parker declared with unironic bombast.[25]

Oak Park, locals insisted, was more than just a suburb.[26] The village's pride buoyed a long history of civic engagement and a confidence that the growing number of citizen groups and community associations could navigate any challenge and preserve what made Oak Park special. The town even created a nonpartisan Village Managers Association that chose local candidates solely on their competence.[27]

Oak Park's pragmatic and reform-minded political climate was coupled with a genteel affluence. The business district attracted shoppers from nearby towns, and private social clubs and an exclusive golf club sprang up for the more well-to-do. Catholic congregations had to fight to build churches in the town, and Jewish congregations struggled as well. In the 1930s one Jewish congregation purchased a building on Lake Street, with plans to expand and create a synagogue. Local laws required that at least half of the neighbors approved such an expansion, and the synagogue did not receive the requisite neighborly support. The congregation instead purchased a plot in adjacent River Forest, but faced antisemitic opposition there as well. A second congregation, having watched this ordeal, used a straw buyer to purchase its property. Both synagogues and the local Catholic congregations remained excluded from the Council of Churches, Oak Park's umbrella organization for local religious institutions.[28]

Figure 8. Lake Street in downtown Oak Park, circa 1951.
Courtesy of Oak Park Historical Society.

Like its neighboring communities, Oak Park faced questions of racial integration in the years after World War II. In 1950, two prominent Black scholars—Dr. Percy Julian, a pioneering chemist, and Dr. Anna Julian, a well respected sociologist and civic leader—purchased a home for their family in Oak Park. Racial epithets were whispered about Julian, whom the *Chicago Sun-Times* had recently named "Chicagoan of the Year." The water commissioner refused to turn the Julians' water on, and the couple received threatening phone calls. On Thanksgiving Day, arsonists twice attempted to burn the house down.[29]

The suburbs next to Oak Park all steadfastly opposed integration, but in the wake of the attacks against the Julian house, something different happened in Oak Park itself. Residents spoke out against the arson, and civic groups reminded the community that they were lucky to have such preeminent scholars in their neighborhood. One woman compared the attacks to those in Nazi Germany, decrying not only the arsonists but the quiet acceptance the attacks received. More than three hundred Oak Parkers signed a petition calling for the Julians to be protected. Other similar events, including the firing of a Black violinist by the Oak Park Symphony, led to more social-action committees, and a growing commitment to change.[30]

But, as in other suburbs across the country, that commitment to change was tempered by the practical concerns of suburban life: good schools, safety, and property values.[31] "Something does seem to happen to Democrats when they get to suburbia," William H. Whyte sardonically noted in his classic 1956 book *The Organization Man*, which studied the residents of south suburban Park Forest.[32] Oak Park's reputation, and perhaps that reputation's impact on real estate values, seemed to hold significant weight for residents. After the arsons at the Julian home, some were more upset by the bad publicity the attacks garnered for the suburb than by the arson itself.[33]

Many of the Chicago's white ethnic neighborhoods bitterly resisted integration, and by the mid-1960s, Dr. Martin Luther King Jr. was compelled to bring the civil rights movement to Chicago. In the summer of 1966 he led a march for open housing into Marquette Park on the Southwest Side, and was immediately met by thousands of white counterprotesters who shouted racial epithets, waved Confederate flags, and even wore Nazi-style helmets. Dr. King was struck in the head by a large rock thrown by someone in the crowd. Two weeks later, the American Nazi Party held a rally in Marquette Park. Standing behind a large swastika, the party's leader, George Lincoln Rockwell, spewed antisemitic and racist vitriol before seven hundred cheering supporters.[34]

Oak Parkers watched as other communities struggled to navigate these demographic shifts, and typically, they determined to be different. Not wanting to fall prey to white flight or allow rampant violence and crass racism to take hold, the village decided to try a limited, managed plan for integration. The Village Board created a Community Relations Commission to foster racial cohesion, protect potential Black purchasers, and remind white Oak Parkers that explicit racism violated Oak Park's established mores of decorum. A focus on home ownership and decorum appealed to more moderate elements of the community, who—though perhaps less sure about integration—did not want to see white flight destroy their property values. The plan allowed them to couch their economic concerns in moral tones and progressive rhetoric, and to project an image of Oak Park as a model city—an image that remained important in the community.[35] "The people of Oak Park choose this community, not just as a place to live, but as a way of life," the town's 1973 Diversity Statement proudly declared.[36] Still, most of Oak Park's streets dead-ended at Austin Boulevard, creating a physical barrier between Oak Park and Chicago's West Side; and the pace of racial integration was, perhaps intentionally, quite slow. "We're in favor of change," one Oak Parker explained, "but stable change."[37]

* * *

At the high school, Kulle was indispensable. He came in when he was sick, and covered for his colleagues when they took vacation. The school's leadership took notice, and when the head night custodian took ill in 1963, administrators asked Kulle to fill in. "He is a very intelligent and hard-working member of our staff," the assistant superintendent wrote of Kulle. "The other men respect him, and he has shown good judgment." Kulle's English was still a work in progress, but he handled the added responsibilities well. When the ailing head custodian retired a few months later, Kulle was officially appointed his replacement.[38]

To make extra money, Kulle occasionally helped colleagues with small projects at their homes. One winter evening, he came to the home of Robert Elliott, the school's principal, to do some electrical work; as the hour grew late, the family invited him to stay for dinner. As they ate, someone complained about the temperature outside, and Kulle interjected: "*This* isn't cold."

He told the Elliotts about the invasion of Russia, about the historically bitter temperatures, about not having proper clothing. He and his

Mr. Reinhold Kulle is Head Custodian.

Figure 9. Kulle at Oak Park and River Forest High School, 1966.
From *Tabula*, OPRF's yearbook.

comrades had entered empty houses to find something warm to wear, he explained, but others had gone through them already and taken the warmest clothing. All that was left when he arrived were slips and women's underwear, which they took—a small defense from the brutal cold.

His description left a deep impact on the Elliotts' young daughter.[39]

Kulle's steady work meant that his family could afford to move into a home of their own. Their first house was a few blocks north of the Eisenhower Expressway on Harlem Avenue, the busy four-lane street separating Forest Park from Oak Park. The house was just around the corner from Otto's Restaurant, to which the Kulles could walk for schnitzel, steinhauer thueringers, calf's liver, sauerbraten, and herring, and the kids could enjoy strudel or German chocolate cake for dessert.[40]

A few years later, the Kulles moved into a small bungalow in a friendly working-class neighborhood. A big green field with several softball fields and a public pool was at the end of their block, a five-minute walk away. It was perfect for Rainer, who, like his father, loved playing sports.[41]

Like Kairys, Lipschis, and Schellong, Kulle lived simply and quietly. He paid his bills, doted on Ulricke, and cheered for Rainer at wrestling matches. He avoided politics and stayed out of trouble. In his spare time, he gardened. He slipped into obscurity, just another blue-collar worker in Middle America with a thick accent and an untold past.

* * *

By the 1950s, the Allies had largely abandoned their pursuit of Nazi criminals. The pursuit had at first been a high priority. The Russians convened the first war crimes tribunal at Krasnodar in 1943, and in the war's immediate aftermath the International Military Tribunal at Nuremberg tried leading Nazi officials, including Hermann Göring, Julius Streicher, and Rudolf Hess. In 1947 the prosecution of Ilse Koch—the notorious "Bitch of Buchenwald," who was alleged to have fashioned lampshades out of human skin—captivated public attention. But after a flurry of postwar trials, the efforts to bring Hitler's men to justice lost steam. Nazis no longer posed a threat, and Cold War enmities quickly became the top priority.

Even when Nazis were discovered, the US government was not always interested in taking action. In 1949, former Croatian Interior Minister Andrija Artukovic brazenly walked to an Immigration and Naturalization Service office in Los Angeles seeking permanent resident status. Government officials realized that a high-ranking Nazi official was living in the country illegally, but took no steps toward removing him. Yugoslavia requested that the State Department send Artukovic back; when the request was ignored, Yugoslav officials went public, and the INS and State Department finally opened deportation proceedings. Yugoslavia also requested Artukovic's extradition, citing a 1901 treaty between the United States and the Kingdom of Serbia.[42]

Artukovic staged a long battle against his deportation, arguing that he had been a simple figurehead, that there was no evidence he had personally committed murder, and that he would be subject to "physical persecution" in Yugoslavia. His attorneys protested that the extradition treaty was no longer valid since the Kingdom of Serbia had been dissolved after World War I, and that the United States had no treaty with the current Yugoslav government. Artukovic found consistent support from his congressman, James B. Utt, a right-wing Republican who introduced bills to help Artukovic gain legal standing. In 1955, Utt spent an hour on the House floor denouncing "the persecution of Andrija Artukovic."[43] By the end of the decade, both the deportation and the extradition efforts had been defeated in court. The "Butcher of the Balkans" was allowed to stay in California.[44]

Though the world's governments had largely moved on, a small collection of individuals across the Atlantic continued the hunt for Hitler's men. There were countless guards and SS men who had escaped justice, and the names of several Nazi leaders—Adolf Eichmann and Josef Mengele among them—loomed large for survivors like Tuviah Friedman and Simon Wiesenthal, and for the handful of others pursuing justice.

In 1960, Israeli Prime Minister David Ben-Gurion made a shocking announcement: Mossad agents had captured Adolf Eichmann, one of the main organizers of the Nazi genocide, outside his small home on Garibaldi Street in Buenos Aires.[45]

Condemnations were immediate—not of the Argentines, who had harbored Eichmann for a decade—but of the Israelis, who planned to put him on trial. Argentina protested the "illegal abduction," and the United Nations—saying nothing of the ratlines Argentina had provided to Eichmann and other Nazis—passed a resolution calling on Israel to make reparations.[46] Politicians and writers questioned whether Israel had legal authority to try Eichmann, but Israel began the trial in April 1961. The television and radio broadcasts drew large audiences.[47]

Eichmann's conviction was unsurprising, but his ensuing appeal brought sweeping pleas for mercy. The *Omaha World-Herald* argued that granting Eichmann clemency would help to "shame lingering antisemitism." The *Detroit News* begged Israel to show that "magnanimity is still achievable," and the *Boston Herald* wrote that commutation of Eichmann's death sentence would show that Jews "carried reverence for human life."[48]

Americans were profoundly ambivalent about the efforts to bring Nazis to justice, especially when doing so was in any way connected to the Soviet Union. In 1961, Soviet prosecutors formally asked the State Department to extradite Karl Linnas, an Estonian concentration camp administrator living on Long Island. The allegations shocked Richard Siebach, who carpooled to work with Linnas. When Siebach asked Linnas about "being a warden" of a concentration camp, Linnas admitted only to having been a guard.

The State Department rejected the extradition request, noting that the United States did not recognize Russia's occupation of Estonia, so the Soviets tried Linnas and two other defendants in absentia. Soviet prosecutors called former guards and survivors to the stand, and produced significant evidence of mass executions that had occurred under Linnas's command. During executions, Linnas had personally inspected victims' bodies to ensure that they had been killed, shooting them again if he found any signs of life. At the end of the three-day show trial, Linnas was sentenced to death.[49]

The Mossad, Friedman, Wiesenthal, and a slew of self-styled "Nazi hunters" continued scouring the earth for the men who had once sat atop the Nazi hierarchy. There were rumors and errant chases, hints of Josef Mengele in South America and assassination attempts against Alois Brunner in Syria, but even after the Artukovic and Linnas cases, few eyes focused on the United States.[50]

That would soon begin to change. Writing about Eichmann for the left-wing *Jewish Currents*, Morris Schappes claimed that "in the United States, in West Germany, in Austria there are war criminals crying to be tried."[51] Over the next few months, information trickled in to both

Schappes and Chaim Suller, the editor of *Morgen Freiheit*, a Yiddish-language communist daily. Among the tips they received was a series of newspaper reports about war crimes trials, including those of two men living in America: Linnas, and Boleslavs Maikovskis. Schappes and Suller asked the investigative journalist Charles R. Allen Jr. to look more deeply into the issue.

Allen told Schappes he was too busy, and that he doubted the claims. Several congressmen had raised the issue a few years earlier, and there was some smoke about a Romanian bishop in Michigan, but it hardly seemed likely. Schappes was insistent, and eventually Allen agreed to take a look.[52]

When Allen examined the documents, he was taken aback. After having an expert at Columbia University's Russian Institute authenticate the documents, he checked archival records from the Nuremberg war crimes tribunal, and identified sixteen suspected Nazis living in the United States. He tracked down fourteen of them for interviews. Beginning in September 1962, he published a three-part series for *Jewish Currents*, and reprinted the pieces the next April as *Nazi War Criminals in America*. The investigations triggered a series of large rallies. Flyers declared that there were "25 NAZI WAR CRIMINALS who have found a haven in our country" and that "THEY MUST BE BROUGHT TO JUSTICE!"[53]

On May 19, 1963, the Chicago-based National Committee against Nazism and Nazi Criminals brought Allen for a rally at downtown Chicago's legendary Sherman House hotel. Two hundred members of the Anti-Bolshevik Action Committee hurled antisemitic curses as they picketed outside. Allen was growing accustomed to protests from émigré groups and neo-Nazis. Weeks earlier, several men had accosted him after a large rally in New York, chanting Nazi slogans, calling him a communist, and tailing his car when he tried to leave.

One of the Sherman House picketers, a thirty-four-year-old Latvian woman named Dagmara Vallens, took a seat in the third row. When the audience stood to applaud one of the speakers, she opened a leather handbag and released ten mice, creating a frenzy of screams and panic. Then several men stood up and removed their shirts, re-vealing swastikas and Nazi uniforms. Allen and others began swinging fists at the men, who were from the American Nazi Party. Allen broke one of their jaws.

In an interview with the *Chicago Tribune*, Vallens implausibly claimed that the release of the mice was accidental. She explained that a boyfriend had handed her the bag because she loved mice, and that she had not had time to stop home before the rally. She also claimed to be the Chicago correspondent for a Latvian-language newspaper in Toronto, though she could not provide any details about the sup-posed paper. When a reporter asked whether she hated Jews, Vallens responded simply: "Those in there."[54]

That same year, an East German book alleged that NASA's Wern-her von Braun had been a high-ranking member of the SS, connected to the brutal slave labor at Mittelbau-Dora. The book, though, con-tained fabricated scenes, and was written off as Communist propa-ganda. Neither the West German press nor the American press gave it much credence. Still, von Braun's Nazi past became fodder for sati-rists. Several years earlier, the release of a biographical film about von Braun, *I Aim at the Stars*, had been met with jokes suggesting that the subtitle should have been *But Sometimes I Hit London*. The titular char-acter of Stanley Kubrick's 1964 film *Dr. Strangelove* was an ex-Nazi sci-entist who seemed a parody of von Braun and other Paperclip scien-tists. In 1965 Tom Lehrer recorded a satirical song about von Braun, calling him "a man whose allegiance is ruled by expedience / Call him a Nazi, he won't even frown / 'Ha, Nazi Schmazi,' says Wernher von Braun."[55]

The von Braun parodies and rallies like the one at the Sherman House created a brief public stir, but most of the Nazis living in Amer-ica remained undisturbed. Kairys, Lipschis, Schellong, Kulle contin-ued living quiet lives. They went to work, played with their kids, and tended to their gardens.

But now, for the first time, someone was looking.

6

MRS. RYAN

In a working-class community hundreds of miles east of Chicago in Queens, New York, Joseph Lelyveld walked up to a small home. The twenty-seven-year-old *New York Times* reporter was checking out a tip from Wiesenthal, who had learned that a vicious Nazi camp guard and convicted war criminal known as the "Stomping Mare of Majdanek" was living in the Maspeth neighborhood under her married name, Ryan. Lelyveld made a list of the address of every Ryan in Maspeth, and—on the afternoon of Friday, July 10, 1964—started ringing doorbells. He asked the first Mrs. Ryan he met whether she knew of another Mrs. Ryan, likely with a German accent, who had come over recently from Austria. She directed him to 72nd Street, the home of Hermine and Russell Ryan.

A large, tall woman opened the door holding a paintbrush, her hair in curlers.

"Mrs. Ryan, I need to ask about your time in Poland, at the Majdanek camp, during the war."

"Oh my God," she said through sobs. "I knew this would happen. You've come."

Ryan tried to convince him that she had been little more than a small cog in the Nazi machine. "All I did is what guards do in camps now," she told the young reporter in heavily accented English. "On the radio all they talk is peace and freedom. . . . Fifteen or sixteen years later, why do they bother people?"

When Lelyveld returned to the newsroom, an editor approached him with a sad, concerned look. "I was sorry to hear about your father," he said softly. Having spent the day in Maspeth, the young reporter had not yet heard that his father, Rabbi Arthur J. Lelyveld, had been hospitalized after being beaten with a tire iron near Hattiesburg, Mississippi, where he was working with the "Freedom Summer" to register Black voters.[1]

After finally reaching his father by telephone, Lelyveld hurried to read all he could about the Majdanek camp. It did not take long to learn about Hermine Braunsteiner Ryan, whose cruelty and brutality featured prominently in survivors' accounts. Known as "the Mare" because of her penchant for stomping prisoners to death with her jackboots, survivors remembered her ripping babies from their mothers' arms and murdering them on the spot. Later, when her name appeared in the *New York Times* and the *Jewish Daily Forward*, a survivor told the INS that everyone in Majdanek knew of Hermine Braunsteiner.[2]

As Lelyveld finished preparing his article, Russell Ryan called. "My wife, sir, wouldn't hurt a fly." Lelyveld listened as Ryan, who apparently had not known of his wife's Nazi past until a few hours earlier, grappled with the revelations. "There's no more decent person on this earth," he insisted. "She told me this was a duty she had to perform. It was conscriptive service. She was not in charge of anything."

Lelyveld felt sorry for him.

Ryan pleaded with the reporter over the phone. "Didn't they ever hear the expression 'Let the dead rest'?"[3]

Ryan's phone call set forth a pattern that would become common in the wake of Nazi revelations. First, denial and disbelief. Then, downplaying and justification. Finally, insistence that forgiveness was the most moral response.

Russell Ryan was not alone in his request to "let the dead rest." The twentieth anniversary of the war's end loomed, and with it came significant legal ramifications; the West German criminal code contained a twenty-year statute of limitations on murder cases. Other amnesties for some Nazi crimes had already come into effect, and unless the West German Parliament stopped the statute, all West German prosecutions related to the Holocaust would end in 1965.

The statute was popular in West Germany. As early as 1946, German clergy had questioned the justice of international war crimes trials. In America, too, some questioned the validity of the trials. Supreme Court Justice William O. Douglas called them victor's justice, as did prominent articles in *The Atlantic*. Senator Joseph McCarthy castigated the program as "Communist influenced."[4]

At first, postwar German jurists were unsure whether Nazi actions could be subject to prosecution, because they had had legal sanction at the time of their commission. And German legal theory placed more responsibility on the ordering of a crime than on its execution, making the "desk murderers" more responsible than those who had pulled the trigger or pushed victims into gas chambers. In 1949 a leading German bishop preached that the only way to move forward was "forgiveness of sins." "Forgiveness came early, indeed," the legal historian Lawrence Douglas remarked.[5]

By the early 1960s, a majority of German citizens favored the amnesty, and major political parties proclaimed their support as well. The "guilty few" had already been prosecuted, the thinking went, and lower-level camp guards and members of auxiliary police battalions had been simply following orders. Grotesque allegations like those against Ilse Koch further desensitized the public to more commonplace examples of violence and murder.[6] And anyway, the statute's supporters argued, it would be impractical and unreasonable to prosecute every person who was affiliated with the Nazi regime.[7] "We must be prepared to live with a few murderers," declared Justice Minister Ewald Bucher.[8]

In reality, very few Nazi persecutors ever faced justice. Though upward of one million Germans participated in Nazi atrocities, fewer than seven thousand defendants were convicted between 1945 and 2005. Even those who were found guilty rarely faced serious sentences. Kulle's former commandant, Johannes Hassebroek, saw his initial death sentence reduced to life imprisonment, and then to fifteen years in prison, before being released early in 1954. Less than a decade after the war, he was living freely in Braunschweig, working as a sales agent.[9]

The pursuit of justice was also impeded by active opposition. The German police leaked information to suspects, allowing them to get away. Judges tipped Nazis off to secret investigations, and the German Red Cross used a dedicated newsletter to alert SS veterans' groups of pending arrests. When the German prosecutor Fritz Bauer was informed of Adolf Eichmann's presence in Argentina, he quietly contacted the Israelis, sure that German authorities would otherwise warn the architect of the Final Solution. In other Nazi cases he asked local vegetable vendors to send telegrams for him, so that there would be no accessible records in police files.[10]

As the date for the statute of limitations neared, Simon Wiesenthal and Tuviah Friedman lobbied for more time to prosecute Nazi murderers. Friedman met privately with Justice Minister Bucher, while Wiesenthal organized world leaders to demand the extension of the statute of limitations. Wiesenthal published two hundred responses, including a short telegram from then Senator and former Attorney General Robert Kennedy that said simply, "Moral duties have no term."[11]

Wiesenthal understood that the confrontation was not between Jews and Germans, but between Germans and themselves. Many of the judges and politicians leading Germany were the sons of Nazis, or had Nazi pasts of their own. Even Ewald Bucher, the justice minister whom Friedman was unsuccessfully lobbying, had been a member of the Nazi Party and the SA.[12]

Germany wanted to move on.

In Israel, a small team of Mossad agents staged a daring plan to stop the statute. Posing as an Austrian businessman, a Mossad agent befriended Herberts Cukurs, the notorious "Butcher of Riga," who had been an active and vicious participant in the slaughter of Latvia's Jews. The agent asked Cukurs to become his partner in a supposed tourist business, and after a months-long operation he lured Cukurs into a vacant home in Montevideo, Uruguay, where a Mossad team was waiting. Cukurs's body was found a few days later. Next to it, the agents had placed a sheet of paper with a verdict condemning Cukurs to death for the murder of thirty thousand men, women, and children. They signed it "Those Who Will Not Forget."

As news of the Cukurs assassination spread, the horrific crimes the Nazis and their collaborators committed were recast in the public. The publicity buoyed the temporary defeat of the statute. The West German legislature retroactively pushed the twenty-year clock forward from Germany's 1945 surrender to the January 1, 1950, formation of the Federal Republic. In 1969 they would again delay the implementation of the statute of limitations for another ten years before it was defeated altogether. But despite the success of the Mossad mission and the delays in implementation of the statute of limitations, a profound ambivalence about revisiting the past remained.[13]

* * *

The day after Lelyveld's article appeared in the *New York Times*, the INS opened an investigation into whether Hermine Braunsteiner Ryan had lied on her immigration forms. Although she had been convicted in Austria after the war, and despite the clear evidence of her guilt, the case lingered for years. Finally, in 1971, the INS secured the revocation of her American citizenship, and began extradition proceedings.[14]

Though the Ryans were not well off, they managed to hire an expensive law firm. Anthony DeVito, the case's lead investigator, theorized that the money came from an international Nazi network. Documents he had kept in a locked safe seemed to have gone missing as well, and someone was making threatening phone calls to his wife and his witnesses. Something was not adding up. For now, though, he kept his increasingly conspiratorial suspicions to himself.[15]

Still, it was hard not to wonder, especially as reports of other Nazis living in America emerged. On a 1971 research trip to Latvia, Dr. Gertrude Schneider was told by the Latvian minister of culture that there were "lots of Nazis" in the United States. When Schneider—herself a survivor of the Riga Ghetto and the Stutthof concentration camp—expressed disbelief, the minister produced documentation showing that two men whom Latvian courts had convicted in absentia years earlier were now living in America. Schneider passed the documents about the men, Boleslavs Maikovskis and Vilis Hāzners, to a reporter from the CBS television news affiliate in New York, and appeared on the station several times over the next few years to discuss America's Nazis.[16]

That same year, Frederick Forsyth published *The Odessa File*, a thrilling novel about a reporter trying to take down a secret Nazi organization, codenamed ODESSA, that was protecting members of the SS. The book sold well, and was rereleased as a mass-market paperback. A film adaptation would soon be underway. DeVito was convinced that ODESSA was not just a thing of fiction but was alive and well, even within the highest ranks of the INS.[17]

The money for Braunsteiner Ryan's defense had not come from ODESSA, but its origins were hardly less noxious. According to Simon Wiesenthal, one source of funding was the Patriotic Legal Fund, registered in Marietta, Georgia. The Patriotic Legal Fund was affiliated with the National States' Rights Party, a segregationist, white supremacist, and neo-Nazi group led by Klansman J. B. Stoner.[18] Stoner was suspected of involvement in a slew of bombing attacks against Black and Jewish targets, including at The Temple—a prominent Atlanta synagogue known for its civil rights advocacy—and the 16th Street Baptist Church bombing in Birmingham, in which four young Black girls were murdered. He had served as defense attorney for Dr. Martin Luther King's assassin, James Earl Ray, and the FBI had even investigated Stoner's involvement in the assassination itself.[19] The money also seemed to be connected to George Dietz, a former member of the Hitler Youth and a leading producer of neo-Nazi materials.[20]

In court, government attorneys described Braunsteiner Ryan as a "cruel, brutal and sadistic woman." But on the witness stand she announced that she had not done anything for which she was ashamed, and that while she was "shocked and appalled" by what she had seen, there was nothing she could have done. "I was too little," she protested. Her husband portrayed her as a victim as well, testifying that she had quit her job out of fear that other employees might kill her, though he could not produce any specifics. Later, he claimed that the Nazi camps were little more than "rehabilitation camps."[21]

Almost a decade after Lelyveld first knocked on the Ryans' door, the *New York Times* sent a reporter back to Queens to ask residents what they thought of their now infamous neighbor. As the reporter walked up the street, a little boy held his hands over his eyes, counting in a high-pitched voice as his friends raced through backyards in search of good places to hide. A young mother pushed her infant in a stroller, and a middle-aged man worked on his car's engine in the driveway. With kids playing stickball in the street and small maple trees lining the sidewalk in front of rows of redbrick homes, the reporter could not help but note the quintessentially American nature of the setting. He approached a group of women to ask about the former Nazi camp guard turned American housewife who lived on their block. "I find it impossible to believe the accusations against her," one angrily scoffed.

Braunsteiner Ryan's neighbors recounted endless stories of her decency. She had lent a helping hand when a neighbor's dog had puppies, and was kind with the kids in the area, too. She kept a clean house, walked through the neighborhood with groceries, and worked in her garden. After a young boy broke the Ryans' window, she had refused to let the family pay for the damage. Her neighbors in Maspeth could not imagine that she was capable of committing the atrocities of which she was accused. "Nobody could have changed that much," one said in exasperation.[22]

Four of the Ryans' friends testified that Hermine Braunsteiner was of good moral character, with a reputation for honesty. One said she was "exceptionally kind and considerate," the kind of person one hoped for in a neighbor. Prosecutor Vincent Schiano asked each witness whether it mattered to them that Braunsteiner Ryan had mistreated prisoners at a Nazi concentration camp.

All four said no.[23]

The media coverage of the case elicited a slew of phone calls from Nazi hunters. One, Otto Karbach, had already provided DeVito with a list of eyewitnesses who could help with the case. And in 1972, at a restaurant on Manhattan's East Side, Karbach slid another list across the table to DeVito. This one had fifty-nine names of Nazis living freely in the United States. "We are counting on you," Karbach said.[24]

Other calls followed, bringing documents and files with evidence on Boleslavs Maikovskis and Tscherim Soobzokov, two of the names on Karbach's list. But more investigative delays followed, enraging De-Vito, whose clashes with his bosses at the INS intensified.[25]

On May 1, 1973, a US District Court ordered Braunsteiner Ryan's extradition to West Germany. Afterwards, the US attorney overseeing the case mentioned that his office was investigating another fifty alleged Nazis living in America. The disclosure was jarring, in part because the INS seemed to be making so little progress on any of the cases. DeVito and Schiano complained to reporters that their efforts to track down Nazis were being stymied by their bosses. They wondered publicly whether it was incompetence, a reticence to revisit the past, or something more nefarious at play. As tensions simmered at the INS, it seemed clear that progress was only going to come from outside the immigration office.[26]

7

A REAL GENTLEMAN

Just after 3 p.m., the night crew filtered into the high school, pushing against the throngs of students heading home or trotting off to practice. It would be an eventful shift. That evening, March 8, 1971, would be The Fight—Joe Frazier vs. Muhammad Ali at Madison Square Garden, one of the most anticipated boxing matches in history. Andrew Heneghan, who worked part-time on Kulle's crew, made sure his transistor radio was ready so that he could listen as he cleaned classrooms on the school's fourth floor.

Kulle gathered his crew for their preshift meeting. He stood up straight and doled out orders like a sergeant. The men knew their assignments—which classrooms, hallways, or bathrooms were their responsibility—and they knew Kulle's expectations. No one wanted to let him down, mess up, or be late, or have him find a room not properly set up or find dirt on a floor. They listened quietly as Kulle finished his instructions and dismissed them to their posts. Heneghan headed upstairs.[1]

As the staff fanned out across the hundreds of classrooms, bathrooms, and gyms, Kulle walked through the school's main hallways. He poked his head into classrooms and offices, checking in on teachers and administrators with a firm handshake and a friendly smile.

"Are you satisfied with your custodian's work?"

"Is your classroom as clean as you wanted?"

"Are you low on any supplies?"

If a teacher complained, Kulle would read their custodian the riot act. The room would be perfect the next day, and Kulle and his staff member would be back to exchanging pleasantries.[2]

After a dozen years in the building, Kulle was every faculty member's go-to. He knew where everything was, an impressive feat in a four-story behemoth of a building that occupied an entire city block. Science teachers could count on him to escort students down to the school's drafty basement to grab beakers, acids, and other materials for experiments. Guidance counselors sought him out when a career fair or college test was approaching, and Kulle would invariably prepare the "extra touches" for which he had become famous among the faculty.

They did not always even need to seek him out. One day, he saw a colleague frantically setting up a career fair. When the man anxiously explained that he was running behind, Kulle immediately reassigned his crew to take over the setup.[3]

Sometimes, Kulle's staff felt he could be too demanding. One colleague complained that Kulle had forcefully rushed the crew as they cleaned the carpet in the library. Kulle brushed off the complaint. Some of his staff members were out, he explained to administrators, and he had simply asked the others to help out; it was nothing he would not do himself. It was true. If another custodian was absent, Kulle simply took on their responsibilities. But he had little tolerance for insubordination. When he learned once that someone had complained about him to a supervisor, Kulle berated the offending colleague. "You'd better wake up," Kulle yelled, "or I'll show you. I gave you your job. You talked behind my back." The scared colleague requested that the administration ask Kulle to treat him and the other employees with respect and not threaten them.[4] But the administrators knew that Kulle got results, and combative interactions were, for the most part, infrequent. His staff was among the best in the building, and the school was renowned for its cleanliness.

Kulle rarely missed a day of work. He worked through injuries—the time his hand had slipped through a glass window when he was cleaning it, or the time a few months later when he had stepped on a wooden board and nails had punctured his shoe, lacerating his foot.[5] While the other supervisors kept to their offices, Kulle continued washing the hallway floors with the power scrubber and cleaning the library carpet on his hands and knees. A staff member even complained that Kulle's drive and hard work diminished opportunities for overtime, but Kulle took pride in keeping the building clean, and the faculty, administration, and staff respected him for it.[6]

As teachers emptied from their classrooms, Kulle walked to the fieldhouse, which Oak Parkers were quick to point out was one of the largest built in an American high school. He stopped to chat with the German women who worked in the girls' gym building and the pool area before heading over to the electricians and carpenters. Before going upstairs to check on his staff, he went to the auditorium to make sure the theater students had everything they needed, and that the hallways were quiet for their rehearsals. The rehearsals took place during his shift, and the students often became friendly with him on their breaks between scenes. When the rehearsals ended, Kulle made sure the students had safe ways to get home, sometimes even calling their parents to double-check that they had arrived safely. If a student was rowdy during a play, he would look them in the eye, commanding them through a thick accent: "You will be quiet now." Watching their classmates cower in fear, the theater students could not help giggling.[7]

By the time Kulle climbed the stairs to the fourth floor, Ali and Frazier were well into the fight. Kulle could hear the broadcast over Heneghan's transistor radio, and stopped in for periodic updates. He and Heneghan's father had worked together on the custodial staff years earlier, and Kulle had taken a liking to the young man, who was working part-time to help pay his college tuition. Heneghan was studying to be a history teacher, and his strong interest in European history gave Kulle a chance to talk about the home he had long ago left—about life in Germany before the war, and life after it. He often leaned against a bookshelf as he and Heneghan discussed anything from sports to President Nixon. But if Heneghan asked about the war itself, Kulle was quieter. He had mentioned the Eastern Front, getting wounded, and something about motorcycles; but Heneghan did not want to pry, and it was clear that Kulle did not want to say much more.

As the heavyweight battle wore on, Kulle returned to Heneghan more frequently. With Ali's politics pushing further and further to the left, especially on the Vietnam War and civil rights, the fight had taken on a political and social dimension not seen since Joe Louis and Max Schmeling faced off in the 1930s, symbols of the simmering tensions between Louis's United States and Schmeling's Germany. Kulle was rooting for Frazier, and as the fight entered the fifteenth round he returned to Heneghan's room for the final minutes. Frazier landed a strong left hook, sending Ali to the mat. Ali got back up, but a few minutes later it was over—Ali's first professional loss.

As the fight broadcast concluded, Kulle reminisced about the Louis-Schmeling fights that had captivated the world decades earlier. The German heavyweight, Kulle told his young companion, had been "the best in his day." Heneghan was surprised to hear Kulle talk so openly and fondly about Hitler's favorite boxer.[8]

At 8 p.m., Heneghan and the other part-time staffers left for the night, and Kulle and the other custodians finished preparing the building for the next morning. It was only a few hours before the first teachers would be arriving for another day of instruction in the area's best-maintained high school building.[9]

* * *

One day, Jim Eitrheim, an English teacher and the school's theater director, saw Kulle barreling toward him. Why, Kulle demanded, had Eitrheim removed him from the auditorium during plays? They were friends—good friends—but Kulle's frustration was palpable. Eitrheim was confused. Kulle had never worked directly with the production of plays. Eitrheim tried to explain that he had no say in how Kulle was assigned, that perhaps the decision had come from Kulle's boss, the director of buildings and grounds. But Kulle did not seem convinced.

The next day, Eitrheim wrote a memo to the administration about the tense interaction. Kulle, he began, "is honest, conscientious, hard working, and a real gentleman." Kulle was an excellent custodian and an incredible asset in his current role, but Eitrheim had another idea he wanted to run by the administration. He seemed to think the school was misusing Kulle's abilities. With rebellion against authority an increasingly salient issue in the United States, OPRF had been trying to implement a stricter discipline system, and there was something different about Kulle—a sternness and quiet power that he alone seemed to have. "While I do not decide if he should be present at all public functions," Eitrheim noted, "could I suggest if a security force of any kind is needed during a play that this school could find no one on the faculty or staff more capable."[10]

* * *

On his weekend rounds, Kulle would often find Rich Deptuch, the beloved head of the school's math department, working in his classroom. Deptuch had left a much better-paying job to become a teacher, and had bought a house located a short walk from the high school. To earn extra money, he joined recent graduates and some other young teachers on the summer paint crew, which required coordination with Kulle. The men took a liking to one another, and Deptuch sometimes joined Kulle for lunch. On other days, Deptuch and the other painters ate quickly so they could spend the second half of their lunch break playing basketball, or heading up to a lounge on the fourth floor where the special education department kept a ping-pong table.

One day, as the painters were volleying back and forth, Kulle came charging into the room. "How could you do that? Now I have to do the whole floor again!" Kulle scolded, pointing to the floor he had just finished buffing.

The next day, it was as if Kulle had forgotten the whole thing. But Deptuch now knew to check the floors before grabbing a paddle.[11]

At the end of each summer, the Deptuchs hosted a picnic to close out the painting season. The Kulles were among the twenty or so OPRF couples to join, and Kulle always seemed to make time for Deptuch's young daughters.

After a few years at home, Deptuch's wife began working night shifts at the hospital down the street from their home. After dinner, Deptuch would take the girls to the school so that his wife could get a few hours of sleep before work. They played and made artwork in his classroom as he graded problem sets and crafted lesson plans. Kulle would whisk them down to the cafeteria for a soft drink or candy bar, relishing the role of surrogate grandfather and happy to give Deptuch a few minutes of quiet. Later, when Deptuch was advising the school's student council, he and Kulle worked together to coordinate dances, talent shows, and other events. On Sundays after dances, Kulle helped student council members remove the decorations. If they needed anything, they could bypass the school's bureaucracy and go straight to Kulle.[12]

When community groups used the high school's space, Kulle made sure their events ran smoothly. The West Suburban Special Recreation Association, which hosted a basketball tournament for kids with disabilities, singled Kulle out in a thank-you note to the school, calling him "extremely helpful with our arrangements."[13] The school was Kulle's domain. If there was an event, on the weekend or in the evening, he wanted to be there.

"At night," a local newspaper explained, "he's boss at [the] high school."[14]

8

HOLTZMAN

Elizabeth Holtzman and a trusted staffer were in her congressional office at the Longworth House Office Building, unsure what to expect from the meeting that was about to begin. A whistleblower had requested a confidential audience. Other whistleblowers had come to her before—usually crooks and cranks with wild accusations. She prepared herself to nod politely, assuage the man's concerns, and get back to work.[1]

Though she had been in Congress for less than a year, Holtzman already had a reputation as a fierce and principled champion of liberal causes. The previous fall, the thirty-one-year old Harvard-educated attorney had unseated a fifty-year incumbent, becoming at the time the youngest woman ever elected to Congress. Almost immediately, she had pierced through the boys' club that was the US Congress, pushing for the Equal Rights Amendment and fighting against President Richard Nixon's bombing campaign in Cambodia. Soon she would serve on the Judiciary Committee, recommending Nixon's impeachment. A few years later she would boldly ask President Gerald Ford if his pardon of Nixon was part of a quid pro quo. "Liz the Lion Killer," *Time* magazine dubbed her.[2]

"There is a matter that is troubling me greatly," the man began, his tone serious. "The Immigration Service has a list of Nazi war criminals living in America, and it is doing nothing about it."[3]

Holtzman's mind raced through stories of gas chambers, sadistic experiments on twins, and mass shootings at ravines. She looked at the man in front of her with confusion. He wore a jacket and tie, spoke well, and appeared rational. She knew a few Nazis had come into the country. Newspapers had reported about the failed efforts to extradite Andrija Artukovic, and the meandering case against Hermine Braunsteiner Ryan, but both seemed like anomalies. She looked at her staffer, who seemed equally thrown. She nodded along, trying to appear polite, but the idea that the INS was sitting on a list of Nazis seemed utterly implausible.

Before the meeting ended, the man paused. He was not Jewish, he told her, but Armenian. That the United States was harboring Nazis brought him deep shame. He hoped Holtzman, a member of the House immigration subcommittee, would be able to do something about it. But Holtzman was bewildered by the charges.[4] Over the next few months she tried to put the bizarre conversation out of her head, but a series of reports in the *New York Times* made her question her skepticism.[5] In December 1973, the US attorney who oversaw the Braunsteiner Ryan case committed suicide, and the paper assigned the reporter Ralph Blumenthal to cover the story. Blumenthal quickly learned of the dissatisfaction within INS ranks, and was intrigued. Nazi war criminals living in America would be an interesting thread to pull on an otherwise dry story about a government bureaucrat's death.[6]

Few reporters would have had the wherewithal to pull such a thread. In the early 1970s, the Holocaust was just starting to make its way into undergraduate and graduate curricula, though it remained largely in the purview of Jewish scholars and students.[7] At the secondary-school level there was no systemic or widespread curriculum outside of some instruction of *The Diary of Anne Frank* or of pieces of Holocaust literature.[8] But Blumenthal was uniquely prepared to examine the story of Nazi perpetrators in America. He had read the earlier reports by Allen and Lelyveld, and had attended the Eichmann trial in Jerusalem. Just a few years earlier, while on assignment in Germany, he had even done a Nazi investigation of his own, reporting on the Nazi past of a Catholic prelate in Munich.[9]

On a tip from Wiesenthal, Blumenthal began looking into a Michigan man whom Wiesenthal referred to as "the bishop." This bishop, Valerian Trifa, had been the subject of suspicion for years. At the YIVO Institute for Jewish Research in Lower Manhattan, Blumenthal poured over Romanian newspapers and other archival materials from the 1940s. What he found in the five hundred pages of documentary evidence was shocking. In mid-December he flew to Grass Lake, Michigan, to interview Trifa, now the archbishop of the Romanian Orthodox Episcopate of America. Blumenthal asked Trifa flat out if he had been a member of the fascist Iron Guard organization. No, Trifa said—until Blumenthal produced a picture of him in an Iron Guard uniform. Trifa then acknowledged wearing the uniform, but claimed he had not done anything untoward. Next, Blumenthal pulled out the text of Trifa's virulently antisemitic speech that instigated a pogrom against the Jews of Bucharest. Trifa admitted giving the speech, but claimed he had not written it.[10] One by one, the thirty-two-year-old reporter broke down Trifa's defenses. The day after Christmas, Holtzman and Americans across the country awoke to Blumenthal's headline on the front page of the *New York Times*: "Bishop under Inquiry on Atrocity Link."[11]

First Artukovic, then Braunsteiner Ryan, now Trifa. A few days later, Blumenthal broke the dam altogether. Just before New Year's, he published a detailed report about the state of Nazi hunting in America. There were seven suspected Nazis in New York alone, including a Long Island carpenter named Boleslavs Maikovskis and a former Estonian concentration camp administrator named Karl Linnas. The INS had thirty-eight active investigations, but somehow, all had stalled. The lack of progress was truly mind-boggling. The INS had been inundated with letters about Trifa for decades, but had yet to take any serious action. And although the Soviets had convicted both Maikovskis and Linnas in absentia, the INS was still "investigating" the cases. After the frustratingly slow pace of the Braunsteiner Ryan prosecution, the INS's fledgling efforts on these investigations were too much for Schiano, who abruptly resigned, citing "irregularities." DeVito did the same, claiming that his investigation into Maikovskis was stymied by higher-ups at the INS.

In light of these reports, Holtzman could not help but wonder if the claims of the whistleblower who had visited her office were true.[12] Soon she would have an opportunity to find out. Her subcommittee was holding routine oversight hearings with INS leadership, and she decided to ask whether the INS was really doing nothing with its list of Nazis. Holtzman was sure the INS officials would tell her that no such list existed, but when she asked, INS Commissioner Leonard F. Chapman made no such denial. She almost fell out of her seat.[13]

"Last December," she said, citing Blumenthal's articles as she tried to regain her composure, "the *Times* mentioned there were thirty-eight persons whose names have been submitted to the Immigration Service. Can you tell me whether any of these thirty-eight persons have been deported since this article appeared last December?"

None had been deported, Chapman said.

"Let me ask you this: Have deportation proceedings been initiated against any of the thirty-eight persons named in that article?

"No."

Holtzman pressed on. "Do you intend in the near future to commence deportation proceedings in any case?"

"No."

"I am surprised that no effort has been made," she responded in dismay.[14]

Later that day, Holtzman issued a press release calling the INS's inaction "outrageous."[15] Within forty-eight hours, immigration authorities announced they had enough "new information" to open an expanded investigation into Trifa, though months earlier they had read the same documents as Blumenthal.[16]

Still somewhat new to Congress, Holtzman had no idea whether she was entitled to access the INS's files. But when she asked, nobody said no.

A week later, she was in Lower Manhattan, staring at a series of files stacked on a metal table. The first file contained allegations that an Eastern European immigrant had committed atrocities against Jews during the war. Notes from an INS investigator accompanied the allegations. The official had visited the suspect's home, rung the doorbell, and indicated he was from the INS. He had asked how the accused was doing, how he felt, how his health was. Then he had left.

Holtzman closed the file, and moved to the next one. It was the same. After a few more, she left, feeling nauseous. There had been no serious investigation of any of the suspects. All the INS had done was ask how former Nazi perpetrators were feeling. Later, she would quip that the Immigration and Naturalization Service had become a public health organization for aging Nazis.[17]

Holtzman lambasted the INS for "an appalling laxness and superficiality," and called for the creation of a specialized War Crimes Strike Force that would have full responsibility for Nazi cases. She dismissed Commissioner Chapman's excuses, curtly telling the former Marine that he could "be assured of my continued interest in this matter."[18]

Hoping to placate Holtzman and give the appearance of taking action, the INS released the list of names Otto Karbach had provided, and centralized Nazi investigations in a dedicated office. It was little more than a public relations stunt. The new office had a shoestring budget, minimal staff, and no authority to ask foreign countries for documents.[19]

The publicity generated from Holtzman's pushing, however, elicited more names from Nazi hunters. In 1975 another list of suspects emerged, this one from Michael Hanusiak, the American-born editor of New York's *Ukrainian Daily News*. His book, *Lest We Forget*, named seventy alleged Nazi collaborators from Ukraine.

Hanusiak's list took a circuitous route to the INS, coming via Senator Jacob Javits of New York. Hanusiak did not fully trust the INS, but the INS also had reason not to trust Hanusiak. He was a member of the Communist Party, and his pro-Russian newspaper was rumored to be a Soviet outlet. Sam Zutty, the INS's new head of Nazi investigations, was both curious and skeptical, knowing that Soviet agents could have had a hand in producing the list. Lacking the resources to investigate all seventy names, Zutty decided to focus on the most promising leads. Among them were John Demjanjuk and Feodor Fedorenko.[20]

More names followed. In the mid-1970s, articles in Russian and

Yiddish presses alleged that Yale professor Vladimir Sokolov had been deputy editor-in-chief of a Nazi newspaper in Russia. Accusations had followed Sokolov since as early as 1954, but he had deftly navigated them, telling colleagues that his staunchly anti-Bolshevik wartime writings had provoked a KGB smear campaign. His earlier protestations of innocence had staved off pressure, but the new allegations, including those in Chaim Suller's newspaper *Morgen Freiheit*, quoted articles in which Sokolov had enthusiastically called for genocide of the Jews.[21]

Four of Sokolov's colleagues in the Slavic Language Department penned an open letter expressing their "profound feeling of disgust and outrage at these documented revelations."[22] Yale's administration claimed that the university could not take action; Sokolov had not violated his contract, and at sixty-three he was only two years from retirement. After a private meeting with the provost, Sokolov resigned; in exchange, he received a full year's salary as a severance payment, along with his pension.

The response from Sokolov's supporters followed the same patterns that Russell Ryan had displayed a decade earlier. At first, they denied the accusations. "I couldn't believe such a gentle, tolerable and just man could have done something so unjust," one student said, noting Sokolov's strong reputation among the student body. Sokolov continued claiming that the accusation was part of a KGB plot.[23]

In the face of mounting evidence, Sokolov's colleagues began downplaying his crimes, noting that he had been in a precarious position as an ardent anticommunist, and that he was always motivated by anti-Bolshevism, not antisemitism. They pointed out that he had not violated his contract or broken the law, and insisted that he harbored none of the antisemitism that had typified his vitriolic wartime writing. Sokolov played along as well, protesting that his anti-Bolshevism had been changed to antisemitism by his Nazi editors. "I was under the control of the censor," he told the *Yale Daily News*.[24]

Soon, the discourse on campus turned to the four professors who had first pushed against him, and the question of forgiveness. Calling their letter "hasty," the college newspaper's editorial page accused the professors of showing contempt for due process. Another student praised Sokolov for "leaving behind such an antagonistic atmosphere, so lacking in compassion and so abundant in intolerance."[25]

"What he did 35 years ago horrifies me," one of Sokolov's close friends and colleagues explained, "but the question is do we recognize redemption or not?"[26]

As Sokolov's friends searched in vain for a redemption arc, Jewish communities expressed outrage at the presence of Nazis on American soil. In 1974 the Society of the Survivors of the Riga Ghetto protested in front of Boleslavs Maikovskis's home, and members of the extremist Jewish Defense League (JDL) demonstrated against Artukovic in California. Two years later, on the anniversary of the liberation of Nazi camps, forty Jews staged a two-hour protest in front of the INS's New York office, demanding the removal of Maikovskis and other former Nazis. Worried that the government's failures would continue, the Anti-Defamation League organized its own investigative task force.[27]

Blumenthal continued his reporting. When accused Nazis refused to answer his questions, he walked up and down their blocks to talk to people who knew them. In neighborhood after neighborhood, behind door after door, Americans spoke kindly of the former Nazis living in their midst. Bronius Kaminskas's landlady told Blumenthal that the man who stood accused of shooting two hundred Jews—including sixty-eight children—and sending another four hundred to their executions was a good man. He "no can kill a fly," she protested. Another neighbor warmly recalled Kaminskas riding his bicycle around the neighborhood, collecting materials to make toys for kids.[28]

On November 15, 1976, the CBS television program *60 Minutes* devoted a segment to the Maikovskis case, including an interview with Dr. Gertrude Schneider. The reporter Mike Wallace came to Mineola, New York, but Maikovskis refused to talk to him. A Jewish survivor told Wallace that she planned to testify against Maikovskis because she owed it to those who had perished. But at a local bar, Maikovskis's neighbors told Wallace that the case should be dropped. After all, they explained, it had been thirty years. Maikovskis was a friendly man; he tended to his garden and regularly attended church.[29]

On the western shores of Lake Champlain, the tight-knit Latvian community in Dresden, New York, dismissed accusations that Maikovskis's friend Vilis Hāzners had forced Jews inside Riga's Choral Synagogue and had set the building ablaze. "I can't believe it," one neighbor said. "When somebody is like that, it shows." Hāzners's neighbors called the retiree industrious, noting the hours he spent working on his property and his well-kept garden. Another woman told a reporter that Latvians had not been willing participants in Nazi murders.[30]

In Baltimore, residents praised the impressive garden Karlis Detlavs kept, and called the former Latvian Legion member a "model neighbor." "War is war," Karl Linnas's neighbor said with a shrug when Blumenthal asked about the former concentration camp administrator. "All I know is that he is a nice man and a good neighbor."[31]

The situation was baffling. In the *New York Times*, the prominent psychologist Robert Jay Lifton noted the "ease with which each man shifts from enthusiastic participation in genocide to proper middle-class life." While the Jewish community focused on the former, Lifton wrote, "neighbors see, and want to believe in, only the latter."[32]

* * *

Despite the growing intrigue, the INS made little progress. There were curious notations on some of the files, and Holtzman grew increasingly suspicious that other government agencies were somehow involved. There was good reason for her suspicion. Late in 1976, Blumenthal reported that Edgars Laipenieks, an alleged Latvian collaborator, carried copies of letters from the CIA on his person at all times, and bragged that he would never be deported.[33] By the end of the year, Anthony DeVito was publicly accusing his bosses of being part of ODESSA.[34]

DeVito's claims were retold in *Wanted! The Search for Nazis in America*, a provocative book by *Village Voice* reporter Howard Blum. With dramatic flair and conspiratorial intrigue, Blum wrote of the

investigations into Tscherim Soobzokov, Valerian Trifa, Andrija Artukovic, and Boleslavs Maikovskis. But the center of the book was De-
Vito's fight against a supposed pro-Nazi network inside the American
government. A prefatory note to the reader declared that the book
was "a true story," though there were no citations or footnotes. De-
Vito's former colleague Vincent Schiano rejected many of the claims
in the book, saying that his former friend "exaggerates and out-and-
out lies."[35]

Still, in the wake of Blumenthal's investigative reporting, *Wanted!*
created a public stir. A few weeks after the book's release, Holtzman
and Congressman Joshua Eilberg called for investigations and hearings.[36] The public pressure seemed to have an impact once again. At
the end of January, the INS filed a denaturalization case against Frank
Walus in Chicago, accusing him of having beaten and murdered Jews
as a member of the Gestapo. The case was brought largely on the basis
of an accusation from a disgruntled former tenant and a decades-old
grainy photo. Presiding over the court was the eighty-three-year-
old Judge Julius Hoffman, infamous for his cynical and antagonistic
conduct during the "Chicago Seven" trial a few years earlier.[37]

In February the INS initiated deportation proceedings against Hāzners. It soon came out that Radio Liberty, the federally funded radio
station that broadcasted pro-American messages inside the Soviet
Union, had been buying scripts from Hāzners. Under pressure from
Jewish groups and Jewish members of Congress, Radio Liberty announced that it would stop featuring Hāzners's pieces.[38]

New deportation proceedings against Artukovic followed in April,
and the INS filed denaturalization charges against both John Demjanjuk and Feodor Fedorenko later that year.[39] The filings did not quell
concerns about the INS's handling of Nazi investigations. Cases were
sloppily prepared, attorneys often lacked the necessary historical
knowledge, and coordination between government agencies proved
challenging. The INS never managed to bring a successful case against
Trifa, even with all of Blumenthal's sleuthing. Attorneys mishandled
evidence in the Hāzners proceedings, and a judge dismissed the case
against Karlis Detlavs for lack of evidence.[40]

Members of the Jewish Defense League tried to take matters into their own hands. Someone who claimed to be the head of the group's Chicago chapter sprayed Walus with mace as he left court, and the JDL led multiple demonstrations outside Maikovskis's home. Mainstream Jewish groups denounced the JDL's actions, worried that they would have an adverse effect.[41]

The Holocaust, though, was taking an increasing role in American public discourse. A Jewish assemblyman in Brooklyn proposed mandating Holocaust education in New York City schools, and the New York City Board of Education produced a four-hundred-page curriculum titled *The Holocaust: A Case Study in Genocide*. The Philadelphia school system began implementing a Holocaust curriculum of its own, and several academic conferences on the Holocaust received significant press coverage.[42]

The attention was quickly met with opposition. The German-American Committee of Greater New York demanded that the proposed Holocaust course be dropped; the group's president reportedly complained that there was "no real proof" that the Holocaust had happened in the first place. M. T. Mehdi, president of the American-Arab Relations Council, dismissed Holocaust education as "an attempt by the Zionists to use the city educational system for their evil propaganda purposes."[43] In Philadelphia, the German-American Citizens' League requested a moratorium on the teaching of Holocaust studies. The tension was particularly palpable in Chicago, home to one of the country's largest German communities. There, the *Abenpost-Sonntagpost* newspaper collected thousands of signatures on a petition requesting that local officials limit Holocaust education, supposedly to prevent anti-German prejudice.[44]

Following Wernher von Braun's death in June, many of the public obituaries avoided mention of his Nazi past, but the *Washington Star* referred to his NASA employment as a "Faustian" bargain, and the *Washington Post* noted that he was both a "space pioneer" and a "rocket builder by appointment to Adolf Hitler."[45] Several letters debating von Braun's legacy appeared in the *Star*, and more precise details about his Nazi past would come out in the next few years.

In the fall, as the congressional hearings Holtzman called for were set to begin, the new INS commissioner announced the creation of a Washington-based Special Litigations Unit (SLU) to run the Nazi cases. Martin Mendelsohn, a Washington attorney, was made head of the new organization.[46] "I am dismayed at what has been happening," he declared after sitting in on the Hāzners proceedings.[47]

It was this surge of interest that brought Simon Wiesenthal to Triton College, a few miles west of Oak Park, in November 1977. Listening to Wiesenthal's lecture that night, OPRF school board member Leah Marcus pondered what at the time seemed like a terrifying hypothetical. What would Oak Park do if a Nazi was found in its midst?

* * *

In May 1978, the Government Accountability Office (GAO) finished its investigation, dismissing DeVito's accusations of a "widespread conspiracy." It did confirm Holtzman's suspicions, however, that the CIA had employed former Nazis. The report blamed the government's failures on a lack of expertise and a lack of will. Finding former Nazis had simply not been a priority.[48] Holtzman remained determined to make it one. Since 1975 she had been working on a bill to close loopholes left open by the postwar immigration laws, and to make easier the deportation of former Nazis.[49]

There seemed to finally be some momentum. In April 1978, 120 million Americans tuned in to NBC's four-part television miniseries *Holocaust*. The series, along with an attempt to hold a neo-Nazi rally in Skokie, a heavily Jewish suburb of Chicago, had a striking popular impact. The destruction of European Jewry was at the forefront of public discourse. Plans for a presidential commission on the Holocaust were soon underway.[50]

At the end of May, the INS won a rare victory. Despite the best efforts of Frank Walus's attorney, Robert Korenkiewicz, Judge Hoffman stripped Walus of his citizenship. There was just one problem: Walus had spent the war on a work farm in Poland. He had not been a Nazi.[51]

As Holtzman readied her bill to appear before Congress, a series of more aggressive confrontations ensued. Rabbi Paul Silton, who had recently brought Charles Allen to speak at his synagogue, led twenty campers and staff members to stage a protest at Hāzners's home. Silton had chosen the day purposefully. It was Tisha b'Av, a fast day in the Jewish calendar commemorating a series of destructions and calamities in Jewish history.

"We have to do something about the past," Silton declared, "not just pray about it."

A group of residents challenged the demonstration, holding signs reading "Go home, Jew Gestapo" and "Jews are a vengeful people." A man identifying himself as "John Christian" denounced the charges against Hāzners as Communist propaganda; identifying himself as a member of the white supremacist Christian Defense League, he defended Hāzners as a "good and gentle man, incapable of atrocities."[52]

On August 4, 1978, someone fired shots through Maikovskis's back door, striking him in the leg. Police found a JDL insignia on his porch, but the group denied involvement. A spokesperson told reporters, "The tragedy is he was just shot in the leg. A man like that deserves to die." The executive director of the American Jewish Congress condemned the shooting, saying, "This violence beclouds the issue and inspires sympathy for those accused to [sic] heinous crimes. It diverts public anger and lends plausibility to the claim of vindictive persecution. Those who want to really see war criminals punished must join in condemning this cruel, pointless and stupid act."[53]

A month later, another tense scene developed in Paterson, New Jersey, as the JDL and throngs of protesters marched toward Tscherim Soobzokov's row house. Soobzokov sat defiantly on his porch as chants led by the JDL grew louder and closer: "How do we want Soobzokov? Dead!" Soobzokov's friends and other immigrants booed and jeered, holding signs of support for the accused Nazi. Soobzokov would receive other, more prominent support in the coming years, both from his congressman, Robert Roe, and from the conservative firebrand Patrick J. Buchanan.[54]

The House of Representatives passed Holtzman's bill in September, and the Senate followed a month later. President Jimmy Carter signed the bill on October 30, 1978, and it became Public Law 95-549. Known colloquially as the "Holtzman Amendment," the new law amended the Immigration and Nationality Act to deem ineligible anyone who—on behalf of or in coordination with the Nazi government of Germany—"ordered, incited, assisted, or otherwise participated in the persecution of any person because of race, religion, national origin, or political opinion." Former Nazis could be denaturalized and deported if they had participated in Nazi persecution or had procured their visa through fraud.[55]

In a press statement, Holtzman declared, "The sorry record of our government over the past 30 years in allowing known Nazi war criminals to live undisturbed in this country has been amply documented. This action confirms my belief that it is not too late to make our stand against war crimes clear and unequivocal."[56] Mendelsohn worked closely with Holtzman to determine the best ways for the SLU to support the cases the INS already had in litigation, traveling across the country to meet with the US attorneys bringing them to trial. But even with Mendelsohn's steady hand at the helm, the new Special Litigations Unit had little chance at success. It was understaffed and underfunded, and the INS's files were often missing, incomplete, or gone to what Mendelsohn called "File Heaven."[57]

There were also two major flaws in the INS approach to Nazi cases. The prevailing strategy relied on eyewitness identification, but the events in question had happened thirty years earlier. Additionally, judges—and sometimes INS attorneys as well—lacked the requisite historical background. The judge in the Fedorenko case did not seem to recognize the distinction between slave labor camps and killing centers, and accepted several ahistorical claims made by the defense, including that Fedorenko had still been a prisoner of war while serving as a guard at Treblinka. In dismissing the case against Fedorenko, the judge even referred to the former death camp guard as a "victim of Nazi aggression."[58]

Mendelsohn urged the solicitor general to appeal the decision. It should not have mattered that Fedorenko had once been a prisoner of war, that he was on good behavior in the United States, or that the judge had concerns about the credibility of the eyewitness identifications. Fedorenko had lied on his visa, and had admitted to being a guard at Treblinka. "There were no neutrals at a death camp," Mendelsohn keenly noted.[59]

Mendelsohn ably worked to right the ship, but there was too much stacked against the Special Litigations Unit. In front of Holtzman's subcommittee in 1979, Assistant Attorney General Michael Egan admitted that the SLU had "not worked out as we had hoped," and reluctantly transferred Nazi investigations to the Justice Department.[60] A newly constituted unit opened as the Office of Special Investigations (OSI), a branch of the prestigious Criminal Division. Armed with a legal mechanism and a dedicated enforcement agency, OSI staffed up, ready to hit the ground running and make up for lost time.[61]

9

STANDING GUARD

After more than fifteen years at OPRF, Kulle had become something of an institution. He had no formal contract, but there was no need. He adored the school, and the feeling was mutual. OPRF compensated him well, and he earned more money than many of the teachers.[1]

As his English improved, Kulle formed strong friendships with his colleagues, inviting them out to Oktoberfest celebrations and giving recommendations and reviews of Chicago's German restaurants. Students in Herr Schoepko's German classes occasionally tried to practice with Kulle in the hallways. He would engage politely and briefly, before returning to his work. A more awkward encounter came when the theater department asked whether the set for their production of the *The Sound of Music* looked authentic. He shrugged; it was not worth explaining that he was a German citizen from a town that was now in Poland, and that the play's story took place in Austria.[2]

Kulle's children were starting families of their own. Rainer married a Polish immigrant named Bozena and they settled in nearby La Grange. Her parents lived close by, and the Kulles grew friendly with them as well.[3]

Ulricke married too, but in 1975, a few days after Christmas, her husband was killed in a car crash.[4] Their son Juan was only ten, their daughter Patricia just seven. Kulle took the next few days off of work, one of the first times he had ever done so, and did his best to act as a second father to his young grandchildren.[5]

Six months later, Rainer and Bozena welcomed a daughter, Michelle. The Kulles moved nearby and were over most days to play with Michelle and care for Rainer, who was suffering from Crohn's disease and kidney issues. Michelle had health issues, too, including open-heart surgery when she was just three. Kulle and Gertrud helped pay the medical bills, and were a constant presence at Michelle's bedside as she recovered.[6]

Kulle was not the only Nazi in the neighborhood. Albert Deutscher and his wife lived about a mile away in a small white bungalow. In Ukraine, Deutscher had shot and killed hundreds of unarmed Jews, including children. In the suburb of Brookfield, the couple cared for the elderly widow living next door, taking her shopping, caring for her lawn, and visiting her frequently. If anyone on the block needed someone handy, they knew to knock on Deutscher's door.

His neighbors never suspected a thing.[7]

**

In April 1976, the National Civic League named Oak Park its "All-America City," largely because of the "unusual racial diversity" that the Oak Park Housing Center fostered. "We know we're a good city," Village President James McClure Jr. commented, "but it's nice to have the efforts of the population recognized."[8]

Not everyone in town was impressed. "The integration programs work for the board," H. Vivian Halliburton told *Chicago Tribune* reporter and future presidential advisor David Axelrod, but it was much too early for Oak Park to celebrate its successes. Only 6 percent of the village's residents were minorities.[9]

A longtime columnist for the *Chicago Defender*, the city's pre-eminent Black newspaper, Halliburton had good reason to question Oak Park's commitment to its ideals. That same year, her run for elementary school board had been narrowly defeated in an election rife with improprieties. The Illinois Board of Elections had refused a recount, though it had agreed that "errors may have cost her the election." Her loss had kept the school board from integrating.[10]

Race was central in the election, and local neo-Nazis had littered

Oak Park with antisemitic and racist leaflets. They had done so periodically in the decade since Oak Park's open housing movement had begun, and on the eve of Yom Kippur, Nazi propaganda appeared on a stop sign just blocks away from River Forest's West Suburban Temple Har Zion.[11]

Halliburton had had enough. She told Axelrod—the son of a Jewish refugee from Eastern Europe—that while there were parts of Oak Park that Blacks could not move into, "if you were a Nazi, you could still move into the community without problem."[12]

* * *

That fall, the National Socialist Party of America (NSPA) sent leaflets to a dozen Chicago suburbs. "WE ARE COMING," the leaflets declared in large letters, with a swastika looming at the side. Formed a few years earlier in Chicago's Marquette Park neighborhood, the NSPA was led by Frank Collin, the former Midwest coordinator of George Lincoln Rockwell's American Nazi Party (ANP).[13] Rockwell had eventually changed the group's name to the National Socialist White People's Party, believing that many Americans who agreed with the party's ideas might bristle at the use of a swastika. Collin, who created the NSPA after Rockwell was assassinated, bore no such qualms. Even by the standards of neo-Nazis, he was crass. He purchased a building near the spot where Dr. King had been attacked, and placed a swastika and an American flag on either side of the entrance. The building, named Rockwell Hall, was just blocks from Western Avenue, the dividing line between Marquette Park and the mostly Black neighborhood of Englewood. Banners with the words "STOP THE NIGGERS!" and "Nigger go home" were frequently affixed to the exterior, and Collin's group was suspected in a slew of violent attacks against Blacks that summer.[14]

Publicity was vital to Collin's strategy. He had spent the better part of a decade staging rallies and various antics to attract attention, sometimes getting into brawls with Jewish and Black groups, which he then spun as evidence that white Chicagoans were under attack. The NSPA relied on the ten thousand dollars or so in annual donations the publicity helped drum up, including money from one major anonymous donor in Oak Park.[15] Struggling to gain traction in the city, and locked in a series of lawsuits over permit applications in Marquette Park, Collin turned his attention to the northern suburbs.[16]

Most suburbs ignored the leaflets and the accompanying petitions Collin sent requesting permits to march. Only Skokie, home to a large community of Holocaust survivors, responded. When rumors spread that Nazis were coming, the survivor community was outraged, and Skokie's Catholic mayor, Albert Smith, along with the village board, passed three ordinances designed to keep Collin out. The neo-Nazis challenged the ordinances in court, and the protracted legal battle garnered Collin the very publicity he had initially sought.[17]

As the case wove through the legal system, Collin continued antagonizing Jews and Holocaust survivors. In the fall of 1977, the NSPA descended on Triton College to protest Simon Wiesenthal's appearance. Dressed in Nazi brownshirts, they gathered outside the building in which Wiesenthal was set to speak. "[Wiesenthal] perpetuates the myth that six million Jews were killed by Hitler," Collin declared to a growing crowd, referencing a scourge of Holocaust denial recently published by Northwestern University engineer Arthur Butz.[18] A second group booed Collin, and Triton police officers nervously eyed the hostile crowd.[19] Then a white-haired man raced through the tangled web of bodies, wrapping his arms around three of the neo-Nazis and bringing them to the ground. Other neo-Nazis repeatedly struck the man with four-foot-long black wooden clubs.

Inside the building, waiting for Wiesenthal to take the stage, Leah Marcus and her son began to hear screams and yells from the melee. Sergeant Ron Dietz rushed out of the lecture hall to respond to the chaos outside, leaving Marcus and the other audience members startled and confused. He was grabbing arms in a vain effort to pull Nazis and counterprotesters apart when one of the neo-Nazis, seventeen-year-old Thomas Krajewski, jumped him from behind. Dietz wriggled free from Krajewski, who then jumped another officer. Collin ordered his men not to stand down, but Triton police regained order, and arrested Collin, Krajewski, and the white-haired man. The two neo-Nazis were ordered to pay a fine.[20]

In May 1978, the Seventh Circuit Court of Appeals struck down the Skokie ordinances as unconstitutional, and the US Supreme Court rejected Skokie's appeal. The Skokie controversy brought Collin increased notoriety, and rival Nazis seized the opportunity to take him down. Collin had long been dogged by accusations that his real name was not Frank Collin but Frank Cohn, and that he was the son of a Jewish survivor of Dachau. While Collin was away from Rockwell Hall, several of his deputies found a significant cache of child pornography in his room, including photographs of Collin posing with his victims. Collin was sentenced to seven years in prison for child molestation. Leadership of the NSPA fell to Harold Covington, and then to Michael Allen, leader of the NSPA branch in St. Louis.[21]

In 1980, largely continuing Collin's strategy, Allen announced plans to rally in Oak Park. "It will be 1923 Germany all over again," he warned an *Oak Leaves* journalist, referencing Hitler's Beer Hall Putsch. Bombastic and threatening, Allen explained that he had chosen Oak Park "because it is a racially changing neighborhood," knowing that the paper would quote him and provide him with free publicity.[22]

It worked. On August 27, 1980, the *Oak Leaves* reported that the Nazis were coming, and an anxious but indignant frenzy took over Oak Park.

When Allen and a deputy showed up at Village Hall to request a permit to march, Oak Park was ready. Three years earlier, scores of Oak Parkers had gone to Skokie to counterprotest Collin's attempted rally there. Now a large crowd of anti-Nazi protestors were heckling Allen, and the village president read a statement about Oak Park's commitment to racial diversity. The police chief told Allen he could not guarantee the Nazis' safety. Oak Park was unanimous in its disgust for the neo-Nazis, but there was still the question of how to handle the rally itself.[23]

On September 3, 1980, Norman Roth walked up to the podium in Village Hall. The longtime labor activist quoted Justice Robert H.

Jackson's opening statement at Nuremberg, and argued that the First Amendment did not protect the Nazis' planned march. Other speakers followed, imploring the Village Board to deny the Nazis a permit.[24]

The local synagogues held emergency meetings. In the sanctuary at Oak Park Temple, David Sokol, one of the village trustees, listened as his fellow congregants expressed their fears with a sense of resignation. Sokol knew the discussion was futile. He and the other trustees had already met with the police chief and the head of the Parks Department, and had agreed that they could not prevent the rally. The Skokie case made the decision easy; trying to stop the rally would give the Nazis more attention, and would cost the village thousands in litigation. They had no choice but to allow the rally. The police would take away any signs that could be used as weapons, the bathrooms would be kept locked, and large pebbles would be cleared from the park. They would give the neo-Nazis as little press as possible.[25]

On Monday, September 15, reporters from the *Oak Leaves*, the *Wednesday Journal*, and some of the larger television channels from Chicago were present at the Village Board meeting to see whether Oak Park would allow the march. The trustees knew that the local weekly newspapers were typeset and sent to printers on Tuesdays. The city outlets had deadlines, too, if they were to include the story in the Tuesday papers or on their broadcasts. The trustees planned to stall their announcement until late at night, after the reporters' deadlines had passed.[26]

The meeting opened with public testimony. One woman asked the Village Board to stop the rally because it would incite violence. Roth again implored the board to take a clear stand against Nazism, stressing the importance of educating both older and younger generations about the Holocaust. Another resident asked the board to prevent the rally so that Oak Park could "retain its positive image."

The board began to stall, discussing everything from zoning appeals to the appropriate number of overnight parking spaces, and to "questions regarding the height of the eye-beam on which the gates were hung." Around 1 a.m., after most of the press had left, the Village

Board offered the neo-Nazis permit for September 27, just twelve days later, leaving Allen little time to advertise. The *Wednesday Journal* was unable to publish more than a seven-sentence story in its September 17 issue.[27]

Community leaders urged Oak Parkers to ignore the Nazis and avoid becoming Michael Allen's pawns. The two local synagogues issued a joint statement that they would not dignify "the vile actions of the American Nazi party by protesting their presence in Oak Park, and thereby draw attention to their viciousness." Sokol decided to take his kids to Michigan.[28]

Others wanted a stronger response. One Black woman stressed the importance of showing the Nazis that they did not instill fear, and others argued that a counterprotest would show "solidarity with our fellow residents." A veteran who had been to Dachau shortly after its liberation asked the *Oak Leaves* to print the history of the Nazis, the Holocaust, and the silence of the world. Another Oak Parker yearned for the days when he could have used "a little tar and some feathers."[29]

On the day of the rally, a diverse group of forty-five Jews, Blacks, and Christians gathered at the Unitarian Universalist Church to discuss the legacy of the Nazis. Sokol's wife, Sandra, attended. They watched a film about the neo-Nazi rally in Marquette Park that had replaced the rally planned for Skokie several years earlier, and they invited Holocaust survivors and their relatives to speak. Norman Roth explained that the group's goal was to take a collective stand against antisemitism and other forms of hate. Though they disagreed on tactics, everyone in town agreed: no Nazi was welcome in Oak Park.[30]

✳ ✳ ✳

The rally itself was a flop. The *Oak Leaves* called it "ludicrous," noting that there were 11.5 police officers for each of the thirteen neo-Nazis who came. The *Wednesday Journal* called it "cheap theater." Allen's group was twenty minutes late, and their public address system did not work. The Cook County Sheriff's Department helicopter circling overhead did not help with the sound either. Roughly one hundred members of various leftist and antifascist groups from across the Chicago area counterprotested; some even brought their own portable loudspeakers. The lunch tables that the neo-Nazis had intended to stand on were turned on their sides as a defense from the eggs, stones, tomatoes, dirt, and firecrackers hurled their way. Some neo-Nazis encircled Allen, protecting him from these "flying salads" with homemade shields. A neo-Nazi photographer was struck by a dirt-filled wad of newspaper that jammed his camera. Three Oak Parkers were seen giving the *seig heil*, and they quickly asked police to escort them to their cars, fearful of their neighbors' response. The *Wednesday Journal* described seeing "12-year-old boys bellow the foulest obscenities and hurl whatever was near-at-hand at the ranging band of misfits who think they are Nazis." The village spent nearly thirteen thousand dollars; the neo-Nazis quickly left after forty minutes.[31]

After the rally, a local journalist channeled the disgust many Oak Parkers felt seeing Nazis in their town: "Tired, dirty, and heartbroken, I strolled home, wondering how it could happen here."[32]

Over the next few weeks, Oak Parkers applauded their village's rejection of the Nazis, but H. Vivian Halliburton again thought that Oak Park's self-praise was premature. She wrote to the *Oak Leaves* that "the distance between a Nazi march and a quiet parlor conference—planned to keep blacks off the school board of a village or to fully participate in any meaningful way in the community—is a mere heart beat away!" She ended her letter with a biting critique. "How many Oak Parkers really hated what the Nazis stood for? Or was it merely that they showed so little class?"[33]

* * *

Three years earlier, tucked in the back pages of the *Oak Leaves*, a simple profile of a local high school janitor had described him warmly as a "refugee from East Germany" who kept the floors clean, the kids in line, and the school running on time. The profile was part of a recurring feature highlighting the "very interesting people" in town. "There's something in Reinhold Kulle's voice that tells you he means it," it

Figure 10. Neo-Nazi rally in Oak Park, 1980.
Courtesy of Oak Park Historical Society.

Figure 11. Oak Parkers protesting the neo-Nazi rally, 1980.
Courtesy of Oak Park Historical Society.

began. The article was accompanied by a posed picture of Kulle: shoulders slightly hunched, with a faint smile, and a short-sleeved work shirt tucked into his dark pants. His name was stitched in cursive above the pen in one breast pocket, and he had a small notebook in his other breast pocket. Though he had gained a few pounds, he was still fit: his shoulders broad, his body solid. The huge ring of keys he typically carried for access to every room in the building was just out of sight.

At high school dances, Kulle explained in the article, he walked around to make sure students were not drinking. It was important to set a strict tone at the outset. "When you stop it the first night, then that's all you have to do." Although Kulle was often in close contact with students, he did not get to know them well. He had learned somewhere in his past "not to get too close to the students because those relationships might interfere with his enforcement of the school's rules." When Kulle spoke, the *Oak Leaves* reported, "you are obliged to believe him."

Kulle oversaw the work of thirty custodians, and each evening he made sure the building was ready for the following school day. "Without supervision," the former SS recruit trainer told the paper, "the job would never be done."

The high school was Kulle's domain. "Whether it's an evening class or a little theater event, Kulle is usually there, standing guard," the paper explained.[34]

10

THE OFFICE OF SPECIAL INVESTIGATIONS

A hush filled OPRF's auditorium. The lights dimmed and audience members took their seats. Just offstage, Mary-Terese Cozzola waited for the curtains to rise. Though student-run theater performances like this one were typically held immediately after school, the director—senior Becky Carroll—had successfully petitioned the school to allow an evening performance. The play Becky had chosen, *The Diary of Anne Frank*, was just too important for matinees.

Mary-Terese and the rest of the small cast scanned the growing crowd. They had heard rumors that neo-Nazis were planning to disrupt the performance. It was no idle threat. Over the past few years, Nazi propaganda had shown up on stop signs, car windshields, and even some doorsteps in town. The cast had discussed canceling the show, but the first two performances had gone well, and everything seemed calm now. Mary-Terese had worked hard to prepare for her role as Anne, copying speeches and lines from the play into her own diary, which she used as a prop in the production. Anne's story resonated deeply with Mary-Terese. Had she been born in a different place, with different parents . . . she shuddered at the thought. She was just a few years older than Anne had been; her own father had gone to Europe to fight in that war. The auditorium was filled with friends, classmates, and members of the community; the neo-Nazis were nowhere to be found.[1]

As the story of the Holocaust unfolded on stage, Kulle was just outside, pacing the halls of the Student Center.

* * *

In May 1979 the Justice Department tapped the former Nuremberg prosecutor Walter Rockler to help establish the new Office of Special Investigations, with Mendelsohn serving as his deputy.[2] Joining the leadership team was fifty-one-year-old Charles Gittens, the first Black agent in the Secret Service. A skilled communicator with decades of investigative and operational experience, Gittens would spend the next twenty years as deputy director for operations. He forged law enforcement partnerships in Europe, hired skilled investigators from other agencies, and handled OSI's relationship with Congress.[3]

Having started nearly thirty-five years after the end of the war, OSI was racing against time. Even the youngest suspects were almost sixty years old, and denaturalization and deportation trials rightfully took a long time. OSI's leaders would later compare their task to an aging runner's attempt to set a world record. "In 1980, you have to run a four-minute mile. And then the next year, even though you're a year older, there's even less time now. You have to run it in 3:59. And you get older and older and older and you have to run faster and faster and faster."[4]

OSI's young staff attorneys quickly made up for lost time. In November 1979, Neal Sher and Norman Moscowitz represented OSI in its first trial, a denaturalization proceeding in Philadelphia against the Ukrainian Nazi collaborator Wolodymir Osidach. Then, in Florida, OSI sought to denaturalize Bohdan Koziy, another alleged collaborator from Ukraine, who now owned a tourist motel in Fort Lauderdale. Other trials followed in New Jersey, Baltimore, upstate New York, and Michigan as OSI worked through the INS's long list of unresolved cases.[5]

In early 1980, ABC News aired *Escape from Justice: Nazi War Criminals in America*, advertised as "the most comprehensive examination of Nazis in America ever televised."[6] The documentary opened with a searing depiction of the 1941 Bucharest pogrom that Valerian Trifa had helped to provoke. It showed meat hooks that had impaled the town's Jews, including a five-year-old girl. The hour-long special brought Trifa, Fedorenko, Laipenieks, Artukovic, and Hāzners to living rooms across the country.[7]

Deputy Director Mendelsohn was Rockler's presumed successor, but Rockler was rankled by Mendelsohn's close ties to Holtzman; and in a surprise move that frustrated Jewish groups, he transferred Mendelsohn out of the unit. Instead, higher-ups at Justice eyed Allan Ryan, an attorney with the solicitor general's office.[8] Ryan was deeply troubled by the thought of Nazis in United States, and he followed OSI's creation with great interest. He shared Mendelsohn's dissatisfaction with the INS's reliance on eyewitness identifications, and their failure to provide historical context about the role of camp guards.[9] Ryan was also no stranger to Nazi cases. He had handled the government's appeal of the Fedorenko decision, arguing that guard service at a Nazi camp alone proved Fedorenko's participation in persecution.[10] The appellate court had agreed.

Ryan sought a meeting with Rockler and Phillip Heymann, the head of the Justice Department's Criminal Division, to discuss this approach. He listened intently as Heymann told him Rockler's appointment was temporary, and asked whether he would be interested in becoming OSI's next director. With a successful Nazi case under his belt, Ryan was one of the leading experts in the field. Though it would mean giving up a prestigious title and job security, he wanted the new position.[11] As he moved over to OSI, Fedorenko filed an appeal, arguing that there was no direct evidence of his personal wrongdoing.[12]

Meanwhile, Ryan visited Holtzman, hoping to prove to her, the Anti-Defamation League, and other Jewish groups that despite his being Catholic, he was right for the job. The meeting was tense at first. Holtzman kept Ryan standing until he promised he was not going to drop any of the cases. She was impressed by his ideas, and by his plans to make the investigations international in scope. In time they would become close, and would come to laugh about their uncomfortable first meeting in Holtzman's office.[13]

One of Ryan's first tests came when Robert Korenkiewicz and Charles W. Nixon appealed Judge Hoffman's decision in the *Walus* case, providing new documentary evidence that seemed to exonerate Walus. The evidence was procured in part by Jerome Brentar, a Holocaust denier who would emerge as one of the staunchest opponents of OSI, and who would provide financial support to many accused Nazis.[14]

Ryan ordered an extensive review, and OSI spent the better part of a year tracking down witnesses in Poland, Germany, and Israel. After nine months, OSI dropped the charges, publicly apologized for the INS's errors, and even reimbursed some of Walus's expenses. It was a politically risky decision, especially so early in the office's tenure, as many casual observers would not differentiate the INS from OSI. But OSI's mission was to pursue truth and historical justice, not rack up courtroom victories.[15]

Ryan was disturbed that the INS had brought the *Walus* case forward. Despite the nature of the work, the SLU had not employed any formally trained historians, and had instead relied on investigators borrowed from other agencies, and graduate students fluent in German. OSI began to change that approach in 1980, hiring Dr. Peter Black, who had helped on the Maikovskis case while finishing his dissertation, as the agency's first historian. Over the next few years OSI would hire other historians, each with specialized expertise on a different aspect of the Holocaust. OSI was determined not to repeat the mistakes of the INS.[16]

* * *

After thirty years in the United States, Liudas Kairys had settled in. He had even been promoted to group leader at Cracker Jack's receiving department. But in the late 1970s a newspaper in Soviet-occupied Lithuania described him as a member of the SS, and a communist newspaper in Chicago reprinted the allegations. Kairys nonetheless drew praise from his neighbors. "Louie is a hard-working man," one of them told the *Chicago Sun-Times*.[17] But as the rumors gained steam, the government opened a formal investigation. *Draugas,* the Lithuanian daily, promptly declared that "Kairys was never a German or SS soldier. And he was not guarding any concentration camps."[18] In 1980 OSI formally initiated denaturalization proceedings. Kairys denied the allegations, claiming that he had been forced to dig fenceposts, fix railroad tracks, and make barracks for the Nazis, and charging that the American government was targeting him just as the Soviets and Nazis had done before.[19]

OSI, however, had obtained records from Soviet researchers proving that Kairys had served at the Trawniki training camp and at the Treblinka killing center. At a pretrial hearing in April, OSI attorney Michael Wolf told the court that the government had also matched Kairys's fingerprints to those in his SS personnel file. In response, Kairys claimed that he was being framed by the KGB, though technicians from the FBI crime lab dismissed the possibility. Not only were the fingerprints a match, but a forensic analysis proved a 1942 photograph of Kairys in his SS uniform to be legitimate as well.[20]

At John Demjanjuk's denaturalization hearing the following February, throngs of Ukrainians came to show support, and ten Ukrainian parishes in Cleveland publicly offered prayers. One Ukrainian told the *Cleveland Jewish News* that the community was "not getting involved on the merits of the case—the guilt or innocence of Demjanjuk," but that they wanted "recognition that the Ukrainians are not the bad guys; we are victims of the Holocaust."[21] In court, a group of Ukrainian children wore collarless embroidered blouses to "show our heritage" and "demonstrate our moral support for the Demjanjuk family." One Demjanjuk supporter derisively told a Jewish reporter that they were "doing it for the same reason you are wearing the little hats"—a reference to Jewish skullcaps or *kippot*.[22]

OSI was also building a case against Albert Deutscher, and in December 1981 it formally accused the train car repairman of being a member of a Nazi paramilitary group in the Ukraine, of lying on his visa application, and of participating "in the shooting and killing of many hundreds of unarmed Jewish civilians including women and children."²³ A few hours after OSI filed suit, Deutscher told his bosses that he was not feeling well, and received permission to leave work early. A few minutes later, he ran in front of an oncoming train. In a macabre understatement, a railroad spokesman said the likelihood of an accident was "a little bit remote."²⁴

Just over a mile from Kulle's house, Deutscher's family and neighbors expressed shock. One neighbor called the accusations "ridiculous." She had lived next to Deutscher for years, and he had helped her care for the yard after her husband's death, often cutting the grass or shoveling the snow before she even got home. Another widow said he did the same for her. One woman called the Deutschers "very sweet," and "probably the nicest people on the block." Though someone described Deutscher as aloof and distant, other neighbors expressed hope that the government had it wrong. One rejected the accusations altogether. "I don't believe any of that. I met him. I know him. I like him. I don't believe that."

Deutscher's grief-stricken son Alfred told the *Chicago Tribune* that his father "cared about people." He denied reports that the death was a suicide, explaining that his father "was ready to sell everything he had to prove he was innocent." The police investigator was incredulous, noting that Deutscher had been running in the middle of the track, and that the train's engineer had blown his horn twice. Deutscher's son, though, was steadfast. "No way on earth could he have been involved in those killings," he said of his late father. "His conscience would have killed him first."²⁵

***

As the number of cases mounted, Baltic and Ukrainian immigrant communities eyed OSI with growing distrust. Most of the early defendants were from Eastern Europe, as getting into the United States had been much more difficult for German Nazis like Kulle than for Eastern European collaborators. Osidach, Koziy, Fedorenko, Demjanjuk, and Deutscher were Ukrainian. Maikovskis and Hāzners were from Latvia, Kairys was from Lithuania, and Karl Linnas—whose citizenship had been stripped in 1981, two decades after the Soviets convicted him in absentia—had served as the administrator of a concentration camp in his native Estonia.

Émigré communities claimed they were being targeted and even persecuted by the Justice Department's newest branch, and Ryan met with community leaders to assuage their concerns. He assured them that OSI was only interested in identifying war criminals, and tried unsuccessfully to enlist their support in sorting "the heroes from the collaborators." But the allegations forced a difficult reconciliation with their countrymen's sometimes willing participation in Nazi brutality, and threatened to undermine broader American support for the efforts to liberate their homelands from Soviet occupation.[26]

Latvian-American periodicals showed little interest in discussing Latvian participation in the Nazi genocide, but the growing number of accusations rendered continued silence and denial impossible. Newspapers shifted to downplaying collaboration with the Nazis, arguing that it "had to be understood only as desperate attempts to militarily protect the Latvian nation," as part of a mission to protect Latvia from the threat of Communism.[27]

The Captive Nations movement instead wielded its own historical narrative—one in which the Eastern European fatherlands were alternatively victims of Soviet and German occupation. Father Joseph Prunskis, director of information for the Chicago-based Lithuanian-American Council, even testified in a pretrial hearing in the Kairys case that no Lithuanian had been involved in Nazi murder. Some Nazi collaborators were being hailed as national heroes, their wartime activities portrayed as anti-Soviet resistance. Across Lithuania, plaques, streets, and schools bear the name of Jonas Noreika, despite his principal role in the massacre of the Jews in the town of Plungé weeks before the Nazis' arrival, because he helped organize anti-Soviet partisans after the war.[28]

Leading groups of the Captive Nations movement had another reason to fight against OSI. Organized in the aftermath of the war and comprised largely of right-wing nationalists, they were rife with Nazi

collaborators. The Anti-Bolshevik Bloc of Nations had direct connec-
tions to the Hitlerite regime, and counted a half dozen Nazi collaborators among its ranks. And though anticommunism was the movement's leading doctrine and many of its participants simply wanted to
end Soviet occupation of their homelands, the movement's Nazi roots
were never far below the surface. One organizer of the 1960 Captive
Nations parade was Austin App, a bitter antisemite and Third Reich
apologist who would soon emerge as one of America's foremost Holocaust deniers.[29]

Ethnic newspapers discouraged cooperation with federal investigators, and a wide swath of overlapping networks and organizations
emerged to oppose Nazi-hunting efforts. *Darbininkas*, a Lithuanian
newspaper based in Brooklyn, ran an article titled "How to Defend
Oneself from Attacks by OSI." Ethnic newspapers also promoted legal
defense funds for accused Nazis, including the Chicago-based Fund
for the Defense of Lithuanian Rights and the New York–based Latvian
Truth Fund.[30]

In a January 1982 meeting with Justice Department officials, émigré
leaders demanded that any evidence procured from behind the Iron
Curtain be considered unreliable. The Soviet Union, they claimed, was
using OSI to attack and discredit anti-Soviet activists.[31] They crafted
an entire origin story for this conspiracy theory, charging that the documents provided to Dr. Gertrude Schneider on her Latvian research
trip were part of an elaborate KGB operation to frame Maikovskis, Hāzners, and others.[32] In June, Liudas Kairys's attorney claimed before the
US District Court for the Northern District of Illinois that a longtime
KGB officer had told him Russians had a program of "falsely accusing
[Baltic immigrants] of being Nazi war criminals," with "a special section whose job it was to prepare false documents."[33]

It was, of course, not true. Émigré groups often exaggerated the
extent to which OSI relied on or even used Soviet documents. When
OSI did receive evidence from Soviet prosecutors, the office made significant efforts to authenticate the records, performing forensic anal-
yses and corroborating the documents with information from other

sources.[34] Even after an FBI expert testified that the fingerprints on Kairys's visa application matched the fingerprint on his Nazi files, Kairys's attorney claimed incredibly that the KGB could have taken the INS file, lifted the fingerprints, and created an entire false SS file under Kairys's name.[35]

It made little sense. OSI's defendants were rarely involved in the kind of anti-Communist activism that would have attracted the Soviet Union's attention, and even Kairys acknowledged that he "never made myself political."[36] A longtime friend of Kairys who worked as an editor for *Draugas* testified that "the Soviets are accusing all of us, the emigrants, of participating in war crimes"; but when OSI attorney Norman Moscowitz asked the witness whether he knew of anyone who had been accused other than Kairys, the witness reluctantly answered, "I do not."[37]

American judges rejected these conspiracy theories, but extremist groups like Willis Carto's Liberty Lobby wholeheartedly embraced them. Originally positioned as conservative and anti-Communist, the Liberty Lobby quickly veered into white supremacy and antisemitism. An unabashed admirer of Adolf Hitler, Carto would later establish America's first Holocaust denial organization, at one point declaring Jews "Public Enemy no. 1."[38] The accusation that OSI, a group perceived to be Jewish, was working with Soviet spies to attack Christians and undermine America fit in with Carto's antisemitic worldview, and his weekly *Spotlight* amplified the false claims against OSI to its readership of more than three hundred thousand. One of the group's earliest and strongest supporters was Congressman James B. Utt, Andrija Artukovic's staunchest defender.[39]

Meanwhile, the growing team at OSI was busy interviewing survivors, researching massacres, and filing legal briefs. After working through the INS backlog, they began developing cases of their own, and a Supreme Court decision made their burden of proof much more manageable. In 1981, Justice Thurgood Marshall upheld Feodor Fedorenko's denaturalization and deportation, writing that "an individual's service as a concentration camp armed guard, whether voluntary

146-2-47-427
146-2-47-P.2
BFalbaum:mp

$\overline{(-}$ $\text{DE } 158)$

Washington, D.C. 20530

September 3, 1981

Ms. Donna M. Cooper
Chief of Documents
Room 2426
Department of State
Washington, D.C. 20520

Dear Ms. Cooper:

In connection with an official investigation, this Office is
interested in obtaining any available information you may have on
the following subject:
Reinhold Kulle - Born: March 5, 1921 in Jungfernsee, Silesia,
Germany (now Poland).

Should you have any questions regarding this request, please
contact Bertram Falbaum or Al Matney at (202) 633-5027.

Thank you for your cooperation in this matter.

Sincerely,

Charles L. Gittens
Deputy Director (Operations)
Office of Special Investigations
U.S. Department of Justice
P.O. Box 28603
Washington, D.C. 20005

Figure 12. The Office of Special Investigations request for Kulle's files.
Courtesy of National Archives.

or involuntary, made him ineligible for a visa."[40] The approach Mendelsohn and Ryan had advocated for was vindicated. OSI would not
have to prove personal wrongdoing, which was an almost impossible
task; murder was too frequent for the Nazis to have documented which
guard killed each of the millions of victims. Instead, OSI would only
have to prove that the defendant had been in a Nazi unit, or at a Nazi
camp, where persecution occurred.

Among the unit's best assets was the Berlin Document Center (BDC). At the end of World War II, an agent from the US Counter Intelligence Corps received a tip that a convoy of trucks was carrying potentially valuable cargo. He arrived at a paper mill near Munich and found mountains of Nazi documents, which had been sent to be destroyed as the German defeat loomed. The files, which formed the basis of the BDC, were a historical treasure trove. They included a nearly complete index of Nazi Party members, the personnel files of more than half of the members of the SS, a half million files from the Reich's Race and Settlement Office, and documents from the Gestapo and other Nazi groups.[41]

During the 1950s and 1960s, officials at the BDC compiled lists of concentration camp guards, and OSI's investigators set off to see whether any of those men were in the United States. At the INS, investigators compared the list of camp guards with immigration records, using the immigration service's sound deck system to search through the names phonetically.[42]

In the summer of 1981, several names hit, and OSI investigators began DORAs—"dead or alive" checks. On September 3, 1981, OSI Deputy Director for Operations Charles Gittens sent a series of form letters to the State Department requesting "any available information" on the recent hits: Josef Baumgartner from Hungary, and Jakob Hetzel, Nikolaus Roth, and Erich Peischl from Yugoslavia.

And another, a former camp guard from German Silesia: Reinhold Kulle.[43]

11

"I LIED"

It wasn't just any letter. It was from the Department of Justice, which had questions about the war, and wanted to talk.[1]

The summer usually brought calm. Just weeks earlier, the senior class had bidden Oak Park & River Forest High School a final farewell. Leah Marcus had handed out diplomas, greeting graduates with handshakes and heartfelt congratulations.[2] Kulle was one year closer to retirement—to being at home with Gertrud, spending his days in the garden, and having more time with the grandkids. After the ceremony, the custodial staff broke down the chairs and cleaned up from the event. Soon the building would be quiet again.

But at the end of July 1982, the Kulles received formal correspondence from Neal Sher, deputy director of the Office of Special Investigations. OSI had scheduled a meeting with Kulle, and because he was not a US citizen, Kulle had no choice but to go. After a few days of phone tag, Gertrud told OSI attorney Bruce Einhorn that Reinhold would take OSI up on its offer to provide an interpreter.[3]

On Saturday morning, August 14, Einhorn waited for Kulle at the Midland Hotel in downtown Chicago.[4] He placed an American flag on OSI's side of the table. Kulle might not have noticed, but the symbolism was important to the twenty-nine-year-old curly-haired prosecutor. Einhorn, a Jewish kid from Brooklyn and the descendent of a prominent American rabbi, would be standing over a Nazi. "For the first time in [Kulle's] miserable life," Einhorn reflected, "there was a Jew representing the United States."[5]

Einhorn had a file of documents gathered over the past year from the Berlin Document Center and the INS. They were more than OSI could have hoped for. The files included not only Kulle's SS personnel file but the marriage application Kulle had filed with the Reich Security Main Office. They had Kulle, in his own handwriting, detailing his Nazi history, proudly recalling his time in the Hitler Youth and Waffen-SS, and assuring Himmler that there were no Jews in his bloodline. They even had photos of Kulle in his SS uniform.[6]

This case was much simpler than the other cases Einhorn was working. In Ohio there was John Demjanjuk, whom OSI had at first thought was the notoriously vicious Treblinka guard Ivan the Terrible. That case had garnered significant press coverage and intense controversy from the start—issues that would only mount when it turned out that Demjanjuk was not Ivan the Terrible, but had been a guard at the Sobibor killing center. Einhorn was also awaiting word from a California judge in the case against Edgars Laipenieks. The Latvian collaborator who had once bragged that he was untouchable struck a different tone now that OSI was in pursuit. In court he disputed that he had materially misrepresented his past when filling out his visa application.[7] The Kulle case, on other hand, was among the most straightforward Einhorn had seen.[8]

OSI's chief historian, George Garand, had been assigned to the Kulle case but was unable to fly to Chicago with Einhorn, so Peter Black had arrived in his stead. Traveling was part of the job, but Black was anxious to return home to his wife and four-month-old son, Aaron.[9] Ahead of interviews, OSI historians had prepared a historical brief for Einhorn. Even the most knowledgeable attorney could not be expected to know where each and every atrocity had occurred, and it was the historian's job to make sure nothing went unnoticed during the interview. This first contact would not only set the tone for the investigation, but was often the best chance to get the suspect to talk. Suspects sometimes made accidental admissions, or unwittingly referenced having been at a place where an atrocity had occurred. OSI had found that German concentration camp personnel were much more willing to talk than were Nazis from Eastern Europe. If Kulle brought up anything Einhorn was unfamiliar with, Black was there to flag his attention.[10]

OSI had three main tasks as it built a case against Kulle. First, it would need to prove that this Reinhold Kulle was the Reinhold Kulle who had been a guard at Gross-Rosen. Second, it would need to prove that Kulle had not disclosed his SS service on his visa application. Finally, it would need to prove that Gross-Rosen had in fact been a place of persecution.

When Kulle arrived, Einhorn was almost relieved by his appearance. Now sixty-one, Kulle still had a powerful frame, his hair thinning on top. Most importantly, he looked exactly like the photos OSI had of him in his Nazi uniform. Kulle had come without an attorney, and the interview began just before 11 a.m.[11]

Einhorn walked through Kulle's childhood in Silesia. "Have you always gone by that name?"[12] "Where and when were you born?" "What was your father's name?" More questions, straight from Kulle's SS files, followed. "Have you ever had the measles?" "Did you ever have scarlet fever?" "You are approximately 170 centimeters tall?" The questions seemed innocuous enough. They were confirming, though, that the Reinhold Kulle of Gross-Rosen, Silesia, was the Reinhold Kulle of Brookfield, Illinois.

Kulle freely acknowledged having volunteered for the SS, joined the Death's Head Division, and trained at Radolfzell. He described his uniform, his service in occupied France, and the wounds he had suffered on the Eastern Front. He answered before Black could translate the questions into German. Einhorn repeatedly reminded Kulle to wait for the translation, but Kulle continued answering in English. It was clear that by now Kulle's English was quite fluent.

Einhorn asked Kulle whether he had received any decorations for his service in the invasion. Yes, Kulle said, but they had been lost when the family fled Silesia. He did have a picture to show Einhorn: one of him in his uniform, with the Death's Head insignia, and with patches and stripes that denoted the medals he had received. The photograph was one of the only items Kulle still had from the war, a remnant he had managed to keep and protect for nearly forty years. Einhorn looked at the photo, and then up at Kulle.

"I take it this photograph means a great deal to you," he said.

Kulle dismissed the remark. "It doesn't mean anything today."

Though he freely acknowledged his military service, Kulle was coy about anything connected to Nazi persecution. He claimed not to know whether his wife had ever been a member of the Bund Deutscher Mädel, and claimed he had not known what the Death's Head Division was. He told Einhorn that once he was transferred to Gross-Rosen, he was no longer a member of the Death's Head Division, though he admitted that the Death's Head insignia was not removed from his uniform. He clearly understood that admitting to persecution could spell trouble, but once he had acknowledged that he was the same Reinhold Kulle who had been born on March 5, 1921, in Jungfernsee, in the Breslau District of Silesia, his protestations were of little value.

Kulle tried to portray his time at Gross-Rosen as strictly military duty, saying he had nothing to do with the prisoners and was only at the camp to train recruits. Einhorn ignored the comment, pressing ahead with the timeline, turning to the end of the war. Kulle explained that he had given himself up and had never been never questioned or arrested. It was now after 1:30 p.m. They had been at it for two and a half hours, and Einhorn called for a break.

Peter Black headed for the washroom. Kulle followed, walking to the urinal next to him.[13] "I want to ask you something," he said.

Black stood silently, taken aback.

Kulle explained that he wanted to be cooperative, to tell the truth, but he was not sure whether he should admit to having lied on his visa.

Black tried to suppress the utter awkwardness of the encounter. Kulle seemed genuinely concerned about doing the right thing, and was looking to Black—who had been helping him communicate—for guidance.

Black had to tread carefully. Telling Kulle outright to confess could deem any confession inadmissible. But he did not want to scare Kulle off, either.

"Well, you know, you're under oath. When I get put under oath," Black said, trying to frame his response as a hypothetical, "I have to tell the truth."[14]

Black excused himself, washed his hands, and hurriedly tracked Einhorn down.

"He's ready to confess," he told his colleague excitedly.

Einhorn was ecstatic. After three years in the unit, he was about to hear a Nazi confess for the first time. Maybe Kulle would even apologize.[15]

"Mr. Kulle," Einhorn began when the interview reconvened, "a moment ago, off the record, you indicated that there were some matters you wanted to explain."

"Yes."

"Did you tell me specifically that you had lied on your immigration papers and that it is that fact which you would now like to explain?"

"Yes," Kulle said. "I did not say that I was in the SS. I said that I was in the army."

"What else did you fail to reveal to those officials when asked?"

"I did not admit that I was with the SS. I did not say that I had been with the—that I had been transferred to the concentration camp Gross-Rosen, because that was all connected with the SS question."

Kulle tried to explain that he had concealed his time in the SS "because I knew that I didn't do anything wrong." He had not lied about anything else. "I never killed anybody," he pleaded with Einhorn. "I only did that which the German government demanded of me."

The admission would be incredibly helpful in court, but Einhorn was unsettled by how genuine the apology was. It would have been one thing if Kulle displayed no remorse, if he proceeded through the interview as callous, hardened, and cruel. Kulle clearly felt bad about lying on his visa. But what of his camp service? What of the years he had spent overseeing slave labor in a Nazi camp? Kulle had given excuse after excuse. He seemed absolutely unbothered by his years at

Gross-Rosen. "It showed a contempt for what he had done to weak, desperate [people]," Einhorn would recall later.[16]

Kulle could tell that Einhorn did not understand him, that he was not convinced. "I joined [the SS]—I did that in order—because it was the only way that I could get away from home," he said. "My relationship with my stepfather was very bad, and in order to get away from home I joined the Waffen-SS."

Kulle's explanations did little to quell Einhorn's frustration. Kulle could have joined the Wehrmacht or volunteered for another type of service if he had really wanted to get away. No one had forced Kulle to join the SS, to work at a concentration camp. Einhorn allowed himself one tough, almost rhetorical question.

"Why did you join the SS as opposed to some other organization that would have sent you away from home?"

Kulle could not find a satisfactory response.

* * *

As the interview continued, Einhorn asked Kulle to verify a series of documents. The first was the form Kulle had filled out for the US Consulate. Kulle could no longer remember completing the forms, but told Einhorn that they were in his handwriting. Next came a series of files from Gross-Rosen, listing Kulle's name, birth date, birthplace, and rank, and then Kulle's marriage application. It included the brief CV that Kulle had written of his life, detailing his membership in the Hitler Youth, which he had denied earlier, and Gertrud's involvement in the League of German Girls, which he had also denied earlier.

"I am honest," Kulle kept insisting, as he acknowledged that the documents were accurate.

Then Einhorn handed Kulle one of the pages from the marriage application, and asked whether it too was accurate.

"No," Kulle said.

"Didn't you just tell me that the document was accurate?"

"Yes, OK," Kulle replied. "I was no full-time SS guard."

"Did you work occasionally as an SS guard at Gross-Rosen?"

"Yes," Kulle admitted. "Not very often. I had to do it, but not on a full-time basis."

With the documents in front of him, Kulle could not deny that he had been a guard. He told Einhorn about the daily schedule, that his pistol was "always loaded," and that he oversaw slave labor. Still, Kulle tried to downplay his past. He had not been allowed to shoot when prisoners attempted escapes, he claimed. "I didn't have an order to shoot, not at all."

Einhorn was incredulous. "If an inmate trying to escape was getting away from you while you were following him, what would you do?"

"Let him run," Kulle said.

"Did you allow prisoners in your charge to escape in such a manner?"

"No," Kulle admitted.

Though Kulle claimed that his perimeter duties had kept him far away from the prisoners, he told Einhorn that he "brought them food after I had come back from vacation. I knew a lot of them. I brought them hens. I was always good to everyone. That is the truth, that is the truth."

"Did you know their nationalities?" Einhorn asked.

"Polish people, yes."

"Did you assist any Russian prisoners?"

"No."

"Did you ever assist any Jewish prisoners?"

"I did not—no, I did not know anything about Jewish inmates."

"Are you telling me that, to your knowledge, you never guarded or came into contact with a Jewish prisoner while at Gross-Rosen?"

"I never had any contact with a Jewish prisoner."

"Were Jewish prisoners sent out in *Kommandos* for forced labor?"

"No," Kulle responded. "There were mostly—there were more healthy people in the *Kommandos*. Mostly Poles or Russians."

It was precisely the response Einhorn was expecting. "Are you saying that Jewish prisoners were treated even worse than other prisoners at Gross-Rosen, and, as a result, were weaker?"

Somehow, Kulle was still claiming that he had never seen mistreatment at the camp, did not know whether medical experiments had been performed on the prisoners, and did not know whether the prisoners had been forced into slave labor. He swore up and down that SS guards were not permitted to punish prisoners under any circumstances. Einhorn quickly turned to Kulle's living quarters, in SS barracks 150 meters from the camp: "Did you ever have any prisoners who worked for the SS at the SS barracks?" Yes. "Were you a part of the company that these prisoners were forced to work for?" Yes.

When Einhorn asked about the forced evacuation to Mauthausen, Kulle again downplayed his role, claiming he had been aboard the transport but had no duties—that all he had done was bring the prisoners water while the train was stopped. Yes, he had been armed, but only with a pistol. And yes, the prisoners' cars had been uncovered despite the winter weather, but some of the prisoners had blankets. Einhorn asked whether Kulle had ever approached the prisoner cars, and Kulle said no.

"Didn't you tell me that you went to get water for the prisoner?" Einhorn asked.

Kulle backtracked. Yes, he had gotten them water, but he had handed it to them without entering the train car or even looking inside.

Finally, as the interview neared its end, Einhorn produced Kulle's visa application. It was in English, which Kulle said he could speak perfectly well. Einhorn wanted to get him to admit one more time, on the record, that he had lied. Kulle obliged. "I think I lied to the American government," he said. "And I feel sorry, sorry about this." Einhorn did not interrupt him, and Kulle kept talking. "Where I lied was on the application for visa. I have lied in the sense that I did not reveal that I was in the SS."

After nearly six hours, the interview was over.

Later that night, over a beer, Einhorn kept going back to the apology. In the moment, he had pressed on; but it would bother him even decades later. Kulle seemed to think his gravest sin had involved paperwork, not the nearly three years he had overseen slave labor at a brutal concentration camp. Einhorn chuckled, and shook his head. "I guess that's a Nazi's definition of a confession."[17]

* * *

Back in Washington, Einhorn and his colleagues prepared to begin formal deportation proceedings. After receiving the interview transcript and making sure there was no additional documentation nor any other leads they needed to pursue, they prepared a memorandum for higher-ups at the Justice Department, detailing strengths and possible weaknesses of the case. It did not take long for them to receive official approval to proceed.

The final step was to craft an order to show cause, which would notify Kulle of a deportation hearing, and lay out the grounds for his deportability.

To gear up for a trial, Deputy Director Sher assigned Ronnie Edelman to join Einhorn as cocounsel.[18] Edelman had transferred to OSI after seven years prosecuting cases for the Justice Department's Fraud Section, and was an expert litigator.[19] As third chair, Sher added Eli Rosenbaum, a young attorney who had a nearly encyclopedic knowledge of the Holocaust.

The son of refugees from Nazi Germany, Rosenbaum seemed destined for OSI. As a young boy, he had been riveted by a TV adaptation of the *The Investigation*, a play about the Frankfurt Auschwitz trials of the early 1960s. He had read Simon Wiesenthal's books, and found efforts to bring Nazis to justice inspiring.[20] His parents, though, rarely spoke about the Holocaust. One day when Rosenbaum was twelve, he and his father were driving in a blizzard. His father had returned to Germany as a noncommissioned officer in the US Army's Psychological Warfare Branch, and was telling the boy how bad the food had been, and other stories that kept his son entertained. Then he got more serious. "You know, I was sent to Dachau by my commanding officer the day after its liberation." Rosenbaum asked what his father had seen. The older man remained silent, his eyes focused on the road. His mouth opened, as if he was trying to speak, but no words came out. Rosenbaum looked over his shoulder, and saw tears on his father's face. It was the first time he had seen his father cry. They never spoke of Dachau again, but it had been an awakening for the young boy.[21]

Rosenbaum had planned to work for the business his father had co-founded shortly after arriving in the States, but after finishing his MBA at Wharton, he decided he was not ready for the business world. He instead went to Harvard Law School and studied under Archibald Cox, Richard Parker, and Alan Dershowitz. On a trip to Philadelphia during his time in law school, he saw a blurb in the *Jewish Exponent* about a new unit dedicated to tracking Nazis down. He had read *Wanted!* and been shocked by the revelations of Nazis in America. When he returned to Cambridge at midnight, he called the Justice Department, assuming they had twenty-four-hour operators. Somehow, he got Martin Mendelsohn's phone number. Rosenbaum's professors strongly recommended him, and in 1979 the twenty-four-year-old became OSI's first summer associate.

At the end of that summer, as he drove back to Boston from Washington, his own eyes were now filled with tears. Rosenbaum had spent the last few months in the middle of a Nazi-hunting operation, surrounded by classified documents, and he wanted—needed—to continue that work. Mendelsohn made it clear that they wanted him back, but the only route to full-time employment was through the Justice Department Honors Program. It would be challenging, with thousands of applicants for just a few slots. But Mendelsohn and others fought hard for Rosenbaum, and he joined OSI the following year.[22]

Rosenbaum had a knack for investigations, and tended to glom onto cases, working day and night to find every shred of available evidence. On his first day at OSI, he approached Deputy Director Neal Sher about Arthur Rudolph, who had managed NASA's Saturn V moon rocket program after coming to the United States from Germany as part of Project Paperclip. At a bookstore in Cambridge, Rosenbaum had found *Dora*, a recently published memoir written by a survivor of the Dora concentration camp, and he was aghast at the atrocities described in it. He returned to the same bookstore days later and found

The Rocket Team, a book about the rocket scientists of the Nazi V-2 program. The footnotes shocked him; the scientists who had overseen the V-2 program at Dora and directed the slave labor that produced the rockets had been interviewed in Alabama. Those men—von Braun, Rudolph, and others—were now in the United States, part of Project Paperclip.

Sher encouraged Rosenbaum to work on other investigations instead; Paperclip cases rarely went anywhere. Rosenbaum agreed to work the Rudolph case only on his own time. Within a few years he had compiled such a strong case against Rudolph that he, Sher, and Allan Ryan flew to interview the scientist in San Diego.[23] Feigning interest in rocket science, they peppered in questions about slave labor, and Rudolph was not shy about answering.[24] He freely told the attorneys that he agreed with "a lot of things" Hitler had written in *Mein Kampf,* and happily showed off mementos he had brought to the United States from his Nazi days. Sher asked him about the slave labor, about the prisoners, about the brutal conditions. "I know that people were dying," Rudolph admitted. Largely because of Rosenbaum's dogged determination, Rudolph eventually agreed to leave the country.[25] The case also led to more revelations about von Braun, whose reputation suffered as a result. Von Braun's defenders tried to downplay his Nazi past, casting him as an apolitical scientist despite his personal knowledge of and involvement with the slave labor facilities at Mittelbau.[26]

When Einhorn and Black were preparing to interview Kulle in 1982, Rosenbaum was already in Chicago as well, as a junior member of the OSI team on the Kairys case. During their lunch recesses, Rosenbaum and his colleagues frequented the Berghoff, an iconic German restaurant down the street from the courtroom, and Rosenbaum struck up what would become a close and lifelong friendship with Sher. In the evenings, though, he was quick to return to his hotel room to make sure he was as well prepared as possible for court the next day.[27]

In November, just weeks before filing the order to show cause against Kulle, OSI received a posttrial brief from Kairys's attorneys, which argued that the lack of an eyewitness "fatally undermines the government's case" against Kairys.[28] It was a particularly galling argument to be made about a killing center. Kairys and his SS comrades had already murdered almost every eyewitness.

At the end of November, OSI mailed the order to show cause to Kulle's home. The eighteen counts against him all coalesced around two basic charges: fraud and persecution. Not including his SS service in his visa application constituted a material misrepresentation, making him deportable under the Immigration and Nationality Act of 1952; and his service as a concentration camp guard meant that he had participated in persecution, making him deportable under the Holtzman Amendment.[29]

On Saturday, December 4, 1982, the *Chicago Sun-Times* had the story: "Deportation Bid on Suburb Man."

12

"BUT I KILLED NOBODY"

For two days, OPRF superintendent Jack Swanson walked through the Oak Park community, almost singularly carrying a bombshell that would soon be common knowledge. So far, the school had been spared any publicity. The *Sun-Times* article had not mentioned OPRF, and the *Chicago Tribune* had misidentified Kulle as a custodian at an elementary school in Brookfield, another Chicago suburb.[1]

But it was only a matter of time. Eric Linden, the lead reporter for Oak Park's weekly *Wednesday Journal*, had already asked him for a comment. Swanson exuded his typical patience and calm, responding that Kulle was "an exemplary employee who will continue to work here at least until some kind of a court decision is made." It was premature to do anything else, he explained. Everyone just needed to let the legal process play out.[2]

On Monday afternoon, December 6, Swanson asked Kulle to come to his office before his shift began. Kulle had kept the school running for decades, and there had never been an issue. A Nazi? Reinhold? There was no way. Everyone knew that Kulle had been in the German Army. He used to joke with the American veterans on his staff about the possibility they had shot at each other back in Europe. But a concentration camp guard?[3]

Swanson could not change the past, but he certainly wished the revelations had not been unearthed. He could never know exactly what had happened a lifetime ago and a world away. But he knew Reinhold, the kind of man he was now. They had become friends. He understood why Kulle had kept his secret—appreciated it even. He dreaded having to ask Kulle about the allegations. His focus needed to be on the future, on students, on the budget. It was his job to do what was best for the school, and Kulle was an irreplaceable asset. He hoped they could weather the storm and focus on work.

Kulle walked in, his collared short-sleeved work shirt covering the slight paunch of middle age. Swanson looked him in the eye, and asked if the allegations were true. Had he really been a guard at a Nazi concentration camp?

Yes, Kulle told Swanson, trying to explain. He had worked at Gross-Rosen, but he had never even fired his rifle. It was just a prison, he added.

And he hadn't said any of this on his visa application?

No, Kulle admitted. He had not.

And he had been in the Hitler Youth?

Yes, Kulle answered. He had joined the Nazi youth movement as a teenager, but he had never been an active participant.

Swanson peered through the large, thin-framed glasses that crossed his angular face. Kulle looked uneasy, as if he knew he was in trouble. Swanson was not finding his answers convincing. But after twenty-three years, Kulle had earned some compassion, some grace. Swanson had to determine how to navigate OPRF through the ordeal to come. He hoped it would all just go away. Kulle had been a young man in the war, doing what everybody else at the time was doing there. And so many years had passed since then.

The man at Gross-Rosen, Swanson told himself, had been a different Reinhold Kulle.[4]

* * *

Two days later, Swanson opened the *Wednesday Journal*. The front page showed a large photo of a new sculpture being unveiled at Village Hall. One witness described the unveiling as "the most exciting thing to happen in Oak Park in a long time." On page 2 there was a story about the resignation of the village finance director. Below it was a picture of

Mickey Mouse, advertising free tickets to a cartoon festival. There was nothing about Kulle. He turned the page.[5]

It was easy to miss, but in six paragraphs on the top left-hand corner of page 3, there it was. "High School Maintenance Man Accused of Being Nazi SS Guard." Eric Linden's lede explained that "an employee of Oak Park–River Forest High School has been charged with being a World War II Nazi SS guard and is in danger of deportation." The story briefly mentioned the case against Kulle, and in an odd parenthetical at the end of the second paragraph, it clumsily attempted to provide historical context for readers. "During World War II, several million Jews, political dissidents and other civilians that the Nazi government deemed undesirable were killed in concentration camps."[6] The story quoted Swanson: "'These are simply accusations,'" he had stressed, adding that Kulle was "'not sure himself what the charges are.'"[7]

But Kulle knew the charges. If the six-hour deposition in August had not made it clear enough to him, the order to show cause he had received in the mail a few days earlier certainly had. It was time for him to hire an attorney. He contacted a lawyer in Oak Park who referred him to Robert Korenkiewicz, the defense attorney who had exonerated Frank Walus a few years earlier.

Even after the local papers reported the story, no one at OPRF seemed to be talking about it. Kulle kept his head down and stayed quiet. That part was easy. He had never talked much at work. He was there to do his job. Swanson had made it clear in his office that the plan was to wait, but it would not be Swanson's decision alone. The school board would have a say too. Kulle had gotten to know—had even befriended—some of them. On the second Friday of every month, members of the custodial staff went to the homes of school board members to deliver packets containing the agenda, briefs, personnel recommendations, and other materials necessary for the board meeting the following Thursday night. Kulle had been delivering materials to school board president Paul Gignilliat and secretary Leah Marcus for several years. What would *they* think?

On Friday, December 17, 1982, Kulle grabbed the board packets and got in his car. On both sides of the peaceful street, set back by long front yards, well-maintained Victorian homes with large front porches blocked the setting sun. On other blocks, wider Prairie-style homes with overhanging horizontal roofs and rows of closely placed windows seemed to grow out of the ground.

Two miles from the high school, Kulle parked in front of Leah Marcus's redbrick colonial home. He walked up the gently sloping stairs to the front stoop, and stood under the white arch in front. He had been here many times in the two years since Marcus's election, but this time would be different. As he approached the door, he could hear muffled intonations from inside. Candles flickered through the white windowpanes on the front of the house: Marcus was lighting Hanukkah and Shabbat candles with her children.[8] She came outside, closing the door behind her.

"Reinhold," she began, staring at the sixty-one-year-old German in front of her. "Is it true?"

"Yes, Mrs. Marcus. It is true. But I did no wrong. I killed nobody."[9]

Marcus was not particularly close with Kulle, but she had found him agreeable, kind, inoffensive, even pleasant. He always smiled quietly as he dropped off the board packets each month, usually on Friday nights when she and her family were celebrating Shabbat. And at the high school he was always willing to help.

Marcus had first learned of Kulle's past from Swanson's phone call two weeks earlier, but she was still stunned. And she was caught in the middle. What would other congregants at her synagogue say? Since she and her husband, Phillip, had moved to River Forest, they had been active members at West Suburban Temple Har Zion. She organized events for Hadassah, the Jewish women's volunteer organization, and was on the board of the synagogue's Sisterhood. They had toasted her at luncheons.[10] Did they know about Kulle? Would they call her to tell her what they thought she should do? Would they whisper their opinions to her during the rabbi's sermon? If the school board did not remove Kulle right away, would the community be disappointed with her? Would anyone say something to her children? And what of her school board colleagues? Would they weigh her responses differently? Would she be perceived as "the Jew"? Would she be put on the spot? Ignored?[11]

Would they understand?

She knew she could handle the pressure. In her old "World of River Forest" newpaper column in the now defunct *Oak Park World*, she had not been afraid to voice unpopular opinions. One of her first pieces had bemoaned the dismissive way a car salesman had "found [her] transparent" as his arm "skimmed past [her] belt on his way to shake [her] husband's hand."[12] Another, which created a local maelstrom, had chastised the owner of a local dry cleaner for his rudeness, calling him out by name, and describing a broader "erosion of civility."[13] When heated letters came back, she had stood her ground. She had no problem taking stands or fending off criticism, but criticism would feel different coming from the synagogue community that was an extended family to her and Phillip.

The Kulle question was complicated. Marcus knew they would have to balance Kulle's legal rights with the obvious moral, educational, and public relations implications of having him on staff. She worried that acting too swiftly might create a backlash or risk a lawsuit.[14] The high school was a precious institution, one she adored deeply. That adoration was the reason why she had run for a position on the school board, and why she attended every graduation ceremony during her tenure on it, giving out eight hundred diplomas and handshakes on balmy June days on the school's football field. It was why, when the English department had given the board a list of Shakespeare's plays for approval, she had read each play herself before assenting.[15]

She had been elected to serve the school's interests, not her own—but that did not make her any less uncomfortable. She called Swanson and requested that someone else deliver her board packets in the future.[16]

* * *

William "Jay Jay" Turner, the only Black member of the school board, was not expecting to see Kulle that night. A different custodian usually

119

brought Turner his board packets, but now Kulle was getting out of his car and walking up to the house. Turner had never met him before, and only recognized him because of the newspaper story a few days earlier. Now Kulle was at his home. It did not seem like a coincidence.

Turner stepped outside and glared at the custodian. What was he doing here? Why had he come?

"He thinks I'm *Untermenschen* [subhuman]," Turner thought. As Kulle neared, Turner puffed his chest out. He did not say hello or ask Kulle why he had come. He did not ask where the janitor who typically delivered the packet was. This was a killer, he thought: "a killer at my door."

Turner looked straight into Kulle's eyes, his back straight, his jaws clenched. "I don't ever want to see your face at my door again," he said.

Taken aback, Kulle handed Turner the packet and quickly returned to his car.

Turner was still shaking after Kulle drove away. Even such a tempered altercation left him uneasy. Kulle was a thug, he told himself. He was sure of that. He had known people like Kulle down South. Turner's father, a sharecropper, had brought the family up to Illinois in 1951 during the Great Migration. The drive had taken three days instead of the eleven and a half hours it was supposed to take, because they had avoided parts of the country they feared would not be safe. But Turner did not think every white Southerner was evil. He wanted to know more about Nazi Germany. How much pressure had there been on Kulle to join the SS? What had Gross-Rosen been like? Was anyone who had served in a Nazi uniform an inherently bad person? Turner was not ready to make a decision about Kulle's employment—not yet. For now, he determined to learn more about the Holocaust, and about Gross-Rosen.

The decision weighed on Turner. Everything on the school board did. The schools in Oak Park had been a godsend for his daughter, who was battling brain cancer; and Oak Park felt more welcoming than Barrington, another Chicago suburb where the Turners had previously lived, and where the only other Black family they knew of was that of the Chicago Bears football great Walter Payton. Turner had first been encouraged to run for the school board by Bobbie Raymond, the former child actress who championed Oak Park's open housing movement. He saw it as a way to give back to the town that had given so much to his family.

There had been naysayers, though, who thought Turner's candidacy was unnecessary. His white neighbors had told him that Reverend Carl Dudley, a school board member and professor at a nearby theological seminary, got along well with the Black community. Did Turner really need to run? they asked him. After his victory, which integrated OPRF's school board, the Turners had suddenly begun receiving invitations to events in the more expensive parts of town. One woman had asked Turner's wife, "Isn't it great that your husband is a board member so you get invited to all the parties?"[17]

*＊＊

Kulle's last stop that evening was at Paul Gignilliat's house, on the corner of East and Chicago Avenues. Large oak trees lined East Avenue, their branches nearly touching each other above the two-lane street that dead-ended at the high school's tennis courts, two blocks south.

Kulle parked near the house and walked around behind it, entering the yard through a gate by the alley. Whenever he came by with the board packets, Gignilliat would join him in the backyard and they would chat briefly—two middle-aged men making small talk about their families and the school. Tonight, though, Gignilliat had more serious questions to ask.

Kulle told Gignilliat that he had been recruited into the SS when he was nineteen, with promises of a farm after the war. He had joined to get away from a difficult home life and an overbearing stepfather. On the Eastern Front, a bullet had struck him in the arm, gone through his chest, and buried itself deep inside his abdomen. He told Gignilliat that he was lucky it was so cold in Russia; otherwise he would not have survived his wounds. The bullet, like so much else from the war, was still buried deep inside him.[18]

* * *

During the next few weeks, school officials began to consider their options. Swanson and Gignilliat were concerned that the story might affect the school's reputation, or become a distraction.

The hearings were set to open in the coming months; and though it was not a criminal trial, Kulle seemed to be owed the presumption of innocence. It was clear that the revelations presented a serious legal issue for him; deportation loomed as a distinct possibility. But Kulle had not violated his contract. He excelled at work, and had taken to helping enforce the school's discipline system with students, something administrators deeply appreciated. In all his time at OPRF, Kulle had never had an issue with antisemitism, racism, violence, or anything of the sort. Even if they wanted to fire him, on what grounds could they do so?[19]

But Kulle's presence remained a source of discomfort, especially for Turner and Marcus. Turner wondered privately whether, if Kulle had lied to obtain his visa, he had a legal right to be working in the United States. There was no formal deliberation among the board members about what action to take, but with Kulle's hearings looming, they assumed they would have an answer either way in the coming months.[20]

13

TRIAL PREP

After decades of practiced quiet, Kulle's secret was now public. He had to walk into his boss's office to discuss his Nazi past, see his name in the local newspapers, and somehow find a way to stay in the good graces of school board members who might fire him at any moment. Then there were the uncomfortable conversations with his colleagues, friends, and grandkids. But none of that compared to what was likely to happen next. He was facing deportation. With a confession under oath and mountains of historical documents tying him to active guard duty at Gross-Rosen, Kulle faced an uphill battle. Any legal challenge against the Justice Department was sure to be both lengthy and expensive.

As Kulle navigated his new circumstances, Neal Sher and Eli Rosenbaum flew to Chicago to meet with Hans Lipschis and his attorney Paul Zumbakis, who announced they would not challenge OSI in court. Instead, Lipschis assented to an order of deportation, and agreed to leave for West Germany within 120 days. Sher held a press conference in Chicago to make the announcement: For the first time ever, a Nazi would be deported from the United States for concealing his participation in the Holocaust.[1]

Kulle, though, was adamant that he had done nothing wrong. When a concerned Rich Deptuch asked about the accusations, Kulle explained that after he was wounded, the transfer to Gross-Rosen had made for safer duty. He admitted that sometimes he had escorted prisoners from one part of the camp to another, but that was it. He had mostly been on the perimeter, away from the prisoners, and had spent his time running military drills with other recruits. He had been just a soldier, following orders from his superiors, hoping to survive the war. Deptuch's daughters were crushed by the idea that Kulle might be deported, and Kulle could not imagine being away from his kids, from his grandkids, or even from the high school.[2]

To bolster Kulle's legal team, Korenkiewicz brought in Charles W. Nixon as cocounsel. Nixon, who had raised his daughter in Oak Park, was one of a handful of attorneys with experience on Nazi cases. Ivars Berzins was the attorney of choice for Latvians on the East Coast, and Zumbakis often represented Lithuanians in Chicago. After working with Korenkiewicz on the Walus appeal, Nixon had built up a large Nazi clientele of his own, including Conrad Schellong, whose case closely mirrored Kulle's.[3]

At Kulle's initial hearing, on January 17, 1983, Korenkiewicz and Nixon asked Judge Olga Springer to dismiss the proceedings, arguing that the Holtzman Amendment should not have applied because it had been written twenty years after Kulle's arrival. Judge Springer rejected the motion. Though the Holtzman Amendment had been written later, it only served to clarify that Nazis were excluded by the 1952 Immigration and Naturalization Act. And anyway, the constitutional prohibition on ex post facto law—the retroactive application of a legal provision—applied only to criminal law, and deportation was not a criminal punishment. Next, Korenkiewicz requested a trial by jury, which Springer dismissed as well.[4]

Korenkiewicz asked to delay the proposed April start date, to allow additional time to find more witnesses. Einhorn coolly suggested that three months was sufficient to prepare for a trial, and Judge Springer agreed. Einhorn assumed that, faced with a sure loss, the best Korenkiewicz could do for his client was to stall.[5] Korenkiewicz then filed a motion for discovery, complaining that the government had not shared all of its records and evidence with the defense. But discovery was not required in immigration court, and Judge Springer dismissed that motion as well.[6]

It was a flailing start to the proceedings. As Korenkiewicz continued to pepper Springer with more motions, Einhorn grew increasingly convinced that he was trying to intimidate her—a concern that
gained weight when Korenkiewicz sued Springer in US District Court
for not compelling discovery. Korenkiewicz was used to the spotlight,
to seeing his name in the *Tribune* and the *Sun-Times*, but Springer had
never handled a case of this magnitude. Now she faced the awkwardness of a public lawsuit as well. The District Court dismissed the suit in
June, but the endeavor forced the delay that Korenkiewicz had initially
sought.[7]

* * *

Einhorn knew that Korenkiewicz would try to portray Kulle as the victim of an overzealous Justice Department—a doting grandfather who
just wanted to live out his remaining years tending to his garden. It
was a common strategy, especially with older defendants, and a judge
might naturally empathize with the senior citizen sitting at the defense
table. OSI wanted judges to meet other senior citizens who would be
more appropriate vessels for those feelings. Though the unit shifted
toward historians and documentary evidence to prove its cases, it
often relied on the testimony of Holocaust survivors to ensure that
judges felt the human toll of Nazi persecution.[8] It found witnesses in
much the same way it found defendants: by scouring the lists of camp
prisoners to locate survivors of Gross-Rosen. Einhorn, Garand, and
investigator Bert Falbaum contacted Dr. Efraim Zuroff, OSI's only
Israel-based researcher, to see whether he could find any living survivors of Gross-Rosen in Israel's Holocaust archives. The survivors
would not be asked to identify Kulle, but rather would be asked to describe their experiences at Gross-Rosen. It was one thing for a judge to
hear about the horrors of Nazi camps from a historian. It was another
to hear the victims relate what had happened to them in all of its horrifying detail.[9]

There was still the difficult matter of Gross-Rosen itself, about
which there was next to nothing written in English. Some postwar

scholarship, written in German, outlined the history of the camp, the treatment of prisoners, the construction of a crematorium, and the use of slave labor. OSI also had rosters from the camp that listed Kulle over a series of years, and communications from the camp comman-dant documenting mass murders of POWs. It found records of food allotments given to prisoners, which demonstrated that Jewish pris-oners had received the smallest provisions. Einhorn's team contacted the Polish Commission on the Investigation of War Crimes to see what other information it had on Gross-Rosen. The director of those ar-chives responded that it had a book about the camp, written in Polish, which would be sent over.[10]

In early March, Zuroff went to the Holocaust Research Center at Bar-Ilan University, and read the survivor testimonials of Flora Izhak, Yisrael Ben-David, and Tzvi Braun. The next day he was at Yad Vashem, the sprawling Holocaust museum and research center on the western slope of Jerusalem's Mount Herzl. There, he read the account of Marcel Lubash, a Jewish survivor who had posed as a Polish gen-tile at Gross-Rosen, imprisoned there after a harrowing escape from a transport to an execution site.[11] Then Zuroff returned to Bar-Ilan for more testimonials—of Dov Mass, Pinchas Pivlowitz, Yitzhak Wagner, and Aryeh Hay.[12] From the US Embassy in Tel Aviv, he cabled Garand with summaries.

Two weeks later, Einhorn cabled back.

YOUR RECENT DISCOVERY OF THE TESTIMONIES OF GROSS-ROSEN SURVIVORS . . . HAS PROVEN MOST PROMISING TO PROS-ECUTION OF THE KULLE DEPORTATION CASE.[13]

OSI asked the Israeli police to interview Lubash, Pivlowitz, and Ben-David, with the intent of using one of them as a witness at trial.[14] If OSI were to bring any of the Israeli survivors to testify in court, an Israeli of-ficial would accompany them to the United States. Survivor witnesses came from all over the world, but no other government had taken that extra step. The State of Israel wanted to ensure that if its citizen survivors were to travel to a foreign country, asked to relive their worst moments, they would not have to do so alone.[15]

* * *

After four months of waiting, Hans Lipschis's 120 days were up. But on the night of his scheduled deportation flight, Lipschis was nowhere to be found. Ralph Blumenthal made some calls to see if he could track down the missing Nazi, but Zumbakis dismissively told the reporter that Lipschis had gone to Europe a week earlier. The attorney insisted that Lipschis's departure was not an admission of guilt, and that Lipschis simply had lacked the financial resources to fight against what the attorney called OSI's "McCarthyist" tactics. Lipschis was an "old, sick man," Zumbakis protested, claiming that the sixty-three-year-old retired factory worker was unfit to stand trial.[16] Once Lipschis arrived in West Germany, officials there announced that they had declined to press charges because there was no evidence that Lipschis had committed a specific crime against a specific victim. For now, at least, Hans Lipschis would remain a free man.[17]

In February, OSI won a deportation order in its long-standing case against Feodor Fedorenko, and in May it won one against Karl Linnas. Both men had been discovered in the late 1970s and stripped of their citizenship in 1981, but it would still be years before OSI could send either of them away. Fedorenko was from Ukraine, Linnas from Estonia—both countries now under Soviet control, which meant sure execution. Both defendants were certain to exhaust the appellate system and tap into Cold War angst.[18]

A translated copy of *Gross-Rosen: A Concentration Camp in Silesia* was delivered to Dr. Charles Sydnor, who was assigned as the expert witness in the Lipschis case. Sydnor had never heard of the author, Mieczysław Moldawa, but he was thoroughly impressed with the book.[19] Moldawa had written it from memory, noting in his introduction that "the SS men were so thoroughly convinced that the witnesses of their activities would never go free, that it allowed them not to pay attention to the prisoners when they were engaged in conversation."[20]

Sydnor checked a variety of sources to vet the book, and gave a glowing report to Einhorn. As both a survivor and a historian of Gross-Rosen, Moldawa would make a powerful witness. OSI contacted the Poles, who agreed to allow Moldawa to travel to the United States to testify.[21]

OSI also contacted various survivor organizations, including a burgeoning group in Skokie known as the Holocaust Memorial Foundation of Illinois. Founded in 1981 in the aftermath of Frank Collin's attempted rally, the group encouraged survivors to attend hearings to support OSI, and sent out a notice asking anyone who was at Gross-Rosen between 1942 and 1945 to reach out to Einhorn.[22]

In May, Einhorn traveled to Toledo, Ohio, to meet a Polish survivor named Marion Wojciechowski. Over the course of several hours, Wojciechowski described his childhood in Połaniec, his arrest and imprisonment at Radom, and his years as a slave laborer at Gross-Rosen. Wojciechowski remembered both Moldawa and Dr. Antoni Gladysz, another Gross-Rosen survivor whom OSI was considering as a potential witness, and he told Einhorn he could vouch for Moldawa's credibility. He also recommended that Einhorn talk to Dr. Antoni Mianowski, the chief inmate physician at Gross-Rosen, who was now living in Chicago.

Wojciechowski's story was compelling. In a memo to colleagues, Einhorn noted: "Wojciechowski was an animated and articulate speaker, fluent in both English and Polish. His memory was excellent, and his narration never seemed contrived or exaggerated. He projects the image of an honest, intelligent man—and would make a credible witness." He asked Bert Falbaum to double-check Wojciechowski's INS files, and asked another colleague to study Moldawa's book for references to him.

The interview with Einhorn was the first time since the end of World War II that Wojciechowski had told his entire story. He had come to the United States as a displaced person in 1950, and had lived and worked in Toledo since gaining his citizenship in 1957. His wife Wadyslawa was also a survivor, having been imprisoned at Ravensbrück during the war. No one had ever asked Wojciechowski about the camps before, and Einhorn noted that the conversation had "appeared to be a cathartic experience."[23]

Ludwig Kozlowski, another Polish survivor, agreed to testify as well. His memories were strikingly similar to those of the other witnesses, and would add credibility and consistency to the case. A fifth survivor witness, a woman who had been transferred to Gross-Rosen at the end of the war, was tasked to Rosenbaum. It would be a powerful testimony, but she was nervous about taking the stand. Rosenbaum readied her—and himself—for trial. Though he had been sixth chair in the Kairys case and had participated in high-level interrogations, Rosenbaum had never actually spoken in a courtroom before, let alone questioned his own witness.[24]

In addition to Sydnor and the survivors, OSI planned to call the officials who had worked at the US Consulate in Frankfurt at the time Kulle procured his visa. Catherine Geoghegan, who had overseen Kulle's paperwork, was unable to come in, and instead swore an affidavit in Oregon. Paul Coffey, who had been the US consul in Frankfurt, would come from Arizona instead and be the government's final witness.[25]

OSI was ready.

* * *

Swanson and the school board members braced for a strong response from the community, but it never came. Korenkiewicz's motions and lawsuit delayed Kulle's hearing until August, keeping the story out of focus. Even *Trapeze*, the high school's paper, did not mention the case. And so, as the spring semester progressed, the school board focused on other issues. They discussed racial disparities in access to honors classes. They talked about the need to hire a more diverse teaching staff. They dealt with purchase orders, and with the school's finances.[26] Despite the December shock, it was business as usual in District 200.

In June, as the deportation hearing was set to begin, Kulle's name finally came up in a school board meeting. In the upcoming school year, he was to receive an 8.5 percent pay raise.[27]

14

IN THE MATTER OF
REINHOLD KULLE

A nervous din of chatter filled the courtroom at the Dirksen Federal Building in downtown Chicago. Einhorn, Edelman, and Rosenbaum settled around their table. Across the aisle, an empty seat waited for Charles Nixon. Though Nixon and Einhorn were becoming frequent courtroom combatants, they remained on good terms, sharing a mutual respect and the occasional Scotch together. Einhorn knew that Korenkiewicz was a skilled litigator with a well-deserved reputation for dynamic courtroom performances. They had met in passing, and Einhorn found Korenkiewicz to be courteous, respectful, and friendly. But when court was gaveled into session, a tenacious intensity seemed to take him over.[1]

At 10 a.m., everyone rose as Judge Olga Springer entered the courtroom.

"Gentlemen, Mr. Korenkiewicz, Mr. Einhorn—are you ready to proceed with the hearing today?"

"If the court please," Korenkiewicz responded, "I am not ready to proceed."

"Your Honor," Einhorn replied, "the government is ready."[2]

Korenkiewicz complained that the government had not honored his various discovery requests. Einhorn reminded the court "that on a voluntary basis the government supplied the overwhelming majority of its case in chief to the defense, and has received nothing in return."

Korenkiewicz turned to OSI's attorneys. "Judge, I notice that [on] the government counsel table, or behind counsel table, are five rather large boxes of material. So I can assure the court that the pittance I received wouldn't begin to fill those boxes."

Judge Springer rejected the request.

Ready to give his opening statement, Einhorn stepped forward, but Korenkiewicz interjected again.

"Judge, are we going to proceed now, in light of my statement that I'm not ready to proceed?"

"Yes, Mr. Korenkiewicz."

Korenkiewicz knew it would be an uphill battle. It was not just that he was up against the federal government. The Walus case had left him skeptical that American courtrooms were prepared to handle Nazi cases fairly, and he worried that once an accusation emerged, no one would sympathize with the accused.[3] To prepare Walus's defense, he had gone to Europe for three weeks, traveling to the farms where Walus had spent the war, talking to men and women who had known him, and even standing in Walus's bedroom. He had taken affidavits, collected documents, and arranged for witnesses to testify. But none of that evidence had mattered to Judge Hoffman, who had sided with the INS and revoked Walus's citizenship. The Walus case had predated OSI and had been brought by a different government agency, but those distinctions did not always register. Even after the Seventh Circuit Court of Appeals vacated Hoffman's decision and the newly created OSI declined to proceed with a retrial, Korenkiewicz had remained deeply skeptical about the fair handling of Nazi cases. He was prepared to fight on every issue to give Kulle a chance.[4]

Einhorn tried to start, but Korenkiewicz was up yet again. The previous day, he explained, he had called Catherine Geoghegan, who had told him that she did not remember Kulle and was "sick of the whole thing." She was unable to attend the hearing, and Korenkiewicz objected to her testifying by affidavit.

After a few more minutes of preliminary debate, Einhorn stepped forward to begin the hearing.

"May it please the court, good morning. I am Bruce J. Einhorn, counsel for the United States." The perfunctory line still filled him with pride. "Beside me are government cocounsel, Ronnie Edelman and Eli Rosenbaum."

His opening statement pulled no punches.

"Together we today begin presentation of the government's deportation case against Reinhold Kulle, self-admitted, nonconscripted, and twice-promoted member of the Waffen-SS and its Death's Head Division, who, between 1942 and 1945, served as a guard and guard leader at Gross-Rosen concentration camp in his native Nazi-controlled Silesia. . . . The issues before the court in this case are serious, but by no means complicated." Einhorn reminded the court that the Fedorenko and Linnas cases had established that guard service alone was sufficient basis for deportation. Kulle had already admitted to twelve of the eighteen charges in the order to show cause. The government would call Dr. Charles Sydnor to establish "Gross-Rosen's status as a place of death and the SS's role as its undertakers," and would also call five former prisoners from Gross-Rosen to "give this court a series of firsthand recollections of persecution, featuring the conduct of Gross-Rosen's SS guards, of whom Reinhold Kulle was admittedly one. . . . If, upon a full hearing, Reinhold Kulle is found to have lied his way into the United States and served as an armed SS guard in the physical subjugation of religious and political prisoners confined to the area of a concentration camp, then he must go, or our laws mean nothing."

Einhorn returned to his seat.

"Apparently our laws do mean nothing," Korenkiewicz announced, rising to begin Kulle's defense. "The thrust of their case is, because he was a member of the SS, because he was a perimeter guard—and that is the fact in this case—he is somehow responsible for something that went on inside this camp. And that is not the case."

Korenkiewicz noted that both Fedorenko and Linnas had entered the United States under a different law than Kulle, had both been explicitly asked whether they had participated in persecution, and had both lied in response. Kulle, he insisted, had not lied. He had never been asked.

Behind Einhorn, several older women took their seats in the court-room.[5]

"Reinhold Kulle is a good man today," Korenkiewicz continued, "and he has always been a good man." He laid out Kulle's life story, telling the court that Kulle was just a soldier with "no reason to believe any prisoner was incarcerated illegally."

Korenkiewicz was going to push on everything; he even criticized Einhorn for suggesting that Gross-Rosen was in Silesia, when Silesia was technically in Germany.

Kulle, Korenkiewicz acknowledged, "was part of a system we find abhorrent today. But I don't think the court can apply American standards to a time back in the late 1930s and the 1940s; and I think always take into account the fact that this was a person who joined to fight, did fight, was rewarded and given medals for honor in the face of the enemy, was severely wounded, had no control over his destiny, but nevertheless personally did nothing bad to anyone.

"Thank you, Judge," Korenkiewicz concluded. "He's not deportable."

Before calling his first witness, Einhorn moved to enter the transcript of Kulle's deposition into evidence. On cue, Korenkiewicz objected, arguing that Kulle had not had a lawyer present when he made the deposition, and that the translator "was not doing his job properly." Dr. Peter Black had translated Kulle as saying that his father was a ship worker, Korenkiewicz snickered, but he was actually a ship owner. "An obvious mistranslation." There were also more instances, he told the court, where Black's translation differed from the facts.

There *were* discrepancies between what had been said at the deposition and the truth, Einhorn thought, but they had nothing to do with the translation. They existed because any time Kulle was asked about Gross-Rosen or about his Nazi past, he had lied through his teeth.[6] Einhorn offered to furnish the recording of the interview to confirm the translation, but Korenkiewicz would not relent.

Korenkiewicz's continued pushes to exclude the deposition transcript wore Judge Springer's patience. Einhorn offered multiple compromises, to no avail. Finally, the judge told them both to move on.

For the rest of the morning, Einhorn marked exhibits for the court—photos, Kulle's SS personnel file, his marriage application, and other evidence—all the documentation he had brought to the deposition. At 11:40, the court broke for lunch.

* * *

The hearing resumed an hour later, and Sydnor took the stand. He had literally written the book on Kulle's SS unit; his 1977 *Soldiers of Destruction: The SS Death's Head Division, 1933-1945* traced the SS-TK's origins and every minute movement it had made throughout the Nazi reign of terror. A witty raconteur with a disarming Southern accent, Sydnor was a gifted storyteller with a knack for relaying complicated and appalling history in an accessible manner. After a decade in academia, he had begun giving commentary on television, and soon had been hired to write speeches for Virginia Governor Charles Robb. In 1980—in the men's room at a conference in Charleston—Peter Black and his colleague David Marwell had recruited Sydnor to join OSI. Sydnor's delivery, his expertise on the Death's Head Division, in which many of OSI's defendants had served, and the fact that he was not Jewish made him the perfect hire for the growing Nazi-hunting unit.[7]

After walking the court through Sydnor's extensive resume, Einhorn moved to introduce his book into evidence. This precipitated another series of objections and caustic remarks from Korenkiewicz: "Apparently we don't need the witness, Judge." After Springer overruled the objection, Einhorn asked the court to recognize Sydnor as an expert. For once, even Korenkiewicz could not object.

Sydnor walked the court through Nazi ideology, the history of the SS, and the growth of the concentration camp system. Theodor Eicke, he explained, had been "among the most uncompromising and violently antisemitic members of the SS." Eicke had adapted strict regulations that became ubiquitous in Nazi camps, including Gross-Rosen. Those regulations had been implemented by men from the SS Death's Head Division, whom Eicke subjected to an "unusually rigorous program of training" and a "systematic program of political or ideological indoctrination." Sydnor explained that Nazi camp guards had typically meted out punishment and torture publicly, in front of all the prisoners and SS men in the camp. Death's Head men like Kulle were uniquely brutal, uniquely violent, and uniquely committed to Nazi ideology.

At 2:40 p.m., Judge Springer paused the proceedings. She realized that she had not yet sworn Kulle in, which should have happened at the start of the hearing. She excused Sydnor, and spoke directly to Kulle. A few minutes later, the court adjourned for the day.

* * *

Early the next morning, RaeLynne Toperoff was reading the newspaper at home in Oak Park, enjoying a day off from the summer program she was teaching. The veteran Chicago Public Schools educator flipped through a dozen pages full of advertisements for back-to-school sales. Then, above a large ad for a new Apple computer, the word "Nazi" caught her eye. Another of Hitler's men had been caught. Good, she thought, scanning the short article.

Then she saw it.

Oak Park?

She thought her eyes were playing tricks on her. "The Oak Park school maintenance man. . . ."[8] She read the line over and over. How had she not heard about this before? She thought about her school-age kids. At which school was this Kulle working?

Toperoff grabbed her phone and called Rima Lunin Schultz, a close friend from her synagogue. After what seemed an eternity, Lunin Schultz finally answered. Toperoff began to explain what she had read, but soon gave up and instead scurried the four blocks to Lunin Schultz's house to tell her in person. They tried to figure out where the hearing was being held. Something they could not yet articulate was compelling them to go to the hearings, to witness the proceedings. From Lunin Schultz's kitchen, they called local leaders, Jewish organizations, anyone they could think of. "Where is this happening?" they kept asking, but nobody seemed able or willing to tell them. Exasperated, Lunin Schultz thought their only chance was to try the Justice Department itself. It seemed preposterous; but a few minutes later, someone answered the phone and asked how they could direct the call.

"I'd like to speak to whomever is involved with the matter of Reinhold Kulle," Lunin Schultz said. They were put through to Einhorn's hotel room, and the attorney told the women how to get to the courtroom.[9] After Korenkiewicz's antics the previous day, he would be glad to have more support.[10]

Toperoff and Lunin Schultz raced the two blocks south to the elevated transit stop at Ridgeland Avenue, and boarded the Lake Street train heading into downtown Chicago. By the time they entered the courtroom forty-five minutes later, the hearing had resumed, and Sydnor was back on the witness stand. Toperoff looked over to the defense table. There he was: this Nazi, this Kulle, sitting in an American courtroom, getting due process, a fair trial, and a prominent lawyer.

On the other side of the courtroom, by the OSI table, several elderly women sat together. Lunin Schultz and Toperoff knew instantly that they were survivors. Without saying a word, they walked over to sit with the women. They looked around the courtroom to see whether anyone else they knew from Oak Park had come. Sure enough, a contingent of Oak Parkers sat on Kulle's side of the room, near a cadre of neo-Nazis. Toperoff and Lunin Schultz stared in disbelief. Their neighbors had walked into the same contrast they had seen—Holocaust survivors on one side, a former Nazi on the other—and had chosen their seats differently.[11]

On the witness stand, Sydnor walked the court through the early history of World War II, focusing on the Death's Head role as a killing unit. OSI wanted to head off any argument that Kulle was just a soldier. Einhorn and Sydnor had a good rapport, developed in part over drinks when they went out "salooning."[12] Einhorn's questions were succinct and factual, Sydnor's explanations detailed but engaging and clear. Korenkiewicz tried to break up their rhythm and stop Sydnor from describing the atrocities Kulle's unit had committed. Each time Korenkiewicz stood up with an objection, the pants leg of his ill-fitting plaid suit fell several inches above his shoe. Einhorn and Rosenbaum had more important concerns than Korenkiewicz's fashion, but they could not help but notice.[13]

Sydnor explained that Death's Head Division recruits had had to be "not only of strong physical caliber" but "absolutely convinced and dedicated National Socialists." Eicke had rejected recruits he did not consider to be ideologically pure.

The direct examination turned to the Nazi invasion of Russia. Sydnor testified that Death's Head units "did summarily execute commissars that fell into the Death's Head Division's hands." Einhorn asked him what the awards Kulle had received indicated about his commitment to Nazism.

"This was a political war," Sydnor explained, "an ideological struggle to the death." The invasion of the Soviet Union had escalated the Nazis' murderous policies, and Kulle had been awarded for his dedicated commitment to those ends. Sydnor recounted the Wannsee Conference, and the Nazi determination to eliminate Jews and other groups they had seen as undesirable. Some camps had functioned to gas or shoot victims. Others, like Gross-Rosen, had functioned to work them to death. Sydnor explained that Korenkiewicz's opening statement had inappropriately "described Gross-Rosen not as an extermination or death center, but as a mere work camp," and that the comment was misleading. Toward the end of the war, Gross-Rosen had initiated the construction of a new part of the camp, to be called New Auschwitz. Sydnor told the court about the crematorium at Gross-Rosen, detailed the prisoners' distinctive uniforms and identifying patches, and walked the court through the camp's daily schedule. Jews, he explained, had received the worst treatment. He was establishing the first prong of the government's case: Gross-Rosen had been a place of persecution.

As lunchtime approached, Judge Springer asked Korenkiewicz how much time he thought he would need for his cross-examination. "Judge, I am not a mind reader," he retorted. Springer, clearly frustrated, recessed the court. Lunin Schultz and Toperoff walked down to the cafeteria with the survivors, stealing awkward glances at their neighbors sitting with the Kulles. Toperoff told the survivors that she was a teacher, and Lunin Schultz mentioned that she was finishing her PhD in history. They had read about the hearings in the paper, they explained, horrified that a Nazi was working in their community.

One of the survivors held Lunin Schultz's arm, tears forming in her eyes, a grateful and knowing expression on her face. "We didn't know if anyone would come."[14]

* * *

When the hearing resumed, Sydnor testified that guards had been selected only if they had extensive experience with firearms and had proven to be hardened, committed Nazis. Einhorn handed him a picture of Kulle in uniform, and Sydnor explained that Kulle's promotions meant that he must have been "performing satisfactorily in every respect, as a member of the guard battalion."

Did guards, Einhorn asked, commit murders in the camp?

Sydnor described a series of massacres, murders, and executions at the camp, and noted that Death's Head guards had frequently participated in such barbarity.

At the end of the direct examination, Einhorn asked Sydnor if he believed as a historian that Kulle had participated in persecution. Sydnor replied, "The concentration camps of the Third Reich were engaged in the business and existed for the purpose of extermination, exploitation, and persecution, and that those members of the SS complements attached to those camps were engaged solely in the business of persecution."

Kulle sat silently.

Addressing Sydnor merely as "witness," Korenkiewicz tried to portray the historian as an expert for hire. "On the subject of what I might call the lurid period in Germany, in how many civil cases have you been an expert witness?" he asked, noting that Sydnor was being paid for his testimony. Einhorn and cocounsel Ronnie Edelman objected, but Korenkiewicz complained: "I have just begun my cross-examination, and immediately [am] being forestalled in that endeavor."

Edelman tried to respond, but Korenkiewicz continued: "Why don't I ask my questions. I am absolutely shocked at the type of objection that is being made." He turned back to Sydnor. "You were paid for all this assistance in . . . those cases, were you not?"

"Yes, sir," Sydnor replied, adding a self-deprecating joke about the amount.

Korenkiewicz turned to the subject of Eicke's regulations for guards. "Didn't Eicke consider it undignified to beat a prisoner, because the prisoner was not worth beating?"

Sydnor tried to give more context—guards could beat prisoners when they felt it was warranted—but Korenkiewicz pushed forward. Sydnor tried again: "May I ask you something, Mr. Korenkiewicz?"

"No, you may not, sir," Korenkiewicz snapped.

Korenkiewicz tried to get Sydnor to say that Eicke's regulations had prevented guards from beating prisoners, but Sydnor held firm. "I am not familiar with a specific instance in which a guard was punished for mistreating prisoners," Sydnor responded. Korenkiewicz then attempted to show a contradiction between this answer and one Sydnor had given in the *Schellong* case, referencing a circular from Eicke prohibiting guards from mistreating prisoners. But Korenkiewicz had his years wrong. By the time Kulle was at Gross-Rosen, Sydnor explained, Eicke had been replaced by Richard Gluecks, who was even more supportive of the mistreatment of prisoners. Korenkiewicz was in over his head, and Sydnor knew it. This was why OSI relied on historians.

Korenkiewicz pushed again, but the historian responded with a long answer citing the postwar testimony of Gross-Rosen's commandant, Johannes Hassebroeck, acknowledging that Death's Head guards had regularly beaten and killed prisoners.

Hoping to regain control, Korenkiewicz asked Judge Springer to limit Sydnor's answers to a simple yes or no.

"Mr. Korenkiewicz," she responded, "we have an expert witness. I am not going to tell him how to answer your question."

"Judge, whenever I don't like the way a witness responds to my question, I will have to object and move that that answer be stricken."

"You can move that it be stricken," Springer responded curtly, "but I will not strike it."

Korenkiewicz began cutting Sydnor off to limit his answers, but Springer chastised him. "You, Mr. Korenkiewicz, are attempting to take my role." When Korenkiewicz tried to defend himself, she responded with a terse warning: "I suggest that you cease."

As the afternoon session neared its end, Korenkiewicz argued that Kulle's membership in the SS did not necessarily make him an evil man. "Not every member of the Totenkopf division was a killer beast," he stated to Sydnor.

"Certainly not."

"Likewise, not every guard in the concentration camp battalion was a killer beast."

"I would say not."

Finally, Korenkiewicz questioned Sydnor's expertise. "When was that that you began this intensive investigation of Gross-Rosen?"

"I would say in February of this year."

"As a matter of fact, in the book *Soldiers of Destruction*, you did not mention the name Gross-Rosen, did you?"

"No, sir."

At 3:25 p.m., a deflated Korenkiewicz suggested that the court recess until the morning.

It had been a long and emotionally exhausting day, but there was one question that Toperoff could not get out of her head: "Why, if it was already determined that Kulle was a known member of the SS, was he still employed at the high school?"[15]

15
BEARING WITNESS

Korenkiewicz waited for the elevator. He knew he might have crossed the line with Judge Springer the previous day, but it was his job to do everything he could for his clients, and he had grown to like the Kulles. They were simple farm folk, good decent people, not unlike a lot of the Polish immigrants around whom he had grown up. Korenkiewicz saw Springer as he entered the elevator. He offered an olive branch of sorts. He hoped she would not take anything he said personally. He intended no disrespect. He told her he would say the same for the record when the hearing reconvened shortly. She assured him that she never took an attorney's comments personally, and that his clarification, though appreciated, was unnecessary.

A few minutes later, Sydnor returned to the stand, and Korenkiewicz resumed his cross-examination. "Dr. Sydnor, before testifying in this case, you have had an opportunity to examine certain documents which refer to respondent Reinhold Kulle, have you not?"

"Yes, sir."

"Did you see any references that Mr. Kulle ever maltreated any prisoner?"

"No, sir."

"Did you see any references that he ever shot a prisoner?"

"No, sir."

"Struck a prisoner?"

"No, sir."

"That he ever kicked a prisoner?"

"No, sir."

"Or in any way bullied a prisoner?"

"No, sir."[1]

The day before, Korenkiewicz had sent Charles Nixon to the Chicago Public Library to take out several leading works on the history of the Holocaust, none of which referenced Gross-Rosen.[2] Korenkiewicz pulled out the books and turned to Sydnor. "None of those works so much as mentions the Gross-Rosen concentration camp, do they?"

"Your Honor," Einhorn fumed, "is defense counsel suggesting that Gross-Rosen didn't exist?" He looked over to the survivors attending the trial. Whatever contempt he felt was nothing compared to what they must be feeling. He steadied himself. He owed it to them to keep his composure.[3]

Korenkiewicz handed Sydnor a copy of Raul Hilberg's *The Destruction of European Jews*, and began asking him what other camps Hilberg had addressed. There was a certain irony in using Hilberg in an attempt to discredit OSI; he was one of OSI's most frequently used expert witnesses. Korenkiewicz cotinued: "I think the government has taken quite a bit of time in this case to paint with a very broad brush a picture of Gross-Rosen as probably one of the most beastly camps extant during the World War II period. I submit that it is not true."

Einhorn could feel his blood pressure rising. Korenkiewicz was skirting dangerously close to Holocaust denial, and doing so in front of survivors. Einhorn tried to remain calm, but Korenkiewicz kept speaking over him.[4]

"Judge," said Korenkiewicz, "I'm trying to establish that Gross-Rosen was in fact a minor concentration camp . . . that no systematic killings of persons occurred at Gross-Rosen."

Einhorn was incredulous. A "minor concentration camp?" It was absurd, he told the court, for "those words to be logically attached to one another." Springer, too, was growing frustrated, but Korenkiewicz kept pushing, asking Sydnor if there were SS men of good character, asserting that any killings at Gross-Rosen had happened in places where Kulle was not located, and arguing that Kulle's promotions were not indicative of persecution. The haphazard cross-examination continued until 3:15 p.m., when court adjourned for the weekend.

* * *

On Monday, August 15, Einhorn called Mieczysław Moldawa, now a sixty-year-old university professor in Lublin, to the stand. Moldawa described the day a black Mercedes had pulled up next to him in St. Anton, Austria. He had been close to the French border, on his way to join a resistance cell when three men in civilian clothes, whom he soon learned were from the Gestapo,[5] exited the vehicle. They asked his name, and ordered him into the back seat.

Moldawa described the terror of his first moments at Gross-Rosen, the SS men jeering, "You better hurry!" as they beat and kicked the prisoners, and the identifying patches the prisoners had received: green for Germans, violet for Jehovah's Witnesses and priests, black for "antisocials," rose-colored patches for homosexuals, and yellow stars for Jews.

In the mornings, prisoners had waited anxiously as the *Blockführer* inspected the barracks, hoping his white gloves would come back clean. If there was even a speck of dust, they would be punished with two hours of "sport": excessive drills, rolling, leapfrogging, and other exercises. On just eight hundred calories a day, the prisoners did not have the energy to add that punishment to their labors.[6]

Einhorn produced a map of Gross-Rosen, and had Moldawa describe his slave labor and indicate where his work units had operated. He asked about the camp's construction, but Moldawa paused, pointing to several areas on the map.

"That was the worst part of the work, because there the prisoners were beaten."

Einhorn asked Moldawa to clarify. "Were any of the forced laborers in that area beaten?"

"Yes, half of us, mostly Jews were killed."

"Who beat and killed the prisoners in that area?"

"It was SS men and Kapos."

There had been no end to the persecution. Prisoners' items—even their food rations and basic camp medicines—had a habit of disappearing, sold by SS guards on the black market to local peasants.[7] The camp hospital, if it could be called that, had little more than paper bandages and aspirin. If prisoners needed a surgical procedure, they were locked into place on the operating table wth leather and rubber straps, serving in lieu of anesthetics.[8] The camp dentist had only been hired to steal gold from dead prisoners' teeth.[9]

Korenkiewicz tried to break up the emotional retelling. When Moldawa recounted seeing guards shoot at prisoners, Korenkiewicz demanded he give the "date, time, and place" of each shooting, and complained that the testimony was "highly prejudicial." Springer overruled each objection, and Moldawa recounted stories of executions and murders perpetrated by SS guards at the camp. "I saw at least thirty [prisoners] being killed," he told the court. Some had been murdered for trying to escape, or for talking back to a guard—others for even less: missing a button, wearing a second shirt, or failing to shave.[10]

Toward the end of the harrowing testimony, Moldawa described the forced evacuation to Mauthausen in open-air coal cars with SS men sitting overhead, periodically shooting into the cars.

Moldawa was involved in groups dedicated to the preservation of Gross-Rosen's history in Poland. Sitting in an American courtroom, he expressed his hope that this trial would raise awareness that Gross-Rosen had been "a place to execute."

Einhorn looked up at the bench. Judge Springer seemed profoundly moved.[11]

***

During a break, Lunin Schultz and one of the survivors headed to the bathroom. A few minutes later, as they washed their hands, Gertrud Kulle walked into the bathroom. Lunin Schultz felt protective of the survivor. Though she had just met the women with whom she and Toperoff were sitting, she felt an almost familial attachment to them. She had come to court to see the hearing for herself, and so that she could report on it to her friends in Oak Park. But now she also felt compelled to be there to support the survivors who were there, to show them that the Jewish people had a future.[12]

The OSI team felt the same way. During breaks throughout the proceedings, the survivors approached Einhorn to thank him for standing up for them. Sometimes they offered unsolicited legal advice, reminding Einhorn what to emphasize and what not to let Kulle say. At other times they came with invitations to Friday night dinners. Einhorn smiled kindly, thanking them for the advice and invitations, and assuring them that his meals were set.[13]

OSI's next witness was Marcel Lubash, whom Zuroff had found through Yad Vashem's archives. Rosenbaum rose, anxious to begin his first examination of a witness.[14]

Lubash had been imprisoned at the Janowska concentration camp, and in October 1943 he had managed to escape from the camp during a forced march to an execution site. For the next two months he was free in Lvov, using papers that identified him as a Christian, until the Gestapo eventually captured him. They had hit him as they interrogated him, and had pulled down his pants to find out whether he was a Jew. Severely beaten and barely able to walk, he had been transported to Gross-Rosen.

Rosenbaum asked Lubash about his background. Korenkiewicz objected that Lubash's experiences in other Nazi camps were not relevant, and that the reason for his imprisonment at Gross-Rosen was also not relevant. Rosenbaum was not intimidated. "Mr. Korenkiewicz," he said, "in your opening you said that Mr. Kulle had not participated in the persecution of any individual because of race, religion, national origin, or political opinion; so you put in issue, I would say, the reasons why some of these survivors, and some of the victims, ended up at Gross-Rosen, where your client was."

Minutes later, Korenkiewicz was up again, complaining that Lubash's testimony was unfairly prejudicial because he was testifying about the killing and brutality that had happened at the hands of Germans. "The court well knows that my client is German and was a member of the German SS," he said. That was, of course, the point: OSI was establishing Gross-Rosen as a place of persecution, and the SS men as its persecutors.

Lubash's memories from Gross-Rosen were nearly identical to Moldawa's. Upon the train's arrival at Gross-Rosen, SS men had marched the prisoners to the camp, kicked them, given them a medical examination, and disinfected them with Lysol. The slave labor, Lubash explained, had been grueling, the climate rainy and cold, the beatings unceasing. He recounted having the SS murder prisoners, including a Russian who had dared to talk back to a guard. Rosenbaum finished the direct examination by asking Lubash about the forced evacuation to Mauthausen. Once again, Lubash's testimony mirrored Moldawa's.

After a lunch break, Korenkiewicz fumed that Lubash and Moldawa had been talking in the hallway, passing documents to one another. Judge Springer asked Lubash if they had discussed the case or Gross-Rosen. No, Lubash explained; they had a common background in architecture, and had exchanged business cards.

On cross-examination, Korenkiewicz asserted that Lubash was at Gross-Rosen not because he was suspected of being Jewish, but because he had attempted to strike a police officer with a pipe. He stayed on the issue for a while, arguing that Lubash had been rightfully interned at Gross-Rosen; it was another attempt to position the camp as a prison for criminals, not a place of persecution. Korenkiewicz questioned Lubash's credibility as well, asking how he had been able to engage in such brutal slave labor if he was barely able to walk, and why not everything that Lubash testified to that morning was in a 1964 testimonial he had given to Yad Vashem. Rosenbaum and Einhorn rose to object, but Springer cut them off, reprimanding Korenkiewicz for arguing with a Holocaust survivor. Korenkiewicz continued anyway, until Springer ordered him to stop. "You have exhausted me," she said.

Korenkiewicz had one last swipe. "If the Court is telling me . . . that you now find this witness sufficiently impeached so that you do not give any credibility to any of his testimony on direct, then I will cease my cross-examination."

"Now Mr. Korenkiewicz, need you be sarcastic?"

Korenkiewicz suggested they recess, adding that the judge was becoming "extremely unnerved." Einhorn stepped in, apologizing that a member of the bar would insult an officer of the court.

Korenkiewicz tried to backtrack. "I didn't mean it as an insult, Your Honor."

"You always say 'I didn't mean it,'" Springer responded. "If you didn't mean it, then why did you do it? I am very resentful of your attempted characterization."

Springer had had enough. She ordered Korenkiewicz to stop asking questions about Lubash's previous testimonials. He moved on, only to assert that Lubash was out for vengeance against the SS. No, Lubash explained; he was merely present to offer evidence.

It had been a difficult day. Lubash had traveled across the world to confront the most trying years of his life, only to be harangued in court.

That night, Einhorn took him to Giordano's, a famous Chicago pizza haven. He watched Lubash closely, almost in awe, as they talked and ate. Lubash was having deep-dish pizza for the first time, and he devoured his slices. "You know," he said, looking up at Einhorn as he swallowed another bite, "life is good."

Einhorn sat quietly, wiping tears from his cheeks.[15]

* * *

Rosenbaum was prepared to call his other witness, an elderly woman who had survived both Auschwitz and Gross-Rosen.[16] But as her testimony neared, she grew increasingly fearful. If she took the stand, her name would be public, and she worried that someone might come after her.

The woman had flown to Chicago with her daughter, who did not think she wanted to testify. Perhaps, the young woman thought, her mother had felt it was the right thing to do; perhaps her father's encouragement had played a role. In the past she had begged for stories, but her mother had rarely discussed the Holocaust at home. Doing so was so traumatic for her that every time she talked about the Łódź Ghetto or the camps, she ended up in the hospital. In Chicago, she and her daughter stayed in their room at the Drake Hotel, anxiously anticipating the call to testify. And as the date neared, the young woman could tell that her mother—who had barely slept since their arrival in Chicago—was too frightened to go to the courtroom.

Rosenbaum sensed that what had begun as nervousness was turning into something closer to terror. After the testimonies from Sydnor, Moldawa, and Lubash—not to mention Korenkiewicz's courtroom antics—he was confident that OSI would win the case. He saw how desperately frightened the woman was, and did not want to cause her more pain. He visited her at the hotel.

"I see the prospect of testifying is taking a great toll on you," he said. "I don't think there's any possibility that anyone is going to come after you, but I don't want you to suffer like this. We're going to win this case. We can do that even without your testimony. I'm here to say I think both of you should go home and not think about us again."

The woman's daughter watched her carefully. She had always seen her mother as a kind of hero. But now, after a very tense thirty-six hours in a stuffy hotel room, she was beginning to understand that her mother was not only a hero but a victim.

"I have one request," Rosenbaum added. "I'd like you to permit me to phone you when we've won the case."

The older woman's brow relaxed, and a broad smile emerged on her face.[17]

* * *

Korenkiewicz had a long drive into the city from the distant suburb of Western Springs, and by the time he walked into the courtroom on Monday morning, August 22, Einhorn was already there, chatting with Judge Springer. The attorneys settled at their tables, and Springer gaveled the court into session. Before testimony began, OSI had two housekeeping items to bring before the court. They had considered calling a survivor named Dr. Antoni Gladysz, but an ongoing heart condition prevented him from testifying in person—an issue they had anticipated since listing him as a potential witness weeks earlier.

There was another matter. Rosenbaum explained that a witness he had planned to call was "extremely concerned about her physical safety and the possibility of reprisals if she testifies in this case." Anticipating objections from Korenkiewicz, Rosenbaum added that the woman was, "as I would hope my colleague would understand, a survivor of various Nazi camps." She had been through enough.

Korenkiewicz asked Rosenbaum to reveal the woman's city of residence, and demanded a physician's note. Off the record, he went further, asserting that the woman had decided not to testify because she had not actually been imprisoned at Gross-Rosen.[18] Trying to quell his fury, Rosenbaum told the court, "Sadly, this is not a country that has yet eliminated antisemitism." The witness, he said, was "simply concerned for her safety."

Korenkiewicz relented, but there was one additional item he wanted to discuss. He had noticed Einhorn and Springer talking, and requested that no such conversations happen without his presence. Einhorn tried to explain that he was thanking the judge for a restaurant recommendation and complaining about the lack of air conditioning, but Springer fumed. Had Korenkiewicz made it to court earlier, she noted crossly, he would have been present for the conversation. Why did he repeatedly impugn her integrity?

Korenkiewicz attempted to smooth things over, but it was too late. "I have been more than fair with you," Springer responded, "and, again, I resent the implication."

A few tense minutes later, Ludwig Kozlowski took the stand. His transport to Gross-Rosen had been as the previous witnesses had described. Screams of "raus, raus" had met him as SS men removed him from the train, beating and kicking him and the other prisoners. When Einhorn asked Kozlowski about how SS guards had treated him, Korenkiewicz rose in frustration. "Apparently," he said, "counsel is trying to show brutality by some *Rapportführer* and his aides, and wants that to be believed by this court to somehow cast light on my client's activities at this camp, and I think that's awfully unfair."

But that was precisely the point, Einhorn explained. Gross-Rosen was a place of persecution, and SS guards like Reinhold Kulle had made it so.

On cross-examination, Korenkiewicz tried to call Kozlowski's memory into question, but Kozlowski was resolute, defiantly testifying that Gross-Rosen guards had wanted to "do away with" him.

"In fact, sir," Korenkiewicz shot back, "you were not done away with, were you?"

Einhorn rose in disgust, calling the question "gratuitous in the extreme." Judge Springer agreed. Korenkiewicz carried on, but the damage had been done. Harassing Holocaust survivors was doing Kulle no favors.

* * *

Though Lunin Schultz and Toperoff were becoming mainstays at the Dirksen Federal Building, most Oak Parkers only followed the deportation proceedings through weekly reports in the local papers. In their initial stories about the hearings, both the *Wednesday Journal* and the *Oak Leaves* relied heavily on interviews with Korenkiewicz, reporting his denials of the accusations against Kulle. A sidebar in the *Wednesday Journal* declared, "Mr. Kulle was an honorable man—part of the system." A large subheading in the *Oak Leaves*, quoting Korenkiewicz, proclaimed, "Kulle is a good man. He always has been." The *Wednesday Journal*'s Eric Linden cited the attorney's explanation that Kulle had joined the SS only "to serve honorably on the Eastern front."[19]

Linden and the *Wednesday Journal* made no effort to hide their pro-Kulle sympathies. At the end of August, the paper reported that Korenkiewicz had no knowledge of any crimes committed by the SS-Death's Head Division, or at Gross-Rosen at all.[20] Toperoff was incensed. Why had Linden not provided context about slave labor at Gross-Rosen? Anyone who read this article was going to think that Kulle was the victim of government overreach. And why was Linden using the word "alleged" when Kulle was not denying that he had been an SS guard? She called to request a meeting with Linden, hoping to persuade him to provide a more balanced report, but he told her that she and her "activist friends" were always agitating about something, and that she should not tell him how to do his job.

Toperoff could not help but worry. There seemed to be a big difference between what was happening in court and how the local newspapers were describing it to Oak Parkers.[21]

16

"I AM ANGRY"

Rima Lunin Schultz and RaeLynne Toperoff stared out the window as the Lake Street elevated train chugged from Chicago's bustling downtown through the city's underserved and impoverished West Side. As the train crossed Austin Boulevard into Oak Park, small brick storefronts gave way to large Victorian homes and structures designed by Frank Lloyd Wright. Even the sun seemed brighter.

The women had assumed that Oak Park would rally against Kulle. The village had built its reputation on its commitment to diversity, won awards for its commitment to integration, and stood proudly against a neo-Nazi rally. But now there was an actual Nazi working in the high school, and no one seemed to care.

They could not understand it. The Kulle case was all either of them could talk about. On Sundays, when they dropped their kids off at Oak Park Temple for Hebrew school, they never made it back to the parking lot. They stopped to quickly tell friends about the hearings, and were still standing in the synagogue's rotunda when their kids scampered out of class two hours later. Lunin Schultz was surprised by how few of their friends had heard about Kulle, but after several weeks of hearings, the story seemed finally to be gaining some attention in the community.[1]

As the first phase of the trial came to a close, twenty members of the high school's maintenance staff wrote a public letter chastising the *Oak Leaves* for reporting in a "sensational manner," and for not including "even one item in support of Mr. Kulle." Had the paper sent reporters to OPRF, Kulle's colleagues wrote, it would have learned that Kulle was "held in high esteem at the high school," and that the "school and community are just a little better because Mr. Kulle has been here."[2] Toperoff put down the paper in a fit of disgust. "The same cannot be said of his Gross-Rosen victims," she thought.[3]

The next week, as if in response to the custodial staff's letter to the *Oak Leaves*, the *Wednesday Journal* sent Eric Linden to the high school. The assistant director of buildings and grounds told him that Kulle remained "respected" and "popular," and that the charges had "not changed that impression." The staff was more concerned about the potential results of the deportation hearing than about the accusations. Kulle's boss told the paper that it was "hard to find any dissenting votes as far as Reinhold is concerned."[4]

Lunin Schultz was following OSI's other cases, especially Conrad Schellong's hearings, and she knew that those situations were difficult. There was no precedent for how a community or an employer should handle such allegations. But Oak Park was supposed to be different. It was, she explained to anyone who would listen, "better equipped to deal with these kinds of issues than other communities."[5]

Each Wednesday, Lunin Schultz opened the weekly papers with trepidation, anxiety, and a pair of scissors, collecting each article and letter about Kulle and placing them in a box. She and Toperoff bristled at Linden's gentle portrayals of Kulle, and at the absence of historical context about slave labor at Gross-Rosen.[6] They were relieved to see, in the middle of September, that they were not entirely alone. Three men sent a letter to the *Wednesday Journal* expressing outrage at the "good guy image" in Linden's recent piece.[7] Lunin Schultz knew one of the men—Norman Roth, from Oak Park's activist community— but she did not know the other two, Tadeusz Lampert and Harry Gaynor.[8] A second letter in the *Wednesday Journal* made her laugh: Stefan Fenichel was questioning why Linden was reporting that Kulle was nice to people at work; Hitler and Eichmann probably liked kids too, he scoffed.[9]

Still, the women knew they were in the minority. Linden said as much when Toperoff called. Kulle's colleagues still supported him, the school continued to employ him, and even the local press was sympathetic. Kulle seemed to have the support of Oak Park's most powerful institutions.[10]

* * *

On Thursday, September 15, Bruce Einhorn flew to Chicago. In the storage compartment of the US attorney's office, he pulled out a series of documents and arranged them in a package to be sent to Korenkiewicz's South Side office.[11] Despite the rulings that Kulle was not entitled to discovery, Korenkiewicz had requested to see the German documents Sydnor used to prepare his testimony, and OSI had decided to give them to him, hoping that it would speed up the trial.[12]

The next night, as the sun set, throngs of community members filed into the sanctuary at Oak Park Temple, wishing each other an easy fast, as Yom Kippur—the Jewish Day of Atonement—began. On breaks from the service, Lunin Schultz, Toperoff, and other congregants talked in muted tones about Kulle. His presence brought about intense pain, especially for those who had lost family in the Holocaust. But that was nothing compared to the pain brought about by seeing their neighbors extol a Nazi in the local newspapers.[13]

When the hearing reconvened on Monday, Korenkiewicz resumed his cross-examination of Sydnor, trying unsuccessfully to get the historian to criticize Moldawa's history of Gross-Rosen. Einhorn objected, arguing that criticisms of Moldawa's book should have been brought up when Moldawa was on the stand. Judge Springer agreed. Korenkiewicz continued throwing barbs at Springer and making snide comments about Sydnor. "I am angry," he declared.

"This is the first time we have had a hearing in three weeks," Einhorn interrupted, and "I would think that three weeks is enough time for any man to calm down." He could not believe that a member of the bar would speak to a judge in such a manner, and he called Korenkiewicz's tantrum "unrighteous indignation."

"He's being a dickhead." Einhorn thought privately.[14]

For the rest of the day, Korenkiewicz argued that Gross-Rosen had not been nearly as hellish as Moldawa and the other witnesses had described. In the afternoon, he asked whether Sydnor thought that Moldawa had "any axe to grind," or whether he was "in any way prejudiced against the Nazis." Later, Korenkiewicz produced a list of four thousand camp deaths, and argued that the list proved that historical estimates of forty to fifty thousand murders were exaggerated. At other times, he suggested that any murders had happened in outlying areas, or subcamps away from where Kulle might have been. He went through a litany of examples of SS-TK men who had been disciplined for a variety of infractions, arguing that Kulle would have risked incarceration himself, had he requested a transfer out of Gross-Rosen. But once again, that was not the case. There was not a single example in any extant Nazi document of an SS man being disciplined for refusing guard service. Kulle could have said no.[15]

Finally, at 6:15 p.m., Korenkiewicz finished his examination and the weary OSI team walked back to their hotel. In the evenings, as his colleagues took a much-needed respite from the day's work, Rosenbaum returned to his own work, reviewing notes, studying documents, and rewriting questions.[16]

At 9:30 the next morning, George Garand brought Marion Wojciechowski into the courtroom to take the stand. Einhorn asked him about his imprisonments at Auschwitz and Gross-Rosen. Wojchiechowski's descriptions of the two camps were strikingly similar to those of the the other survivors. He recalled his arrival at Gross-Rosen: SS guards yelling as the train doors opened, dogs barking, slow prisoners being beaten, and children from the neighboring village throwing stones as they were marched into the camp. The conditions at Gross-Rosen were so bad that Wojciechowski had volunteered for slave labor at a subcamp a few hours away, hoping it might be less dangerous. Later, he had returned to the main camp, where he suffered the same brutal conditions that Moldawa, Lubash, and Kozlowski had described.

On cross-examination, hoping to question the witness's memory,

Korenkiewicz asked Wojciechowski why he had not previously written or spoken of his time in Gross-Rosen.

"I have events of Gross-Rosen always in my mind," Wojciechowski said, choking back tears.[17] Judge Springer recessed the court to give him a respite from the stand. When he returned, Korenkiewicz, in another attempt to portray Gross-Rosen as a prison for criminals, asked him whether his resistance activities had been illegal. Resentfully, Wojciechowski shot back that the entire country of Poland had supported the resistance—a significant exaggeration that Korenkiewicz chose to ignore. The attorney instead shifted tactics.

"Did you think that you were unjustly imprisoned by the Germans?" he asked.

"Yes, I was."

"I take it, therefore, you consider yourself a victim of these Germans, correct?"

"Yes, it is."

"So I take it, then, you became somewhat resentful toward the Germans."

"During the war, yes."

"Never get those three years back?"

"Never."

"Would you like to do that to some other person?"

Einhorn objected, and Springer chastised Korenkiewicz for the question. But he continued on.

"I take it, then, you also felt resentful toward the SS?"

"Yes, I was."

"I take it, then, that you wanted to get revenge against the Germans and the SS?"

"I would say do justice," Wojchiechowski responded firmly. "Put them on trial, let them answer for that what they did."

Aside from his initial interview with Einhorn a few months earlier, this testimony was the first time Wojciechowski had talked openly about Gross-Rosen; and the day was clearly wearing on him.[18] Several times, the court paused so he could have water. Later, he needed to sit. After lunch, Korenkiewicz continued his efforts to rehabilitate Gross-Rosen—but Wojciechowski, still emotional, remained defiant, the floodgates now open.

Korenkiewicz asked him whether there had been a special block for Jews in the camp.

"No," Wojciechowski retorted, "because most of them died already, or they were killed."

When Korenkiewicz asked whether Wojciechowski was sure that Jews had even been permanent prisoners at Gross-Rosen, Wojciechowski again wrested control of the courtroom. "Now, counsel, you say permanent. Normally, if Jew was sent to any camp, then normally he would not live more."

Korenkiewicz demanded that Judge Springer instruct Wojciechowski to answer yes or no, complaining that Kulle's right to a fair trial was being undermined by her refusal to stop the witness. "If all I'm here to do is exercise my vocal chords, I'm not serving my client's interest, and I cannot continue."

"Well, sometimes I think that you enjoy exercising them, Mr. Korenkiewicz," Springer responded.

A few minutes later, Korenkiewicz objected again to Wojciechowski's long answers. He had made the same complaints of Sydnor, he noted, but at least Sydnor "was an obviously intelligent man." A rush of murmurs rose behind the attorneys, as Einhorn disgustedly demanded that Korenkiewicz stop insulting the survivor.

When the cross-examination ended, Wojciechowski stumbled off the witness stand, breathing heavily. He collapsed into the seats behind OSI's table, overcome with emotion. Several Jewish survivors swarmed him, wrapping him in their arms, and holding him as he cried.[19]

* * *

Lunin Schultz and Toperoff were among a small group in attendance the next morning as OSI presented film footage from the liberation of Mauthausen.[20] Kulle had acknowledged having been part of the transport to Mauthausen, and OSI wanted the court to see what that concentration camp looked like. Korenkiewicz objected, noting that the film was taken months after Kulle would have passed through, and arguing incorrectly that there was no evidence that the individuals imprisoned at Mauthausen had been there for persecutory purposes.

Afterward, Lunin Schultz and Toperoff agreed that it was time for a more concrete step. They did not think that the school board would be swayed by their voices alone. Kulle seemed to have the faculty and the local press on his side. They would need a powerful ally too.

On a typewriter at Lunin Schultz's home, they drafted a letter to the Community Relations Commission, Oak Park's diversity watchdog. At the commission's meeting that night, they explained their concern that the community's "major thrust has been to avoid dealing with the past, and to simply say that Mr. Kulle is a good, reputable employee." Lunin Schultz acknowledged that the Kulle question was complicated. Remaining silent would be "uncaring to the victims of the camps," but asking for Kulle's firing would risk violating his rights. Still, Kulle did not belong in a public high school. They urged the commission to get involved, and to request that Kulle be placed on a paid leave of absence.[21]

* * *

With Catherine Geoghegan unable to testify, Ronnie Edelman called John Coffey, Geoghegan's supervisor, to explain the US visa application process. Coffey, who had recently retired after thirty-eight years in the foreign service, discussed the procedures used at the US Consulate in Frankfurt, the questions the consulate asked to determine applicants' eligibility for visas, and the directions it received from the State Department to deny visa applications to former members of the SS. Coffey insisted that every officer at the Frankfurt consulate would have asked applicants if they had been a member of the SS. The only way Kulle could have gotten a visa was to lie. After a short direct examination, Edelman returned to the OSI table.

On cross-examination, Korenkiewicz focused on the exact language on the visa forms. Nowhere, he pointed out, had the forms explicitly said that members of the Nazi Party or the Waffen-SS were excluded. Coffey tried to explain that SS men were excluded by other language, but Korenkiewicz noted that the forms explicitly listed the Communist Party.

Though Korenkiewicz had held firm on the Coffey cross-examination, OSI had done what it set out to do. Sydnor had established that the SS-TK had existed to persecute, and that Kulle had been a voluntary and decorated member of that unit. The survivors established that Gross-Rosen had been a hellish place of persecution, and provided emotional heft to the government's case. Coffey had established that Kulle would have been asked about his time in the SS in Geoghegan's office. With that, the government rested its case. Court would reconvene three weeks later, in the middle of November, for Kulle's defense.

* * *

Since Yom Kippur a few weeks earlier, the Kulle issue had gained traction in the community, though the school board remained noticeably silent. Following Lunin Schultz's lead, Oak Park Temple's board of directors asked the school board to separate the legal and moral issues of the case, and urged them to place Kulle on leave until the hearing's conclusion.[22]

The school board held its second meeting of the academic year on October 4. Science teachers presented some new instructional practices, and Leah Marcus noted that she was troubled about the lack of support for the physical education department. A little after 10 p.m., board members entered the superintendent's office through the door at the back of the boardroom.[23] They had received a few calls to place Kulle on leave, and wanted to review the issue together, doing so in closed session because it was a personnel issue.[24]

The growing calls for Kulle's removal worried Rich Deptuch. Kulle had clearly been a military man, but it just seemed impossible that someone who was so sweet with Deptuch's kids could possibly be capable of the crimes of which he was accused. Deptuch understood why the Jewish community was upset. How could they not be? They saw

Kulle as a symbol of the most horrible things. But Kulle was not just a symbol. He was a colleague, a friend. He bought candy bars for kids, and made sure classrooms were set up perfectly for students. Deptuch hoped the board would let the legal process play out. If Kulle was deemed guilty, that would be it; but he at least deserved the chance to defend himself.[25]

The rising tension put Marcus in a particularly difficult position. Many in the Jewish community wanted her to act swiftly, but she was just one member of a seven-person board. If she pushed hard to remove Kulle, she risked engendering a potential backlash or a lawsuit. And given her position as the board's only Jewish member, it seemed likely that any removal would be seen as her prerogative.[26]

In Swanson's office, the board agreed to continue its current position: there would be no action taken until Judge Springer handed down a decision. With the case wrapping up, and Kulle's employment rights to consider, it seemed the prudent and responsible choice.[27]

17

A DECISION
NOT YET REACHED

"One issue now has us baffled," the *Wednesday Journal*'s front-page editorial declared on October 5. "The case of Reinhold Kulle."

Kulle admits to once serving as an SS guard, but he denies mistreating prisoners.

But before the deportation charge and since, Reinhold Kulle has been known only as a dedicated employee of Oak Park–River Forest High School, as an upstanding resident of the suburb of Brookfield, and as the nice fellow who sets up the chairs for groups that meet after hours at the high school.

We find ourselves, as do all others, despising the Nazi leaders and followers who hurt all humanity with their senseless persecution of concentration camp prisoners. Thus, if Reinhold Kulle did some of these things, it follows he should be punished. And yet, we find ourselves not necessarily rooting for his deportation, even if he is guilty.

And now we have two Oak Parkers raising yet another aspect of this issue: If Reinhold Kulle is not deported, but unsavory aspects of his past are revealed, how does this community deal with the fact that he works at its high school?[1]

***

Once again, Lunin Schultz and Toperoff sat together at a typewriter. This time, their audience was the high school's human relations committee, a parent group meeting that evening. They carefully typed a detailed summary of Kulle's past, arguing that waiting for the end of the hearing would not be satisfactory. With a three-tiered appeals process in place, a final ruling could take years. And the legal matter was hardly the point. One of OPRF's most important educational responsibilities was to foster good character. "Can it be possible that an admitted Nazi SS guard belongs in our high school?" Lunin Schultz asked the group, reading the statement aloud.

The women called out the "shocking insensitivity" of the *Wednesday Journal* editorial. "'Even if he is guilty'—what a statement," they scoffed. "The trouble with Reinhold Kulle is not how he has lived his life since 1957, but how he lived his life during the Hitler era in Germany."[2]

But the human relations committee did not believe the Kulle affair to be within its purview. They had been set up to navigate issues related to racial integration. The Kulle matter might be of importance to the women, but it was not a community issue. Besides, one woman told Lunin Schultz, "I don't want my kids to hear this story. I don't know if I want my children to be exposed to the Holocaust."

"Why not?" Lunin Schultz. "I want my kids to learn the truth about slavery. That's the school's job."[3]

In early October, several Oak Parkers wrote to the *Wednesday Journal* to express dismay at its Kulle coverage. One couple criticized the paper for minimizing the seriousness of Kulle's admissions, writing that the paper was immobilized because Kulle seemed like a nice fellow. The paper added an editorial note in defense of its coverage: "It hasn't been determined in court if he's killed or mistreated anyone."[4]

Other community members wrote to the school board as well, and both local rabbis made statements to the *Oak Leaves*. "I think if [Kulle] were a decent person," Rabbi Joseph Tabachnik said, "he would take a leave of absence. But I don't expect an SS man to do that." Oak Park Temple's Rabbi Gary Gerson said that Kulle had "no place working in a public school." But neither rabbi took his complaints to the school board.[5]

Seeing Kulle's name in the *Oak Leaves* each week was surreal for Rich Deptuch. At dinner parties, friends would casually ask him about his friend, about the allegations, about what would happen. He told them the truth: He didn't know. Deptuch knew the school board was hearing from community members who saw Kulle as a symbol of the Nazi regime, and wondered what he could do to make sure they also knew how Kulle's colleagues saw him.[6]

Despite the increased attention, the board focused on the routine operations of the building. Of pressing concern was the question of computers. In September, teachers and board members held extensive discussions about the purchase of new equipment. Would they choose Apple, or a competitive system? How would they navigate teachers' computer literacy? How long would the terminals last? One board member said that it was "one of the most difficult decisions" he had faced in his time on the board.[7]

Searching for allies, Lunin Schultz, Toperoff, and their husbands attended a meeting with a small new group organized by Bruce and Julie Samuels, who were active in progressive politics and environmental issues in the village. Bearded, with a round, cherubic face and a Brooklyn accent, Samuels bore a striking resemblance to Einhorn. He thought the Kulle issue was a symptom of an ignorance of history, especially Holocaust history, and he hoped to push the high school to improve its curriculum. Samuels's goals were expressed in the lofty name of his group: Coalition for an Informed and Responsible Citizenry.[8]

The issues that concerned Samuels were not just local in nature. Throughout 1983, a right-wing group calling itself the National Democratic Policy Committee was running slates of candidates in school board races across the country.[9] The effort was spearheaded by the enigmatic and cantankerous Lyndon LaRouche, who operated the organization through a series of front groups. Though he had started on the left, LaRouche's views had shifted to the far right by the end of the 1970s, and after a trip to Germany, antisemitism played a larger role in his politics.[10] He promoted conspiracy theories with antisemitic tropes, and engaged in Holocaust minimization and, eventually, denial.[11] By the early 1980s he had a cultish following, particularly in the Midwest, and three LaRouche-affiliated candidates were running in the OPRF school board election in 1983.[12] Samuels was deeply concerned about their candidacies, and had organized the Coalition for an Informed and Responsible Citizenry in response. Toperoff and Lunin Schultz prioritized the issues differently, but it was easy for them to find common ground with Samuels, and they all agreed that there was an urgency to the issues. If the LaRouchites won, neither Kulle's dismissal nor an improved Holocaust curriculum seemed likely.[13]

The group met on October 16 and agreed to start speaking at school board meetings. OPRF was the most important institution in the community. It had a responsibility to act, to model leadership, to show students the importance of separating right from wrong. The coalition wanted to put each candidate on the record about Kulle, and to raise awareness about the dangers of the LaRouchites. But the push concerned school board president Paul Gignilliat, who feared that forcing candidates to take a stand on Kulle could lead Kulle's supporters, who seemed to be in the majority, to vote for the extremists. Gignilliat asked Samuels for a meeting.[14]

A few nights later, a small group gathered in the combined living and dining room of the Samuels' modest bungalow in south Oak Park. Lunin Schultz and Toperoff joined Samuels and a few other coalition members; Gignilliat came with two other school board members, Reverend Carl Dudley and Dick Ratcliffe.

After a few minutes of pleasantries, Lunin Schultz, Toperoff and Bruce Samuels made their case. Gignilliat and Dudley insisted that the board could not discuss personnel issues, and that a policy statement would come after the elections. But Samuels was insistent. The issue could not wait until after the elections. Lunin Schultz eyed the board members. Dudley was growing increasingly irritated.

Lunin Schultz tried another tactic, one that she thought might resonate with the theologian. The school board, she argued, reiterating the argument she had been making for weeks, needed to separate the moral questions from the legal questions. At issue in court was whether

Kulle had lied on his visa; his time as a concentration camp guard was not in dispute. Whatever legal issues prevented the board from firing Kulle aside, there was nothing stopping them from placing him on administrative leave. What kind of message were they sending to the community by continuing to employ a Nazi?

Lunin Schultz could see Dudley's frustration mounting. He took each push, each question, each prod as an attack on his ethics, his decency, his morality. And she had intended them to be so. She *was* calling his morality into question. The board needed to act, or at the very least make a statement. It was a moral imperative, she demanded.

Finally, Dudley's frustration boiled over. "Since the Lebanon War," he said, referencing the bloody skirmish between Israel and Lebanon, "*you* don't have the club over our heads!"[15] The Holocaust, he added, was "no longer pure."[16]

An uncomfortable silence took hold in the room. Gignilliat may have been right that pushing on the Kulle issue would help the LaRouchites, but if a current school board member was willing to be boldly antisemitic while defending a Nazi, Lunin Schultz wondered what difference it would make.[17]

* * *

In October, the school board received an anonymous letter, seemingly from faculty members, requesting that Kulle not be removed. Riddled with antisemitic tropes, the letter had harsh words for Lunin Schultz and Toperoff: "We are concerned that a small minority are acting immorally, ungodly, and unamerican, trying to force their selfish, narrow pointed opinions on the rest of the community." The writers contended that Kulle was being unfairly condemned "because he joined an organization over forty-five years ago when he was 18 or 19 years of age. How easy it can be to join an organization and how difficult to sometime get out. We have heard no shred of evidence that this man did anything wrong, other than being a member of an organization." With a legal case ongoing, the letter said, there was "no justification for a small group to take the law into their own hands." The letter characterized anti-Kulle sentiments as an "undemocratic ... attitude of guilt by association," and asked the school board to judge the case "on the facts presented to the Federal government" and not "on the emotions of a small minority of citizens in Oak Park." Though it argued that Kulle should be considered "innocent until proven guilty," it also criticized the Coalition for an Informed and Responsible Citizenry for being "completely unforgiving."[18]

Lunin Schultz thought the letter almost laughable. If Kulle was innocent, why would he need forgiveness?[19]

One of the first Oak Parkers to speak out publicly in Kulle's defense was Kari Juel, a student at the high school, who declared Kulle "one reason to be proud of [the] school."[20] Toperoff was crushed when she saw Juel's name in the *Oak Leaves*. Their families were friendly, and her son and Kari were close.[21] Juel called Rabbi Gerson's public remarks "unnecessary," and argued that Kulle did not deserve "the mistreatment and verbal abuse that gets printed in the paper. . . . Mr. Kulle is a very kind and friendly man at school and I am sure that he is not proud of his Nazi background."[22]

Lunin Schultz had expected Kulle's family, and even some friends and colleagues, to support him. But now the community's children were standing up for a former concentration camp guard. Juel wrote that "many students, myself included, greatly respect him for who he is and what he has done for our school." Lunin Schultz was left deeply unsettled. What was happening at the high school?[23]

She had barely calmed down the next day when she received a letter from John Lukehart, the idealistic chair of the Community Relations Commission. He thanked her and Toperoff for bringing the Kulle matter to the commission's attention, and attached a letter he had sent to the school board. The letter argued that the charges against Kulle were not just a Jewish issue, but "have an impact on the community as a whole." The commission recognized "the discomfort, the pain, the anguish" that Kulle's presence brought to members of the community. "Mr. Kulle is a public employee, paid with public funds," Lukehart wrote. "He is visible to the community in his present job. Given the above observations, it is the commission's judgment that the Board of Education should put Mr. Kulle on a leave of absence immediately."

Then Lukehart went a step further, beyond even what Lunin Schultz and Toperoff had called for: "The Community Relations Commission further believes that, should Mr. Kulle's involvement as a member of the Nazi SS be substantiated, regardless of the outcome of the present judicial proceedings, the School Board should terminate his employment immediately."[24]

Lunin Schultz and Toperoff had been optimistic about garnering Lukehart's support. He was an eminently kind man, and had dedicated his professional life to pushing Oak Park to live up to its reputation. But few outside the Jewish community had lent support, even in private. The women had begun to feel defeated, but Lukehart understood the Kulle issue exactly as they did, and his letter provided the credibility and support they needed. They were beyond grateful.[25]

At their monthly meeting that evening, Gignilliat and the other school board members saw a growing group of concerned citizens sitting together in the boardroom, including five members of the Coalition for an Informed and Responsible Citizenry, who sat patiently as the board worked through its regular business. There were consent items and landscaping contracts and parapet renovations to discuss. Halfway through the meeting, the board turned to a memo about incentives for early retirement. It was a topic that was increasingly on their minds.[26]

The board did not complete its agenda items until after 11:30 p.m.[27] Public comments usually followed; but before they could begin, Gignilliat announced that the board would adjourn to a closed executive session; anyone who "had indicated their desire to speak concerning a school employee was invited to meet individually with the Board to express their sentiments."[28]

What was left of the small crowd protested. One woman asked why Gignilliat insisted on discussing the situation in executive session when the matter "had become public information." Another woman wanted to "lodge a protest against the procedure of the Board to deny public expression to citizens concerning a subject on moral issues such as the one in question."

Gignilliat and his board colleagues conferred, and offered a compromise. Anyone who wanted to comment broadly about policy could do so in public, but anything specific to an employee needed to be said in executive session.

Quickly, the board was inundated with tough questions. One man asked whether the school "had a policy relating to the employment of individuals who have cooperated with the Nazi Party or the Holocaust." No, the board answered, it did not. Bruce Samuels asked whether the board would consider adding a policy to address employees' affiliations with questionable organizations. Gignilliat said he was not sure what legal authority the board had, but that Samuels could submit a proposal for consideration.

A little after midnight, Marcus thanked the visitors for their patience, assuring them that the school board was "as interested as they in maintaining the character and integrity of the school."[29] It had been a tough meeting. The board was an accomplished group. Its members were leaders in the community, trusted and respected, competent and confident, and unaccustomed to public pressure.[30]

There seemed to be one way out of this increasingly uncomfortable situation. Kulle was already sixty-two. His retirement was just a few years away. They discussed the idea of an early retirement for nearly two hours in executive session before finally adjourning at 1:55 a.m.[31]

The next day, the Coalition for an Informed and Responsible Citizenry issued a summary statement for members to distribute among their friends. It reiterated the arguments about Kulle's continued presence that Lunin Schultz and Toperoff had been making for the last few weeks, and concluded with a strongly worded demand for justice: "Whitewashing the complicity of members of the SS does no justice to history, and gives no guidance for the future." The coalition members were enthusiastic. A dozen Oak Parkers had attended at least one of their meetings, and now several others had spoken publicly or written to the school board. Both local rabbis had been quoted in the *Oak*

Leaves, and five other individuals had expressed interest in attending future meetings. The coalition's summary statement ended with a sense of optimism: "The interest in this issue and its broader implications is growing."[32]

A week after the school board received Lukehart's letter and faced tough questions at its meeting, Swanson asked Kulle if they could talk. Explaining the board's current thinking, he privately suggested the idea of an early retirement. The board could provide some additional incentives. The plan would alleviate concerns in the community without the board having to take a public stand against him. Gignilliat thought it "might be a solution to the problem."

Kulle mulled over the idea for a few days and discussed it with Korenkiewicz, but he did not want to retire, and his ongoing legal fight was expensive. Korenkiewicz had other concerns; a midyear early retirement might look like an admission of guilt. It was "not a good idea," he explained to his client.

Kulle declined Swanson's offer.[33]

*　　＊ ＊ ＊*

On October 21, senior Kalyn Wulatin walked into the high school's crowded auditorium, where faculty members were trying in vain to quiet the cacophony of students' voices. This "Tradition of Excellence" assembly—the first in what would become an annual event honoring the high school's prestigious alumni—featured an especially impressive bunch: Ernest Hemingway, class of 1917; Ray Kroc, the founder of McDonald's, class of 1920; Congressman Bruce Barton, the advertising man who had developed the Betty Crocker character, class of 1903.[34] The assembly had been carefully constructed. No one mentioned Hemingway's bigotries or disdain for Oak Park.[35] There was no discussion of Kroc's resistance to having Black owners of McDonald's franchises,[36] or of the hush money Barton had paid to his lover's husband.[37] OPRF was a special place, the school's faculty kept telling the students, with a special history.

Back upstairs, in her role as editor in chief of the high school's newspaper, Wulatin met with Jeff Currie, the paper's faculty advisor, to discuss upcoming issues. She brought up Kulle, and looked to gauge Currie's response. *Trapeze* was not going to scoop the *Tribune* or the *Sun-Times*, or even the local Oak Park papers, but it had to cover the Kulle story. It would need to find an angle, something that would be unique, something that none of the dozens of other articles about the Kulle affair had done.[38] Any story would also risk affecting the school's image—an image that, if the "Tradition of Excellence" ceremony was any indication, mattered deeply to the community. But Wulatin had no doubt Currie would be supportive, even if the administration would not be thrilled about it. He had supported all of the *Trapeze* staff's ideas, including the week they had published an entirely fake edition satirizing the school.[39]

Currie's only concern was the amount of work this effort would take. Wulatin would have to talk to Kulle, attend the hearings, and make sure to provide the historical context that was lacking in some of the other reporting. She would have to ask tough questions of her teachers, her theater director, and her friends' parents. She was a star journalist, among the best he had ever worked with, but a piece like this one would be too much work for anyone, even her, to do alone. He asked her to work with Dave Newbart, an impressive freshman from one of his English classes.[40]

Wulatin faced an additional challenge. Between theater rehearsals and her work on the school newspaper, she was often in the building at night, and Kulle was always around. He had helped her and a friend find a lost purse in the Little Theater, and had poked his head into the shared office space when she and the yearbook editor worked late into the evenings. Reinhold Kulle was not just her subject, but a person she knew.

One day after school, in the airy, high-ceilinged Student Center just inside the school's main entrance, Wulatin met Kulle to ask him a few questions. During the school day the area was mobbed with students, and with staff members grumbling at them to get to class. But in the evenings it was calm, with only the occasional person walking

through. Wulatin and Kulle sat side-by-side on one of the square concrete benches that was too low to possibly be comfortable. Kulle made
it clear that their conversation would not be an interview, and that he
was not there to be quoted. But there would have been little to quote
anyway. He said little more than what he had told Catherine Geoghegan in the Frankfurt consulate. He talked about the Eastern Front,
about getting wounded, and about his time in the military; but he did
not mention Gross-Rosen, and Wulatin could tell he had no intention
of talking about it.

With the hearing set to resume in just another week, Wulatin would
soon have a perfect opportunity to learn more about the embattled
custodian—and the high school—she thought she knew.[41]

* * *

In the weeks before the school board election, the local newspapers
asked each candidate about their priorities. Gignilliat, who was running unopposed, declined to comment on Kulle. Marcus, also unopposed, said it was a "complex issue" that the board should address
after the hearing's conclusion. Other candidates offered similar statements, adding that Kulle was innocent until proven guilty. Neither the
outgoing board members nor the current candidates had any intention
of making a statement.[42]

But there was simply no avoiding Reinhold Kulle. In late October
and early November, a wave of letters poured into the local papers in
Kulle's defense. They did not seek to vindicate Kulle, but rather argued
that the calls for his removal were the real problem. A recent graduate
pleaded with villagers to remember that "we're all human and make
mistakes," and described Kulle as "pleasant and helpful to all students."[43] Another added, "Few of us can boast of making all the right
decisions when young."[44] Yet another letter writer argued that Kulle
was "caught in a situation not of his choice."[45]

Ronald Napier went a step further, comparing Kulle to US soldiers
in Vietnam who had done their duty to their country and followed orders. Kulle had not committed war crimes, he added, "as some would

have you believe." Napier denounced all Nazi investigations as "witch hunts" done "only at the badgering of . . . a few radical groups." He added—incorrectly—that "the last two gentlemen who were charged with this type of alleged crime (?) . . . just happened to be the wrong men." Begging the community to "show compassion" for Kulle, he bemoaned how "easy it is to jump on a popular issue to condemn someone who is probably too ashamed or embarrassed to fight back." Even the local rabbi, Napier wrote, had managed "to forget compassion," and the command to love his neighbor.[46] One Oak Parker begged the village to not "destroy a life because of emotion," and another implored the town to "leave vengeance to God."[47]

It seemed like everyone who was weighing in saw Kulle not as a man but as a symbol, a prism through which Oak Parkers saw themselves and their community. For the Coalition for an Informed and Responsible Citizenry, Oak Park was a beacon of diversity that could not accept a Nazi persecutor in its midst. But others in the community denounced what they saw as a rush to judgment. If Oak Park was the accepting community it claimed to be, they argued, it could not chase Kulle out of town on an unproven accusation, or deny him the possibility of forgiveness.

Lunin Schultz and Toperoff were glad to have each other, especially as the ire of Kulle's supporters was directed against them. A recent graduate characterized the push to remove Kulle as "cruel and thoughtless and uncaring," chastising Lunin Schultz and Toperoff for being "obsessed with tormenting him." Oak Park, the young woman wrote, should be "the land of opportunity and equality" and "give this man a chance." Otherwise, "before long, people will try to fire everyone for anything they do."[48]

One letter that week was different, devoid of the vitriol in many of the other letters. It was written by Hans Delius, one of Kulle's friends. Delius did not attack Lunin Schultz or insult Toperoff. An OPRF alumnus born in Germany, he thought that castigating Kulle for his time in the SS misunderstood the pressures of growing up in Nazi Germany.

"Reinhold Kulle did not grow up here," Delius wrote. "He was

12 years old when Hitler's thugs took over his native Germany and his exposure to varying points of view was, to say the least, meager." Kulle had been only twenty when assigned to Gross-Rosen, and the "bullet he still carries in his body serves as a daily reminder of those awful years." And now, "40 years later, after long since proving his worth as a human being, a friend, good neighbor, loving husband, father and grandfather, and an outstanding employee, he is undergoing this terrible emotional and financial strain." Kulle was being attacked, Delius lamented, by those "who previously had never heard of him." And though the Justice Department had charged Kulle with being a member of the Waffen-SS, his attackers in Oak Park were holding him "personally responsible for an entire bad period of history.

"I can only say that as a symbol of something evil," wrote Delius, "Mr. Kulle is an extremely poor example."[49]

18

FRIENDS OF REINHOLD

"Are you Liz Holtzman?"

Holtzman had stumbled out of bed to answer the phone in her Washington apartment. "Yes. Who is this?"

"If you want your life to be worth anything," said a man on the phone in a thick accent, "stay out of Bayonne." The phone clicked.

Having to avoid New Jersey wasn't the world's worst punishment, the congresswoman thought as she hung up.[1] Though she shrugged off the call, a concerted effort to undermine Nazi investigations was well under way. At the White House, a few blocks from OSI's Justice Department headquarters, government personnel and National Security Council officials sat down for a meeting with representatives from Americans for Due Process, a Queens-based coalition of Eastern European émigré groups that had been set up to "resist" OSI.[2]

The group had good reason for optimism. For decades, the Republican Party had courted the votes of Eastern European immigrants, appealing in part to hardline anti-Communist sentiments prevalent among those who had fled Soviet occupation. The outreach webbed through a collection of ethnic advisory boards chaired by émigrés, and coalesced under the National Republican Heritage Groups Council, whose affiliates were annual attendees of Captive Nations rallies across the country. The founding chair of the National Republican Heritage Groups Council was Laszlo Pasztor, a member of the far-right, ultranationalist, and antisemitic Hungarian Arrow Cross who had served five years in prison after World War II for crimes against humanity.

Other former Nazis and Holocaust deniers had risen to prominent positions on these ethnic boards and in the Republican Party apparatus. There was a board for almost every ethnic group in the country except Blacks and Jews.[3]

The White House meeting was just one in a series of public and private attempts to curb OSI's progress. Back in April, Rasa Razgaitis, one of the leaders of Americans for Due Process and the daughter of accused Nazi collaborator Jurgis Juodis, had published a letter in the *Washington Post* complaining about the lack of a statute of limitations in Nazi cases.[4] In November, just weeks after the meeting in the White House, a group of attorneys who represented OSI defendants made the same request in a private conference with Justice Department officials. Though the assistant attorney general rejected the request, the leader of yet another émigré group reiterated the argument in a December letter in the *Washington Times*.[5]

Émigré groups had long rejected the accusations against their countrymen, and by 1983 their varied and disparate opposition coalesced under a coherent, organized strategy: explicit appeals to Cold War politics. In *Lituanus*, a Lithuanian quarterly in Chicago, Silvia Kucenas charged that "OSI may be accusing innocent victims on the basis of what the KGB has to say," and that "collaboration between these two governments is not only escalating; it is going out of bounds." Kucenas briefly quoted Einhorn and Bert Falbaum (whose name in the article was further Judaized to "Feldbaum"), but her major sources were two other attorneys who were happy to see attacks on OSI's reputation. One was Paul Zumbakis. The other was Robert Korenkiewicz.[6]

In the *Ukrainian Quarterly*, former Displaced Persons Commissioner Edward Mark O'Connor lambasted OSI as KGB pawns, and praised the Waffen-SS.[7] *Draugas* was even more blatant, publicly identifying Jewish employees of OSI and complaining of "Jewish participation in Communist activities."[8] Decades earlier, this very myth of a "Judeo-Bolshevist" conspiracy, now somehow being wielded in defense of Nazi murderers, had impelled many Baltic and Ukrainian collaborators to murder Jews in the first place.

Lyndon LaRouche, whose extremist group had gained some mainstream support, pounced on the émigré fearmongering. OSI became a constant target of conspiratorial antisemitism in his weekly newsletter; Holtzman was a "Zionist mobster," OSI a "witchhunt body." Every few weeks, there was a different conspiracy theory. At first, LaRouche claimed that OSI was a front for a plot between a Jewish senator and the Federal Reserve. Later, it was "an outpost for Israeli intelligence," and a scheme for the "Zionist lobby" to control American foreign policy.[9]

Even in more reputable circles, any suggestion of collaboration with the Soviets was sure to raise eyebrows. Patrick Buchanan was one of the first mainstream voices to take up the anti-OSI banner. More tempered than LaRouche, less explicitly antisemitic than the white nationalists, and less personally involved than émigré groups, he lent an air of credibility to the push against Nazi investigations, couching his support for Linnas, Fedorenko, and other Nazis in anti-Soviet rhetoric. A former Nixon advisor with a radio show and newspaper column, he chastised the government for wasting money on allegations from four decades earlier, and derided the Justice Department for its "collaboration" with the Soviets.[10] Unlike LaRouche and Carto, Buchanan tried to avoid explicit antisemitism, more deftly positioning his defense of Nazis as "anti-Communism." But it was hard even for him to keep up the veneer at all times. In the late 1970s he praised Hitler's "great courage" and his "intuitive sense of the mushiness, the character flaws, the weakness masquerading as morality that was in the hearts of the statesmen who stood in his path."[11] More articles defending Hitler would follow, as would others criticizing the US entry into World War II. By the late 1980s, Buchanan would drop the veneer altogether and engage in Holocaust denial, writing that Treblinka's gas chambers, which had murdered more than nine hundred thousand Jews, "cannot kill."[12]

Allan Ryan would eventually call Buchanan "the spokesman for Nazi war criminals in America," but in the early 1980s he was not seen as an extremist.[13] He was a syndicated columnist, an author, and soon the White House communications director. He lent mainstream bonafides to the anti-OSI efforts, and gave cover to Nazi apologists. He provided a script, guised in patriotism and Cold War rhetoric, for anyone who did not want to believe the allegations against their friend or neighbor: "KGB collaboration," "fraudulent documents," "the persecution of old men."

At a conference in the DC Hyatt Regency Hotel in 1985, émigré leaders bragged that their "Soviet disinformation" claims had been "the most sensitive and successful" weapon against Nazi hunting.[14]

Decades later, Silvia Kucenas would see firsthand how strongly rooted these conspiratorial beliefs came to be. In the early 2000s she learned that her grandfather Jonas Noreika, the venerated hero of Lithuanian resistance, had been a "Jew killer." She engaged in an earnest decades-long effort to expose his past and to demand that Lithuania reckon with its history. But she was met with the same accusations of KGB collaboration, the same admonitions to protect Lithuania's reputation, and the same refusal to accept the truth of the historical record that had once welcomed her own article in *Lituanus*.[15]

The "Soviet disinformation" strategy was working.

* * *

Many communities did not have to grapple with the fraught moral questions that the Kulle case brought. Albert Deutscher's suicide had kept his case from proceeding past initial accusations, and Hans Lipschis had agreed to leave the country before his case went to court. Their neighbors avoided having to consider what their continued presence in the community would mean. Both Conrad Schellong and Liudas Kairys had denied any wrongdoing, and their friends—some of whom testified on their behalf—glommed onto those protestations of innocence. Schellong, who like Kulle was represented by Charles Nixon, argued that there was no evidence he had personally harmed prisoners, and that he had just been on the perimeter. He did at least acknowledge that Dachau was a concentration camp and, in an almost absurd understatement, testified that it was "not a nice place to be."[16] Kairys claimed he was the victim of a KGB plot, and even had a former KGB spy testify at his trial.[17] Demjanjuk made similar claims through his attorney, Mark O'Connor, the son of the displaced persons commissioner who decades earlier had helped pave the way for Nazis' entry into the United States.[18] In those other cases, friends and neighbors and family members could convince themselves that maybe, just maybe, OSI had the wrong man.

But Kulle had already admitted his SS service and his time at Gross-Rosen, and his employment at a public school added a peculiar wrinkle. Deutscher had fixed trains. Kairys worked at a candy factory. Schellong was a welder. Demjanjuk worked for Ford. Their employers might suffer a brief embarrassment. But a school was different. A school was supposed to be the moral and intellectual center of a community—a place tasked with inculcating values, preparing an active and engaged citizenry, and being a democratizing force. Cracker Jack and the Ford Motor Company could equivocate and wait out the deportation trials while Kairys or Demjanjuk continued working. It was an entirely different thing for a public high school to do the same.

By now, Kulle was a constant topic of debate in the local papers, and both the *Chicago Tribune* and the *Chicago Sun-Times* were covering the trial. Kulle's name had even appeared on WGN News television broadcasts.[19]

Delius called to ask Deptuch what he thought they could do to help Kulle, and Deptuch agreed that it was time to make sure the school board knew how the faculty felt. Other faculty members had approached Deptuch as well, typically hoping to help a friend. On at least one occasion a colleague expressed explicit antisemitism, and Deptuch immediately shut the conversation down and made clear that he would not work with that colleague on anything related to Kulle. It was not his place to decide Kulle's guilt, and bigotry of any kind was absolutely and always unwelcome. He simply hoped that the school would wait until the courts had made a decision.[20]

In early November, Deptuch sat down to draft a response. "Dear Fellow Employee," he began.

By this time, you must be well aware of the problems which Reinhold Kulle has been forced to face during the past year. Recently, on top of the pressure of his deportation trial, Reinhold has witnessed a public debate regarding his continued employment at our school, via the local newspapers. A small, but vocal, group of citizens has approached our Board demanding *Reinhold's immediate dismissal.* Though, initially, I was not worried about the fulfillment of such a demand, the amount of negative publicity directed toward Reinhold in the form of "letters to the editor" makes me begin to believe that those of us who feel differently about this issue perhaps need to relay our positive support to the Board of Education.

Below the letter, Deptuch wrote a petition asking the OPRF school board not to remove Kulle. Stressing the "positive influence" Kulle had on the school, it argued that "accusations of Reinhold's alleged criminal misconduct as a member of the German SS nearly forty years ago should have no bearing on his opportunity to continue to provide such valuable services to the school." The final paragraph contained a reminder that Kulle's "guilt or innocence . . . be decided only in the courts," and urged the school board to wait until a court ruling before making a decision regarding Kulle's employment.[21]

Deptuch made several hundred copies of the petition at a local printer, and distributed them in faculty mailboxes the next day. Over the next week, hundreds of sealed envelopes came back. He did not look to see whether his colleagues had signed the petition or written a note opposing Kulle's presence; but he was confident that if the petitions were anything like his conversations around the high school, almost no one wanted Kulle to be removed.[22]

There were a few exceptions. At a faculty meeting that fall, history teacher Michael Averbach had given an impassioned speech against Kulle. It was not simply a legal case, he had argued, or even a moral one; the school had a pedagogical responsibility to fire Kulle. "How can we tell kids that what they do at sixteen or seventeen matters," he had pleaded, "if we say that what Reinhold did at twenty or twenty-one doesn't?" Keeping Kulle employed would undermine everything the school claimed to be, Averbach had argued. But the majority of the faculty, the staff, and even the administration was solidly in Kulle's corner.[23]

19

THE DEFENSE

On November 15, Kalyn Wulatin stepped into the wood-paneled courtroom and tried to collect herself. Today, while her friends were pretending to have finished their calculus homework, she was at the Dirksen Federal Building in downtown Chicago, reporting on a high-profile deportation case. She saw many familiar faces. RaeLynne Toperoff was a few rows away. Next to her, Rima Lunin Schultz ruffled through her bag for a pen. Wulatin had met with Lunin Schultz several times while voraciously studying the Holocaust to prepare for her article. None of it felt too distant; Wulatin's house had been leafleted by neo-Nazi propaganda a few years earlier, and she had been gripped by the miniseries *Holocaust*, whose images of Sam Wanamaker's Moses Weiss leading Jews out of the Warsaw Ghetto had seared in her mind. Lunin Schultz had encouraged her to attend Kulle's trial, to see for herself who this custodian really was.[1]

At OSI's table, Wulatin watched two young attorneys, one with a beard, the other tall with a thick mustache, making final preparations. A few feet away, Kulle and his attorney were patiently waiting for court to begin. Wulatin had prepared for the day as best she could. She had received permission to miss her classes to report on the hearings, and had spent the last few weeks reading the coverage of the case and doing preliminary interviews. But standing in the entryway of the courtroom, she realized she had not thought about where to sit. The courtroom looked almost like a tense wedding, the choice of seat a statement of whose side she was on. She took an open seat in the last row, where she might remain unnoticed. An older man soon sat next to her.[2]

At 8:40 a.m., Judge Springer gaveled the courtroom into session.[3] Lunin Schultz pressed a blue pen to the small pad on her lap. "November 15th," she wrote and underlined at the top of the page. "Defense Day #1."

"Judge," Korenkiewicz began, "I would move to terminate these proceedings on two grounds. There has been no evidence Mr. Kulle in any way committed acts within the ambit of the so-called Holtzman Amendment, which is the basis of one of the charges in this case, nor did he participate in any acts. The court will recall that no witness identified Mr. Kulle—so much as mentioned his name, in fact. In addition, there was no evidence of any false statement by Mr. Kulle, which is the other basis upon which these hearings are premised."

Lunin Schultz scribbled furiously. By the time Springer denied Korenkiewicz's motion, Lunin Schultz was already on her third page of notes.

The defense's first witness was Bozena Kulle, the wife of Reinhold Kulle's son, Rainer. Bozena told the court that she had left Poland because of persecution and antisemitism, and that she was now stateless. Lunin Schultz underlined the comment in her notes. Did Kulle have a Jewish daughter-in-law?[4]

Years later, Bozena would tell a different story about her emigration to America. In a 2015 interview about the day spa she had been operating since the early 1990s, she told *Hinsdale Living* magazine that she had developed a passion for makeup while in Poland, and had traveled to Rome to study skin care before coming to the United States to "put her passion into practice."[5]

In court, Bozena explained that Kulle had been a godsend for her family as they dealt with a seemingly unending cycle of health scares. Rainer had been in and out of the hospital as recently as the previous week, and though their daughter Michelle's condition had stabilized, they did not yet know her long-term prognosis. Kulle had helped financially while Rainer was unable to work, and had spent almost every day with his granddaughter. "I think he is the nicest man I ever met in this country," Bozena said, "and I'm very proud to be his daughter-in-law."

Korenkiewicz asked Bozena when she had learned about Kulle's SS service. The previous year, she replied, but it did not change their relationship or her opinion of him.

"And what effect, if anything, would Reinhold Kulle's deportation have upon you and your family?" Korenkiewicz asked.

"I just hope that will never happen," Bozena said, "not only for my husband who definitely need their [sic] parents, also for me. But most of all for our daughter, who grew up knowing her grandparents. They were there all the time at her bed during the surgery, and they are there until now. And it's very hard to explain to a seven-year-old why all of a sudden her grandparents are not there anymore. So I just hope that will never happen."

Korenkiewicz looked to the bench. "I have nothing further, Judge."

Einhorn stood up. "Your Honor, I have no cross-examination. Thank you. However, with all due respect to the witness, I would respectfully move that her testimony be stricken from the record as irrelevant and immaterial to the issues in these proceedings."

Einhorn had no intention of questioning any of the character witnesses that Korenkiewicz planned to call. For all his aggressiveness as a prosecutor—he liked to think of himself as a "bruiser"—he could not fault anyone for loving their father-in-law or grandfather, and it seemed cruel to subject family members to a rigorous cross-examination. And a cross-examination made little strategic sense. Bozena and the rest of the family had no firsthand knowledge of Kulle's wartime activities, and asking them tough questions risked making martyrs out of them. "I had one person I wanted to prosecute," he would later reflect, "and it was not Bozena Kulle."[6]

Einhorn was not surprised when Springer denied his request. Judges often allowed character testimony because they did not want to appear uncaring or unfair. Still, Einhorn made clear that he had a standing objection to any testimony about Kulle's character and reputation.

Kulle's grandson, Juan Sierra, was next to the stand. It had been almost a decade since Juan's father had died, and the eighteen-year-old was now working security at a local retail chain and living with his grandparents. He and Kulle were very close. "He is like my second father," Juan told the court. Like his aunt Bozena, Juan said that Kulle had a strong reputation for honesty, truthfulness, and peacefulness. Kulle was "very gentle, kind, loving," Juan testified. "And I know he wouldn't hurt anybody."

Korenkiewicz asked Juan whether learning about his grandfather's past had changed Juan's opinion of Kulle's character or reputation.

"No," the young man said. "It made us even closer."

Lunin Schultz was taken aback. It made them closer? She wrote the sentence down, and stopped taking notes.[7]

"Now," Korenkiewicz asked, looking up at Juan, "what effect, if any one, would your grandfather's deportation have upon you personally?"

"It would be like losing my father all over again."

* * *

Together, the first two witnesses had testified for no more than fifteen minutes. After a short break, Korenkiewicz began calling Kulle's colleagues to the stand. The first was Bob Wehrli, the recently retired chair of the high school's physical education department. Wehrli made for a strikingly All-American witness. After his first year of teaching, he had left to serve as an ensign in the US Navy during World War II, where he had earned a Silver Star for leading four PT boats in a close-range attack against Japanese installations in the Philippines.[8] He had worked closely with Kulle, meeting with him several times a week for nearly two decades as they ensured the cleanliness and operations of the school's fieldhouse. He lauded Kulle for being "always available, always ready to help." Kulle's reputation was a "ten on a scale of ten for honesty, truthfulness, peacefulness, cooperation, friendliness," Wehli explained. "I think he has excellent character."

Lunin Schultz, back to her note taking, underlined the word "truthfulness."

Korenkiewicz asked Wehrli if Kulle was "the type of person who would engage in wanton violence."

"There's just no way I could ever imagine Mr. Kulle engaging in any kind of violence," the gruff former college football star responded.

As he had done with the previous witnesses, Korenkiewicz asked Wehrli when he had first learned of Kulle's past.

"About a year ago," Wehrli responded, "when this persecution all started."

"Persecution," Lunin Schultz wrote, pressing her pen hard into the paper, angrily underlining it twice.[9]

In between witnesses, the older man next to Wulatin began talking to her about the war. She looked down at his forearm. She knew about the tattoos the Nazis had emblazoned on prisoners at some of the camps, but she had never seen one before. It was much larger than she had imagined.

"Auschwitz," the man explained.[10]

The next witness was James Brown, who lived a few blocks north of Lunin Schultz. In his role as athletic director, he and Kulle were in nearly daily contact. He, too, testified to Kulle's stellar reputation: "It's the finest, the highest." Kulle, he testified, "goes out of his way to be nice to people. He really would not have to do that. But he goes out of his way to be nice to people. And I think this is one of the nicest things about Mr. Kulle, is that people love him because of the way he treats everyone all the time so nicely."

The courtroom door creaked open, and Lunin Schultz looked over to see Hans Delius and his wife entering, there to show support for the Kulles.[11] She looked back to the witness stand, where Korenkiewicz was asking Brown whether Kulle could engage in wanton violence.

"I believe that he would not do that at all," Brown replied.

Korenkiewicz then called Jim Eitrheim, the head of OPRF's speech and arts department. Wulatin had been in shows that Eitrheim directed, and she knew his daughter from school. Now Eitrheim was about to testify as a character witness for an admitted Nazi in federal court. This was a whirlwind of a day.

Eitrheim and Kulle had first become close in 1960, when Eitrheim took a summer job on the custodial staff, and the pair worked side-by-side. In later years, Eitrheim's responsibilities in the auditorium had kept them in close contact. He extolled Kulle's professionalism, calling his ability to organize his staff "phenomenal," and praising the school as "one of the best-kept of all the schools in the area."

Over the last few weeks, Wulatin and her friends had talked a lot about Kulle, and about what they would have done had they been in his situation. They were roughly the age he had been when he joined the SS. They talked about how hard it would have been to not be affected by Nazi propaganda, and about Stanley Milgram's obedience experiments. Wulatin thought about Eitrheim's daughter, her classmate, who had probably known Kulle since she was a little kid. She thought about her father's friends, the men around whom she had grown up, and the impossible feelings she would have if she had been in the same situation as her classmate. Maybe there was something to getting a fresh start, to changing. Forty years was a long time.[12]

On the stand, Eitrheim agreed with his colleagues' assessments of Kulle's honesty. Kulle was straightforward, up-front, and "would not take shortcuts with the truth."

Korenkiewicz asked about Kulle's reputation for peacefulness.

"I have never seen Reinhold in any way angry," Eitrheim told the court. "In one instance, a very violent man knocked him down as a result of being told that he had to clean something again, and Reinhold did not retaliate." Kulle had great relations with the students, Eitrheim added, and was "well loved for good reason."

Korenkiewicz began to wrap up. "Has learning [about Kulle's past] caused you to change your opinion of Mr. Kulle's reputation or character?"

"No, it has not," Eitrheim responded indignantly. "I kind of refuse to believe that all people in any organization are identical based on belonging to an organization."

After Judge Springer excused Eitrheim, Korenkiewicz produced approximately thirty additional affidavits, mostly from Kulle's colleagues. One from the high school's vice principal extolled Kulle's work ethic, and claimed—falsely—that Kulle did not have a single complaint in his personnel file.[13]

Toperoff turned to Lunin Schultz. Three men—three leaders at

OPRF—had just testified to Kulle's character, his decency, his honesty, his nonviolence. Did they not understand what had happened during the Holocaust? Or did they not care?[14]

Lunin Schultz shared her friend's dismay. "These are our children's teachers," she said.[15]

* * *

Wulatin had been feeling off for a few days—she would end up missing the next three weeks of school—but she was determined to make the most of the opportunity to see this day in court. Throughout the morning, the old man sitting next to her kept asking if she was OK, a worried look on his face.

"When you get home," he said kindly, "put lots of honey in your tea."[16]

As the morning wore on, Lunin Schultz recognized more and more Oak Parkers in the courtroom. Everyone there had come for one reason and one reason only. And at 10 a.m. it was time.

"Your Honor," Korenkiewicz announced to the court, "as the next witness, I call the respondent, Mr. Reinhold Kulle."

Kulle and Korenkiewicz had gone back and forth regarding which language to use, but Kulle had insisted on testifying in English. Einhorn had arranged for an interpreter to be positioned near Kulle, just in case.

Korenkiewicz tried to present Kulle as a sympathetic figure—a man of good character, whose deportation would cause significant harm. Kulle explained that Rainer, Juan, and his wife, Gertrud, were all dependent upon him, and that in twenty-six years in America, he had never been arrested or in any kind of trouble.

They turned to Kulle's childhood: his father's death, his mother's remarriage, his lack of schooling, and the move to Alt Ellguth in Silesia. Korenkiewicz was presenting to the court the Kulle he had come to know—the hardworking, unschooled farm boy who, with few other prospects, had enlisted in his country's military.

"Why did you join the German SS?" Korenkiewicz asked.

"My stepfather gave me a hard time," Kulle explained. "I never got along with him." There were other reasons, too. "I had some friends joined [*sic*] the Waffen-SS, and he [*sic*] came home on leave, and he was telling me about how the SS was an elite group." The government had also offered him a civil job or a farm after the war, he added. Kulle described his training at Radolfzell, and his initial months with the Totenkopf in France, before turning to the decorations and ribbons he had received for his service, and the wounds he had incurred on the Eastern Front.

Korenkiewicz explained his rationale to Judge Springer. "I want to establish for this court that all the medals received by Mr. Kulle were for combat against the enemy, that no decorations were received for any duties in connection with anything at Gross-Rosen camp, and that Mr. Kulle was, in fact, at all times a combat soldier until he was unfit for further combat." Kulle was simply "an honorable and brave combat soldier," Korenkiewicz insisted.

Kulle's descriptions made his guard duty sound almost boring. "I was just standing as a guard and walk maybe fifteen minutes this way and fifteen minutes this way." Korenkiewicz had Kulle identify the locations of his guard duties on a map of the camp. All of them were outside the protective custody, away from where the prisoners were kept. In Korenkiewicz's retelling, Kulle was little more than a security guard, unaware of the goings-on inside the camp—a bored rube walking in circles for hours on end.

Just before noon, Korenkiewicz suggested the court pause for lunch. As the judge and the attorneys discussed the length of the lunch break, Charles Nixon finally entered the courtroom. He had been absent so much that Judge Springer had forgotten his name. An hour later, when court resumed, he was gone again.

Though Korenkiewicz was on his own, he was having his best day since the hearing began. His examinations were succinct and well-organized, and he had avoided confrontations with Springer. Most importantly, he had shown an entirely different Kulle than OSI had presented weeks earlier. Kulle was unquestionably a devoted family man and an excellent custodian. A Jewish daughter-in-law, a Hispanic grandson, and dozens of colleagues from a diverse public high school clearly adored him. Halfway through his direct examination, Kulle was coming across as a simple soldier, neither a true believer in National Socialism nor a violent man.

Back on the stand, Kulle testified that his main responsibility at Gross-Rosen had been to train SS men for combat duties, and that he was often away from the camp itself.

Korenkiewicz asked Kulle whether he had requested to be transferred to Gross-Rosen.

"No, I did not," Kulle responded.

"Did you want to be a guard?"

"No, I don't want to be a guard."

"While you were a guard did you ever make application to be returned to the front?"

"Yes, I did."

Korenkiewicz had one more series of questions.

"Mr. Kulle, did you have any knowledge of what went on inside the protective custody area of the camp?"

"No, I did not."

"Were you, yourself, ever within the protective custody area of the camp?"

"I never did."

"Mr. Kulle, all the time you were at the Gross-Rosen complex, did you ever see a prisoner beaten?"

"No, I never did."

"Did you ever see a prisoner shot?"

"No, I never did."

"Did you, yourself, ever see a prisoner physically maltreated?"

"I did not."

Lunin Schultz, whose notebook was almost full, switched to a thick black sharpie, her writing more rushed, less legible.[17]

Kulle claimed he had only once had contact with a prisoner. In 1943 he had had a short conversation with a prisoner who was working in the SS barracks; and, he testified, he had given that prisoner a chicken.

"Your Honor," Einhorn interjected, "Mr. Kulle has testified, credibly or not, that he was not inside the camp. He is now answering questions about people ... inside the protective custody area."

Korenkiewicz asked Kulle whether he had ever struck a prisoner, shot a prisoner, shot in the direction of a prisoner, killed a prisoner, or maltreated a prisoner. Each time, Kulle responded firmly, "No, I never did." He insisted that he had "had no duties" on the evacuation out of Gross-Rosen, and even testified that when the train had stopped in the town of Mauthausen, he had not seen any concentration camp.

Lunin Schultz was bewildered.

Later that afternoon, Korenkiewicz asked Kulle about his visa application. "Now, do you specifically remember whether or not there were any questions regarding membership in the SS?"

"There was no question about member in the SS."

"How do you specifically remember that?"

"When this question was answered—asked—I never would fill out paper to come in this country; I would say, 'Goodbye, America.'" Kulle explained that he had looked for a question about the SS in the visa application, because after the war, "SS men in Germany was hunted," and "I was afraid of it." Kulle had left behind his family, friends, and property to come to the United States. He had believed that he would be allowed to stay.

Kulle's friends took a nervous breath as Korenkiewicz finished his examination. Kulle had fared well, they thought, and had come across as the sincere, hardworking, loyal man they knew. He had been a soldier and nothing else. After all this time, the government still had not produced any evidence of him hurting a prisoner, and it seemed as though he had never even gone inside the camp.

* * *

Einhorn walked out from behind the prosecution's table to begin cross-examining Kulle. "Do you remember testifying that during the Nazi invasion of the Soviet Union, you were involved in an SS capture of Soviet soldiers, numbering 250 in all?"

"Yes, correct," Kulle responded.

"What happened to those soldiers after they were discharged and captured?"

"I don't know, Mr. Einhorn."

Lunin Schultz perked up.[18] She knew that those young men had likely been shot in a ravine or sent to a slave labor camp. After Korenkiewicz had spent the day arguing that Kulle was a peaceful and kind man, it was a powerful way for Einhorn to begin.

Einhorn was confident that OSI had already proven its case. Now, with Kulle on the stand, he needed simply to reject the defenses that Korenkiewicz had proffered that afternoon. He went after them, one by one.

Korenkiewicz was implying that Kulle had been sent almost unwillingly to Gross-Rosen and had tried to transfer out. Einhorn clarified, asking Kulle if he had tried to transfer out of the camp while he was assigned there.

No, Kulle admitted.

Later, Einhorn turned to the visa application. "Did you tell me specifically that you had lied on your immigration papers, and that is that fact which you would now like to explain?" Kulle had answered yes. Einhorn asked Kulle if he remembered that answer, and Kulle said he did.

Einhorn continued reading the transcript: When he had asked Kulle what he'd lied about, Kulle had answered, "I did not say that I was in the SS. I said that I was in the Army." Einhorn looked up from the transcript and turned to Kulle.

"Is that the question you were asked and the answer you gave?"

"Yes, it was asked," Kulle responded.

With that, Einhorn turned to Judge Springer. "Your Honor, I have no further questions."

* * *

That evening, Rich Deptuch sat patiently in the high school's boardroom. The LaRouchites had been soundly defeated in the school board election, and three new board members were joining Gignilliat, Marcus, Dudley, and Turner at the helm of the school.[19] The board swore them in and approved a series of expenditures, contracts, and commit-tee assignments. It considered bids from various security firms, sum-marizing them under the ill-considered heading "Daily Guard Ser-vice."[20]

A few seats away from Deptuch, Michael Fleisher and Bruce Sam-uels eagerly awaited their chance to speak. First, though, Gignilliat opened the floor to anyone who wished to discuss the parking situation around the high school. There was a series of complaints from neigh-bors, and the board promised to look into the situation.

Finally, Gignilliat recognized the community members who had come to discuss Kulle. He issued a stern reminder that comments re-garding policy were acceptable, but discussion of personnel issues was reserved only for executive session.

Fleisher stood to address the board. He had been meeting with Lunin Schultz and Toperoff, hoping to help push the high school to remove Kulle. The board had now received two statements urging it to place Kulle on leave: one from Lukehart's Community Relations Commission, and one from a parent group. Fleisher urged the board to consider both statements closely, and to place Kulle on leave until the conclusion of his trial. Fleisher's friend Marjorie Greenwald urged the board to revisit the school's Holocaust curriculum.[21]

Deptuch had known several of the board members for years. He and Gignilliat had built floats together for the school's homecoming parade, spending afternoons working in Gignilliat's garage. Gignil-liat had rewarded Deptuch's daughters with a trip out for ice cream. Oak Park could feel like such a small town sometimes.[22] Deptuch sub-mitted the several hundred petitions he had collected, explaining his concern that the board "not set a precedent by releasing a school em-ployee before a guilty verdict has been declared."

Gignilliat thanked Deptuch for his thoughts, and turned to ad-dress the room. Board members had "wrestled and agonized over the matter," he explained, "knowing of the angst it had produced in the community." But they needed to respect the constitutional rights of individuals. They would listen to public opinion, but they had been "advised to move very cautiously." The meeting returned to parking issues, but the board members knew that the community's patience was waning. After the room cleared out at 10:30 p.m., they went into executive session. They stayed and discussed Kulle for several more hours until finally, exhausted and beleaguered, they once again walked out onto Scoville Avenue in the middle of the night.[23]

* * *

In the morning, Kulle returned to the stand for a brief redirect. Korenkiewicz asked him to clarify his answers to Einhorn. "Did you lie on your immigration papers, Mr. Kulle?"

"I did not lie on my immigration papers."

"Then why did you say yes at your deposition in August 1982?"

"I didn't understand the question."

Einhorn asked for a brief re-cross. He thought back to that balmy day at the Midland Hotel, to Peter Black coming out of the bathroom to tell him that Kulle wanted to confess, to Kulle answering questions in English before Black could translate them into German.

"Mr. Kulle, did you tell me the truth at that interview?"

"Yes, I did."

"And were you aware of being under oath at the time you gave your answers at that interview?"

"Yes."

"And did you once during the course of that interview stop me and indicate that your previous answers or my previous questions were a product of misunderstanding, that you did not comprehend what I was saying or what you were saying?"

Kulle stayed firm. "Yes, I did."

Einhorn handed Kulle a transcript of the deposition. "Why don't you find the place where it occurred."

Kulle looked through the transcript. "I don't find it," he eventually replied.

A few minutes later, the hearing was over. Kulle's fate was now in Judge Springer's hands.

20

A NO-WIN SITUATION

The end of the trial brought Lunin Schultz little respite. The *Wednesday Journal*, covering the defense's case, praised Kulle as a "hard worker" who "helps keep the school building in good shape."[1] She tossed the newspaper aside. "He's not on trial for being a bad custodian," she fumed to herself.[2] The *Oak Leaves* was hardly better. "Kulle Says He Did Not Abuse Prisoners," the headline to Jeff Ferenc's article proclaimed.[3]

Lunin Schultz flipped to the letters to the editor. In the last few weeks, their focus had shifted from whether Kulle was guilty to whether supporting or opposing him was the most moral and just response. One Jewish woman, Dorothy Samachson, had excoriated the support Kulle was receiving as "disgraceful," and said that keeping Kulle employed at the school communicated to students that it was "all right to do whatever you want as long as you get away with it long enough."[4]

Incensed, Kulle's friends had lashed out. Delius had argued that the anti-Kulle coalition was rooted in "self-righteousness and prejudice," comparing it to Joseph McCarthy and Adolf Hitler.[5] Raymond Kinzie, a prominent bank executive, had urged the village to ignore Kulle's detractors, "who feel two wrongs do make a right. . . . I do not know Reinhold Kulle, but I do know a witch hunt when I see one. Halloween is over and so is The Holocaust." The goal of the criminal justice system, Kinzie argued, was not retribution but rehabilitation. "Does any reasonable person really doubt that Reinhold Kulle is fully rehabilitated?"

Kulle's painful memories, Kinzie wrote, were "punishment enough."[6] On the same page, the *Oak Leaves* had also published a second letter from Samachson which criticized Kulle's "soft-hearted defenders" for being tricked by his courtesy. "Why shouldn't he be polite? He's safe and well-paid while others of his ilk have paid for their crimes." It did not matter whether Kulle had personally "prodded victims into the gas ovens." He had "volunteered to support those policies and implement them."[7]

The juxtaposition of his letter with Samachson's had rankled Kinzie, who had written back a few weeks later: "Since my letter defending Mr. Kulle's plight was printed opposite hers, I must set the record straight." After touting his credentials and calling himself a "historian" thanks to an undergraduate degree in history, he had compared Samachson to McCarthy, saying that she, like the senator from Wisconsin, had supported "guilt by association" in calling Kulle guilty simply because he was a member of an organization. "The day our village starts tossing its civil servants out on their ears on mere accusations, we are all in big, big trouble. Dorothy Samachson, you should realize that all that stands between you and the gas ovens is 'innocent until proven guilty.'"[8]

Lunin Schultz was appalled. Was Kinzie really threatening a Jewish woman with "gas ovens"?

A few days later, someone passed Lunin Schultz a fundraising letter that was circulating around the community, supposedly written by Eitrheim and another teacher.[9] "Dear Friends of Reinhold Kulle," it began. "As you know, Mr. Kulle is facing staggering debts to defend himself against our government which has endless resources. Mr. Kulle has exercised the right this country gives to all peoples, the right to defend themselves in court when they believe they are not guilty of charges filed against them."

Lunin Schultz was shaking. He believes he's not guilty?

"Mr. Kulle's attorney feels confident he will win this case against the government, as there has not been one piece of evidence presented linking Mr. Kulle to any mistreatment of peoples or other gross wrong doings, but the case will probably require appeal into the court system."

She could not believe what she was reading. Not one piece of evidence?

"Thus Mr. Kulle faces additional costs he may not be able to raise, unless his friends help him. What a crime in itself, that a man who would be judged innocent, is found guilty only because he was not rich enough to defend himself."

The moral equations had been flipped. Kulle was no longer the oppressor; he was the victim. His friends, the men and women actively supporting a Holocaust perpetrator, had recast themselves as the defenders of the little man. Any internal angst they may have felt about their relationship with Kulle—about what it meant to be friends with a Nazi—could be discarded. They were not supporting a concentration camp guard, the letter implied; they were helping a blue-collar worker who could not otherwise afford to defend himself against the Justice Department's goliath budget. They were not the bad guys, the Nazi sympathizers, the hypocrites who befriended a murderer. They were good liberals, they could tell themselves, who ensured that an aging janitor had the right to a fair trial.

There was an account at Citizens National Bank. The "Kulle Defense Fund."

Lunin Schultz was livid. This community had paid the salary of a concentration camp guard for a quarter century, and it was apparently not enough. The school board had hoped that the legal system would take the decision out of its hands, but the fundraising note made it clear that Kulle had no interest in a quick resolution. The case, it said, would "probably require appeal."[10] It was hardly surprising. Many of OSI's defendants continued litigating even when they had little chance of victory. They could delay a deportation or the cancellation of their Social Security benefits, and make a show of denying the allegations to their family and friends.[11]

Gignilliat finally issued a public statement on December 7. Explaining that the school board had "wrestled and agonized" over the case for the last year, he noted that three aspects of the issue had driven their process. First was the "range of emotions" the Kulle affair had elicited in the community. Next was the board's concern for the "fair treatment of individuals." Last was the board's responsibilities to the best interests of the high school. Trying to assure the community of the board's neutrality, Gignilliat stressed that faculty members had been instructed not to use school facilities or school communications to advocate on either side. He claimed that school officials were reviewing the curriculum on issues of human rights and the Holocaust, and he invited public comments, though he stressed that "action will not be taken until all relevant information has become available."[12]

Jay Jay Turner empathized deeply with the difficult position Leah Marcus was in. She was facing a lot of pressure—much more than other board members—and he admired the way she remained professional. They had a special bond, a way of communicating without needing to speak, and he could feel her discomfort.[13]

Shortly before the next school board meeting, Lunin Schultz, Toperoff, and a few others gathered to strategize. They needed to find a way around the "personnel issue" problem—a way to force the board to discuss Kulle in open session.

Back in October, Bruce Samuels had asked, almost sarcastically, whether the school had a policy about employees' memberships in questionable organizations. What if, Lunin Schultz suggested, they asked the board to adopt a policy against employing Nazis? There was something elegant about the idea. They would not mention Kulle's name or talk about him in any way. The discussion would remain theoretical and abstract, and the board would not be able to hide behind the "personnel" concern. Could this be it?

It seemed impossible that the school board would return with a policy in favor of employing Nazis. The group had little interest in an actual policy—it seemed entirely unlikely that OPRF would be in this position again—but the "proposal" would box the school board into a corner. Michael Fleisher volunteered to prepare a statement to read at the next board meeting. He was young and poised, and had a calm,

Figure 13. Barry Greenwald, Marjorie Greenwald, and RaeLynne Toperoff
meet to discuss Kulle, 1983. Courtesy of RaeLynne Toperoff.

polished presence. Driving home that evening, Lunin Schultz felt a
weight coming off her chest.[14]

* * *

"Dad," Kalyn Wulatin pleaded, "can you call me in sick?"

She knew her mom would say no, but she had been working furiously on her Kulle article for *Trapeze*, and needed more time. With her
dad's permission, she stared at a blank screen on the new Apple computer, and she gathered her notes from her interviews with Einhorn
and Deptuch, the summaries from committee meetings, the letter
Hans Delius had written to the *Wednesday Journal*, and the notes from
her history study sessions with Lunin Schultz.[15]

Wulatin began the article with Hitler, the Holocaust, and World
War II, driving home the point that those "grim happenings" had not
been so long ago. "Many children who died during the war would be as

old as the average teenager's parents are today," she typed, hitting her stride. Next, she wrote of Kulle, who was called "friendly and efficient" by his colleagues, and outlined OSI's case along with Kulle's defense. She was detailed, summarizing the testimony she had witnessed weeks earlier in court, and the evidence that had been presented beforehand. But the bulk of her piece was about Oak Park, about the high school, and about the community's struggle to decide what to do. She quoted Lunin Schultz, who had told her that "by trying to be neutral, the Board is taking a stand." She quoted Deptuch, who had told her that "nobody should condemn him until he is proven guilty." And she quoted Delius, who had written that Kulle had proven "his worth as a human being."

Kulle knew *Trapeze* intended to run a story, and hoped he could convince them not to do so. After school, he walked to the large suite of workrooms attached to English classrooms on the third floor, and begged English teacher and yearbook advisor Steve Gevinson to cancel the article.

"You're looking for *Trapeze*," Gevinson said. "That's next door."

Kulle scurried out, walking past the *Trapeze* office, too embarrassed to try again.[16]

A few days later, the article Wulatin and Dave Newbart had written was all over the school. A sketched picture of Kulle in a collared shirt adorned the cover, the outline of an SS man lurking over his shoulder. "Echoes of the Past Engulf the Present," the headline declared.[17]

* * *

There were few empty chairs at the next week's school board meeting. Lunin Schultz recognized many of the visitors, but the Kulle issue seemed to cast a wide net. Neo-Nazis were an increasing presence in front of the school, passing out booklets denying the Holocaust. Some of them even tried to speak on Kulle's behalf but, lacking Oak Park addresses, they were denied.[18]

The board and the administration took their seats just after 7:30 p.m. and proceeded with typical housekeeping. After agreeing to draft a letter of appreciation to a retiring engineer, the board ceded

Figure 14. Sketch of Kulle that appeared on the front cover of *Trapeze*, 1983.
Courtesy of William Earle.

the floor to the superintendent. But the large crowd certainly had not come to hear him discuss the new geometry textbooks. The meeting continued with a long list of items—everything but Kulle. Finally, after the board accepted an eclectic array of gifts, including an old car for the mechanics class, and one thousand pounds of acrylic plastic, it was time for public comments.[19] Gignilliat issued yet another reminder that the board would hear discussion of policy but personnel issues would be reserved for executive session. Toperoff tried to cover a wry smile as Michael Fleisher rose to address the board.[20]

After acknowledging the difficult position the school board was in, Fleisher admonished the members for not being more scrupulous in their dissemination of information. "Specifically," he continued, a recent board summary had referred to Kulle as "someone who has been accused of participating in the Nazi SS during World War II. . . . We request specifically the change of the words 'accused of' to 'admitted to.'"

Next, Fleisher turned to Gignilliat's recent statement. He continued:

> A great many in our community are feeling emotional stress over this issue. This emotional stress has increased as a result of the board's lack of ability to differentiate the legal from the moral issues. Those members of the community who are close to the events of the Holocaust need a clear public reaffirmation that the board of District 200 clearly understands that the doctrine and practices of the Nazi SS required a total commitment to racism and genocide. We ask the board to pass a resolution by public vote tonight stating that District 200 condemns racism and genocide in all of its expressions and specifically condemns the ideology and atrocities of the Nazi SS.

The board members listened quietly, Fleisher's respectful but firm tone adding to their discomfort. The board's refusal to take action, he asserted, jeopardized "the first obligation of the high school," their responsibility to train students to make informed and moral decisions.

A strong sense of pride washed over Lunin Schultz.[21]

Fleisher pushed for more specifics about the board's supposed desire to improve the Holocaust curriculum. "We would like to know from the board tonight how this review is proceeding. Who is responsible? How will it be conducted? What is the time for implementation? What are the appropriate avenues for our input?"

Leah Marcus remained silent.

Fleisher had the room enrapt as he shifted toward the group's ultimate demand. "We urge action based on a moral principle," he said. Gignilliat's recent statement had reiterated that the board would not act until it had all of the relevant information. "We are unclear as to what 'relevant information' you are lacking. What avenues are you pursuing to obtain this information? When can you expect you will have it?" Fleisher looked up at the stoic faces of the school board members. "If you are awaiting a legal decision by a hearing officer and/or continue to see this as a narrow personnel matter, you have misunderstood the issue," he said. "We request an answer. Should a person who has voluntarily served in the SS be considered a suitable employee of District 200?"[22]

Fleisher handed the board members copies of his statement, which had forty signatures at the bottom, and returned to his seat.[23] A few other speakers followed him, but even as they spoke, his words kept a firm hold on the room.[24]

Some board members grew defensive. Reverend Dudley responded that he would be "disturbed if the board responded immediately to the questions raised under the kind of pressure exercised in the meeting tonight." Marcus added that they were "not in the habit of answering hastily."

The discussion began to unravel, but Jay Jay Turner tried to reestablish order. Thanking Fleisher for his statement, he explained that the school board was a collective unit, and that members did not respond individually. Fleisher and the Coalition for an Informed and Responsible Citizenry had taken time to formulate their ideas together, and the school board needed to do the same.

At 10:15 p.m., Turner moved for the board to go into closed session in Swanson's office.[25] Almost exactly a year earlier in this very room, Swanson had first learned of Kulle's Nazi past from an article in the *Sun-Times*, had called Gignilliat and Marcus, and had had the first of many difficult conversations with Kulle.

In the closed session, Gignilliat and Swanson reported on their lengthy discussions with the school's attorneys. Swanson could tell he was losing the board members' support. As professional and even as Marcus had been, she was never going to sympathize with Kulle. Turner seemed to be moving in that direction as well. Swanson was losing patience. Kulle was just "a simple sergeant," he argued. "Why was he getting blamed for everything the Nazis did?"[26]

It was now past midnight, nearly five hours after the meeting had begun. The board members were all haggard, emotional, and drained. They agreed to continue their discussion the following week, at Gignilliat's office in downtown Chicago. Deptuch's petition, Fleisher's speech, and the continued increase in attendance at school board meetings made it clear to everyone in the room: a decision regarding Kulle's employment had to be made, separate from the outcome of the legal case.[27]

* * *

Lunin Schultz was back at the high school the next day to meet with David Diedrick, the chair of the history department. She hoped they could speak about Kulle and the school's Holocaust curriculum historian to historian, educator to educator. The school board kept insisting that the Kulle affair was a personnel issue, a bureaucratic item subject to legal considerations. But it was quite clearly a moral issue, and a pedagogical one as well.[28]

Holocaust education was still far from commonplace in public schools, but it was no longer entirely radical. A few years earlier, two Massachusetts teachers who had met at a conference sponsored by the Anti-Defamation League had begun working together on a Holocaust curriculum that stressed the choices individuals made. The program, "Facing History and Ourselves," asked students to use lessons of the past to consider problems of the present. It would soon receive a federal grant, become its own organization, receive national plaudits from the US Department of Education, and—in 1982—be published for national distribution.[29] Still, through the late 1970s, Holocaust education remained mostly a Northeastern phenomenon. National textbooks gave it little coverage, and the rise of Holocaust denial posed a distinct threat.[30]

As a broader demand for Holocaust education was increasing, a conservative push for schools to return "back to basics" threatened to undermine curricular reforms. In April 1983, just months before

Lunin Schultz met with Diedrick, President Ronald Reagan's Education Department released a landmark report titled *A Nation at Risk*, which seemed to confirm conservative fears that American schools were falling behind.[31] OPRF was hardly immune from those questions and pressures. The LaRouchites had rooted their insurgent school board candidacies on a "'back to basics' educational philosophy," and had garnered enough support so that Gignilliat, Marcus, and the other mainstream candidates had banded together to fend them off.[32]

In their meeting, Diedrick tried to assure Lunin Schultz to not be concerned. The Holocaust was covered in the world history classes, he explained, which spent two weeks on World War II. Teachers typically showed *Night and Fog* and *The Twisted Cross*, two films that showed the barbarity of Nazi oppression. The Holocaust was also addressed in the psychology and sociology courses, two electives that a handful of students took each year.

Lunin Schultz was worried that the lessons might be missing the mark. She challenged Diedrick, bringing up recent pro-Kulle statements that students had made, arguing that their support for Kulle suggested they did not understand the barbarity of Nazi oppression.[33]

Diedrick was dismissive. It was challenging to get students to connect emotionally to the Holocaust, he explained, because to them it already felt as distant as the Norman Conquest of 1066.[34] Lunin Schultz acknowledged that, but said it was the school's job to connect history to the present. And in the case of the Holocaust, it should not have been too difficult. They had a literal Nazi walking the halls, she said; teachers could easily use the Kulle case as a teaching mechanism. But as she spoke, it was clear to her that Diedrick was not particularly interested in her concerns. Parent committees, the school board, and now the faculty were in agreement: teaching about the Holocaust, Kulle, and antisemitism was not a priority.[35]

* * *

In the middle of December an arctic front swept in, pushing bitterly cold air through northern Illinois. For a week, the temperature barely reached ten degrees Fahrenheit, plummeting to nearly twenty below in what was one of the city's coldest months on record.[36] On Wednesday, December 21, Swanson and the school board met in the offices of Kidder Peabody & Company, Gignilliat's securities and investment banking firm, on the corner of South Wacker Drive and West Adams Street in downtown Chicago.[37] The building was impressive, a thirty-one-story silver skyscraper originally built as the headquarters for Northern Trust.[38] Getting there on this day was no easy feat, as the city was pounded with more than three and a half inches of snow.[39]

The meeting opened with the review of a letter from Charles Peterson, the president of the Oak Park–River Forest Community of Churches, which declared that Oak Park's Christian clergy had no interest in passing judgment on Kulle's guilt, or even in offering advice or demands to the school board.[40] Rather, they wanted to reach out to a community in agony, and consider the lessons of the past. "In relearning those lessons," the letter explained, "we must here ally ourselves with the defenders of Mr. Kulle who have cautioned us against hasty judgment, self-righteousness, or blindness to our own faults." It also called for a renewal of religious tolerance and understanding, concluding "We are all children of the last Holocaust and potential co-conspirators in the next one."[41]

It was an odd note, with a moralizing tone but no condemnation of Nazi atrocities, and no formal stance on the community's biggest moral question. Arguing that the most ominous outcome of the Holocaust was the willingness to see others as expendable, the letter aligned itself with Kulle's defenders, imagining him as the victim deemed expendable. It also seemed to suggest that everyone had been equally affected by the Holocaust, that the line between victim and perpetrator was blurry and malleable. The call for religious tolerance was particularly confusing, as the Community of Churches still excluded Oak Park's Jewish congregations.

At 4:30, Bernard "Bud" Nussbaum, the school's attorney, joined the meeting. He sat quietly as Reverend Dudley recounted his conversation with Kulle earlier in the week. Nussbaum would have to speak soon, to explain the court proceedings and the school district's legal responsibilities. He was prepared, but this issue was more personal to him than to anyone else in that room.[42] Tucked away in a family photo album at Nussbaum's house was a picture of a portable wooden staircase leading up to a large boat, with two sailors ushering a couple onboard. At the very left of the photo, almost out of the frame, stood a woman wearing a light trenchcoat and dark fedora, holding a small suitcase. Next to her was a small boy, his head barely visible under his hat. Other than a skinny leg bent at the knee, the boy's body was cut out of the shot. On the back of the photo an inscription read:

Exodus

Aug 1936

Mutti with Bernard

The photograph had been taken when Nussbaum, then five, had fled Nazi Germany with his mother. His father had already come to the United States to establish enough of an income to support them. Nussbaum's younger brother, Michael, had been too sick to travel. When Michael and a cousin came later, they had been quarantined; only an appeal to the immigration board in Washington had kept them from being sent back to the Reich. Nussbaum had served his new country in the Army, graduated from the University of Chicago Law School, and become a brilliant trial attorney for a major firm.[43]

Now, everyone in the room turned to Nussbaum, the five-year-old refugee from Nazi Germany, for counsel on how to deal with Kulle. For the next few hours, he walked them through the legal implications—the possibility of deportation, the likelihood of appeal—and the school's potential liabilities. Briefs were due in mid-January, he explained, and a decision could come anytime between the end of March and the beginning of July. They reviewed the moral and ethical implications, too: issues of justice, of forgiveness, of loyalty.

Everyone wanted to be thorough. They decided to invite Kulle, to give him a final chance to explain himself. If he brought Korenkiewicz, Nussbaum would join, too. With the semester ending and the holidays approaching, the school board members postponed its next meeting until Saturday morning, January 14. At 9:19 p.m., after more than five hours, they adjourned for the night.[44] By the time they woke up the next morning, Chicago was facing a record one hundred straight hours of subzero temperatures.[45]

* * *

On New Year's Day, the Sunday edition of the *Chicago Sun-Times* dedicated a full page to Kulle. "Reinhold Kulle is an ordinary man with a past steeped in blood," the article began, noting that the "paradox" of Kulle's life was "tearing at the fabric of Oak Park." The *Sun-Times* added little to what Wulatin and Newbart had written, and it even used the sketches of Kulle that *Trapeze* had featured. In the middle of the page, the *Sun-Times* tried to give faces to both sides of the debate. On one side, it featured a cutout of Michael Fleisher; on the other, it used a photo of Tadeusz Lampert, which appeared above a caption that read, "Tadeusz Lampert, once an inmate of a Nazi prison camp in Poland, believes Kulle is innocent."[46]

Lampert was distraught. He had been one of the first Oak Parkers to call for Kulle's firing, writing a joint letter with Norman Roth and Harry Gaynor. In recent weeks he had met with Lunin Schultz, attended school board meetings, and organized his church to stand against Kulle. But his fury ran deeper. When he was sixteen years old, he had taken up arms to defend Warsaw, his hometown, from the Nazi invasion. He had fought in the resistance throughout the war, and had lost many people close to him. That so few Americans understood that Poles, too, were among Hitler's victims made his pain even lonelier. He had found solace in the more universalistic approach of Simon Wiesenthal and had become an avid reader of his writings.[47] He was the "white-haired man" who had charged Frank Collin's band of neo-Nazis at Triton College. His head had been covered in blood when the Triton police wrestled him off the ground to arrest him.[48] And now, the *Chicago Sun-Times* was misidentifying him as a Kulle defender, a Nazi supporter. Lunin Schultz tried to calm him down, but Lampert was inconsolable. She spent hours on the phone with the paper, eventually getting them to issue a correction, but the damage had been done.[49]

Meyer Rubinstein—a former member of the Polish cavalry, now living in Skokie—read the *Sun-Times* report on Kulle with dismay. A boldface subheading in the article implied that perimeter guards were far from the prisoners, far from persecution. But that was not true. Rubinstein wrote a letter to the editor:

> I was prisoner 30510 at the Gross Rosen camp. The Nazis tried to provoke the inmates to escape. They encouraged the prisoners to run toward the perimeter, and then the perimeter guards would shoot the fleeing prisoners on the spot.
>
> The perimeter guards took part when sick prisoners from satellite camps were brought to the crematorium. They would surround the truck until all the prisoners were gassed and burned. I witnessed this atrocity.
>
> The group of Oak Park churches that has refused to take a stand in the Kulle matter is repeating the same mistake of so many churches in the Hitler era.[50]

* * *

Deliberations resumed in the high school's boardroom at 8:12 a.m. on January 14, 1984. Kulle and Korenkiewicz were due in about an hour, but the board members had several matters to discuss before they arrived. One member recounted a harrowing conversation he had had with a former Gross-Rosen prisoner. Gignilliat was struck by the fact that the number of reported deaths at Gross-Rosen was almost the same as the entire population of Oak Park.[51]

Nussbaum had recently talked with Sydnor, and recounted what the historian had shared about the camps that Nussbaum had narrowly avoided fifty years earlier. He reminded everyone that Kulle was an at-will employee, rehired every year, and that OPRF had no obligation to employ him after June 30, though they could employ him beyond that date. If they chose not to bring him back, they did not need to give a reason or an explanation. Their duties to Kulle extended only until June.

At 9:20 a.m., Kulle and Korenkiewicz joined the meeting, and Korenkiewicz gave prepared remarks. The board members then took turns interviewing Kulle.[52]

Jay Jay Turner had been reading everything he could about Gross-Rosen, and had grown convinced that Kulle was responsible for a lot of dastardly things. He was also sure that Kulle would underestimate him. When his turn to interview Kulle came, he stared across the table and asked him whether he had seen prisoners. No, Kulle responded, he had been on the outskirts of the camp. Turner quickly changed the subject. He asked about how Kulle's promotions at Gross-Rosen had impacted his relationship with Gertrud's father. Then, he asked Kulle whether he had ever done anything kind for the prisoners. Kulle told Turner the same stories he had told in court; he had brought chickens to a prisoner once, given water to another.

Which is it? Turner thought. Had Kulle been away from the prisoners, or had he brought them gifts? It was all Turner needed to hear. Kulle was lying, and now he knew for sure. Reinhold Kulle needed to go.[53]

Other questions followed from other board members, but Kulle claimed to remember very little from Gross-Rosen.

Had he ever shot anyone?

"I don't remember."

Had he ever abused or tortured a prisoner?

"I don't remember."

Had he ever killed anyone?

"I don't remember."[54]

Gignilliat found the answers eminently frustrating. Kulle was giving them nothing to go with, and it was certainly not helping his cause. And "I don't remember?" Killing someone seemed like a thing a man would remember.[55]

Finally, Reverend Dudley tried to break through. It had been a tense day, and the stress of the entire situation was wearing on everyone. "Reinhold, how do you feel? Do you feel guilty? Do you feel that the things you did were wrong?"

"Ya, ya, I feel bad. I feel bad about the whole situation," Kulle responded.

"Tell us exactly how you feel," Dudley implored, hoping for some kind of clarity.

"I feel bad, very bad," Kulle said. "I just wished we had won the war."[56]

21

A TERMINAL
LEAVE OF ABSENCE

An envelope addressed to Reinhold Kulle arrived at the high school in January. Inside were two pension estimates from the Illinois Municipal Retirement Fund (IMRF).[1] They would prove instructive. The "policy proposal" against employing Nazis had boxed the school board into a corner, and Kulle's answer to Dudley's question had done him no favors. One by one, school officials were coming to terms with the gravity of the situation. Gignilliat, who had long held out hope that they could weather the storm, now recognized that it would be impossible to retain Kulle. But before they decided anything, the board members wanted to know what impact the potential solutions would have on Kulle.[2]

Back in December the board had promised a response to Fleisher by its January 24 meeting, but as the meeting neared, no statement had been released. Growing impatient, Lunin Schultz and Toperoff distributed a note urging friends to attend the upcoming meeting, hoping their presence would help "bring about a sound policy on this issue." Attached to the note was a petition from Fleisher requesting substantive responses to the questions he had raised at the previous meeting. He planned to speak again.[3]

Finally, on January 18, the school board released a statement. In large part a response to Fleisher, it pushed back on the suggestion that the board adopt a resolution condemning racism and genocide, which "would imply that the board has not previously condemned those heinous ideas and acts." Quoting board policies, the letter stressed the district's commitment to both moral concerns and diversity, and reiterated that an ongoing curriculum review was underway.

At the end of the statement, Gignilliat addressed the board's decision process. These were complicated issues, he explained, and it was precisely because "the board is well aware of the impact this matter has had on our community" that they would "continue to seek counsel as needed, act with prudent deliberation, and resist attempts to precipitate a premature decision." They would announce a final decision when they had all the necessary and relevant information, and when they were sure they could do so without abridging Kulle's rights.[4]

Lunin Schultz could not understand what "necessary and relevant information" they still needed to have. What new information could possibly come out?[5]

But Gignilliat felt that a decision of this magnitude would have to be unanimous, and the board would need the administration's support.[6] They could not just summarily fire Kulle and move on—not after a quarter century of service. As important as it was to end what had become a public relations nightmare for the school, they hoped to somehow avoid hurting Kulle financially. The two IMRF simulations provided some clarity. The first estimated Kulle's pension if he retired at the end of the school year; the second if he waited two more years and retired in July 1986.[7]

Over the next few days, Gignilliat, the school board, and the administration weighed their options. Quietly, slowly, carefully, they crafted a way out—one they would shroud in secrecy for decades.

* * *

January 24 came quickly. After the school day ended and the night staff began their shifts, Swanson asked Kulle to come and talk.

Kulle gave a knowing glance as he entered Swanson's office. Sitting with his longtime friend, the superintendent choked back tears as he explained that the school board had made its final decision. Today would be Kulle's last day at OPRF. Swanson had released employees before—it was part of his job—but this time felt different.

There was one more thing. It would be best if Kulle were not there that night. The board did not want a confrontation. Swanson could no longer keep back the tears; he felt like he was losing a good friend. Kulle's reaction was muted, unemotional. He was disappointed, but not surprised. Half an hour later, as their meeting ended, Kulle asked Swanson to thank the school board for their consideration.[8]

* * *

Toperoff waited nervously for the school board meeting to begin. Word had gotten out that the board planned to make an announcement, and all indications were that it would be of Kulle's removal. To accommodate the large crowd that was expected, the board moved the meeting to one of the school's auditoriums. Toperoff's husband, Gil, sat on one side of her; Lunin Schultz and her husband, Richard, on the other. The Fleishers, the Greenwalds, and other friends were gathered nearby in the same cluster of rows. Herr Schoepko, the school's German teacher and Kulle's friend, settled into a seat behind them.[9] Meanwhile, a man Toperoff did not recognize was pacing up and down the aisle. She could not shake the feeling that he was staring at them.[10]

The room grew quiet. Oak Parkers were still filtering into the few remaining seats. After a few minutes of formalities and consent items, Gignilliat announced that he was going to read a statement, after which the board would act, and that visitors would not be allowed to comment until later in the meeting.

Toperoff took a deep breath, and looked over to Lunin Schultz.

"In recent months," Gignilliat began, "this board has devoted considerable time and attention to Reinhold Kulle's employment in the district. Mr. Kulle was a Waffen-SS guard for two and one-half years at the Gross-Rosen concentration camp in Nazi Germany during World War II."

The unknown man was still pacing in the aisle, and the room was eerily quiet. Gignilliat read slowly and deliberately: "Mr. Kulle was an armed guard at the camp."

Toperoff tensed, waiting.

"The board understands that under present law, no guard at a Nazi concentration camp would be permitted to immigrate to the United States."

Toperoff looked to her husband, and to Lunin Schultz.

"As a member of the noncertified supervisory staff, Mr. Kulle does not have a written employment contract."

The crowd was now becoming animated, whispers growing louder. Toperoff lost sight of the unknown man.

"The law does not compel the board either to re-employ or to terminate Mr. Kulle. The paramount considerations are and have been moral issues, including fairness to Mr. Kulle. Fairness to Mr. Kulle suggested to the board that it do nothing to interfere with his defense during the deportation hearing. The hearing has concluded. The board has obtained all the necessary relevant information, has been deliberate in its consideration, and is now prepared to act."

Lunin Schultz tried to quell her frustration at the revisionist history of the last thirteen months.

"The board is unwilling to show less than utter revulsion for the Nazi horrors. In making a decision, the board rejects any suggestion that to terminate Mr. Kulle's employment involves notions of 'guilt by association.' It is not the board's charge to decide whether Mr. Kulle is 'guilty' in that sense; nor does the board wish to prejudice his employment in the private sector. It is simply that no former guard at a Nazi concentration camp will be employed by this district. In a public school supported by public funds for educational purposes, the goal is to teach that each individual must accept responsibility for personal behavior and its implications for society."

It was strong rhetoric, and the crowd was responding strongly as well. Around Toperoff there were smiles and tears of exhaustion; behind her, groans of frustration and louder murmurs of discontent.

"Accordingly," Gignilliat continued, "Mr. Kulle will not be re-employed as of July 1, 1984, and is placed on terminal leave of absence effective January 25, 1984. Because the performance of his duties has given no legal cause to end his employment status or to cease compensating him, he will continue to receive his salary until June 30, 1984."[11]

Gignilliat moved back from the microphone.

CHAPTER TWENTY-ONE

Toperoff stood up, applauding. "The high school is finally clean," she thought.

Nearby, Norman Roth, Lunin Schultz, and Tadeusz Lampert were applauding as well. So were the Fleishers, the Greenwalds, the Sokols, and dozens and dozens of others.[12]

It was over. Kulle was gone.

A group of Kulle's friends a couple of rows away heckled loudly. "Where do these Jews come from? They rise from the ashes!"[13]

Jeffrey Greenwald, a sophomore, stood with his parents, and heard a scolding voice a few rows behind him: "*Wir bleiben setzen.*"

He turned around to see Herr Schoepko, and leaned over to his father, confused. "We stay seated," his father translated.

Chills went down the boy's spine.[14]

* * *

The announcement had done exactly what the board hoped. Kulle's opponents were happy, and the board would soon be able to move on from the turmoil and return to its work running the school. Though Kulle's colleagues would be upset, Swanson would be able to handle the faculty.

But Reinhold Kulle had not been fired. He would be allowed an early retirement. The board would give him a severance package. School officials would work with the retirement fund and Kulle's lawyers to find the best possible solution for his family. They would do their best to take care of him. It was a compromise among the board and the administration, a way of satisfying those who wanted him gone and those who thought the school still owed him loyalty. And it would all be kept quiet. There would be no additional announcement or public statement. The board would be careful to discuss the topic only in closed session, and the notes from those meetings would be kept sealed for nearly forty years—one of the high school's best kept secrets.[15]

* * *

After school the next day, Gignilliat and Marcus met with a select group of faculty, staff, and students. The school board meeting had ended well after midnight, so many who gathered in the large third-floor lecture hall had not yet read the board's statement. Gignilliat gave an introduction and background information about the board's decision before fielding questions.[16]

The student council president directed a question to Marcus. Earlier in January, *Time* magazine had carried a cover photo of the pope kneeling, forgiving his would-be assassin, Ali Agca. "If the pope can forgive Ali Agca, why can't *they* forgive Reinhold?"

They.

Marcus was keenly aware of why the question had been directed to her. It was not the first time during the Kulle affair that someone had suggested to her that forgiveness was Christian and vengeance was Jewish.

The pope might forgive for himself, she explained, but he had no authority to do so for anyone else. The victims of Gross-Rosen alone were empowered to forgive for what had happened there. Personal forgiveness, Marcus reminded the student, did not exempt Agca from consequences. After all, though the pope had offered his forgiveness, Agca remained in jail. She tried to remain poised and professional, but the question stung.[17]

The following Monday, the board held a larger meeting, and then a press conference. Two other board members joined Gignilliat and Marcus, and the entire faculty was invited. At both meetings, teachers and staff members expressed concerns, though Marcus felt that the faculty was understanding of the board's decision.

"You made the right decision, but it hurts," one teacher said.[18]

Not everyone was so understanding. Some accused the board of caving to community pressure. Marcus responded, with her characteristic diplomacy, that the issue had drawn "pressure from all sides," but Dudley told the faculty that he was confused by the accusation; after all, the board members had acted contrary to what they understood to be the popular view. If anything, he added, "the pressure made us less willing to act swiftly."[19]

Gignilliat stressed that their consideration, process, and decision focused on the school's best interest. In a moment of candor, Swanson told the *Oak Leaves* that the board "knew what decision to make" after meeting with Kulle and Korenkiewicz, though he did not elaborate. Gignilliat declined to disclose what Kulle had said in those private conversations, though he, too, agreed that the meeting was a "factor."[20]

With Swanson, Gignilliat, and Marcus handling the public relations, the school's business office began the separation process. Kulle was friendly with Jonathan Smith, the business manager; Hans Delius's wife Sharon worked in the business office as well. After twenty-four years, it was hard to find any room in the building where Kulle did not have friends. Smith began compiling Kulle's attendance record by hand, tallying the unused sick days he could still be paid for. In the 1983–84 school year, his days out of the building had been almost exclusively for court attendance. Kulle had 30 unused vacation days and 180 accumulated days of sick leave.[21] At eleven dollars a day, the school district owed him $3,237 for his vacation days and $1,980 for his unused sick days; it added $1,200 in "separation pay," which it was under no obligation to offer. The payments were spread out evenly from February through June on top of Kulle's regular salary, which he would continue to receive.[22]

On Monday, January 30, the business office issued a "notice of employee separation" for the high school's chief custodian. In the "reason for separation" section, Smith checked "other." The school's form had no line for what had just happened.

At the bottom of the form, Smith wrote:

The Board of Education has placed Mr. Kulle on "terminal leave of absence." Mr. Kulle no longer works here, but will be paid every two weeks through June 30, 1984. Above action was taken because the Board found Mr. Kulle to be a former guard at a Nazi concentration camp and felt that former SS soldiers should not be employed at this school.[23]

* * *

On February 1, Swanson sent a memo to members of the faculty and staff. He made no secret of the fact that he had not wanted the board to remove Kulle, but he had a responsibility to lead the school through this crisis. "The past week has been a most trying period in the lives of many of us," he began. "We have shared feelings of loss, anger, frustration, sorrow, betrayal and guilt as a result of the Board's decision to release Reinhold." He expressed shock at the "suddenness" of the board's action. The decision had been personally painful. Reinhold, he told the school's staff, was not just an employee, but a colleague and a friend. "I found it exceedingly painful to be the bearer of such news and physically impossible to restrain the tears of compassion for a man I loved and respected."

The memo mentioned the financial burden Kulle faced, and the importance of helping him find other employment opportunities. Swanson reassured the faculty and staff that the district would continue paying Kulle's salary through the end of the school year, that Kulle would be compensated for his unused sick leave, and that his pension would remain intact. He added that Kulle was, gratefully, receiving assistance with his financial burdens.

Swanson wrote that Kulle "never failed to express regret that he was 'causing problems' for me, the Board, and the school." But the school had to carry on—for Kulle, if for nothing else; "It will add to [Reinhold's] burden if this incident is allowed to affect" the school adversely. Swanson reminded his employees of the importance of respecting differences of opinion, and of following the school district's policy against using the classroom to promote any particular point of view. "Though emotion may make this difficult, our professional responsibility must prevail." Once the "grieving process is completed," he concluded, "let the healing begin."[24]

* * *

Though the faculty's response to Kulle's removal was mixed at best, Lunin Schultz, Toperoff, and their friends thought a celebration was in order. What had started as a collection of like-minded individuals had grown into something of a community. They wanted an opportunity to celebrate, to get to know each other better, and to plan for other ways to promote pluralism in the village.[25] As far as they could tell, they were one of the first groups in the country to get a Nazi removed from his job. And they had done it through the power of moral suasion.

Five couples, including the Lunin Schultzes and he Toperoffs, organized a get-together at Nielsen's Restaurant, a large redbrick restaurant and banquet hall on North Avenue. On Saturday night, March 3, 1984, several dozen members of the ad hoc coalition came together to enjoy a smorgasbord and to toast to their successes. The food was plentiful: baked ham, slow-roasted turkey, Danish style red cabbage, meatballs, baked chicken, mostaccioli, and a series of salads, sides, and slaws. There were a few short speeches, and drinks were raised to a successful defense of pluralism.[26]

It was hard to celebrate fully. What they had learned about their neighbors, their friends, and the community was deeply disquieting. But for now, at the very least, there was no longer a Nazi working at their kids' school.

22

A HOLLOW VICTORY

"We have found no cause for celebration," the *Wednesday Journal* admonished in its first story after Kulle's removal. Calling the board's decision a "hollow victory," the paper scolded those who had given standing ovations. Kulle had "had his life shattered," it said, and even his detractors "must know that his life has now become an even bigger hell than it was when the U.S. government filed its deportation case. . . . Unemployment has now been added to Kulle's load. The board's decision marked the ruination of a man's professional life, and that alone should have been enough to subdue the cheers and glad-handing. It was not, but that is history." With Kulle now facing unemployment and economic ruin, the *Journal* opined, the cheers were "deplorable."[1]

Reinhold Kulle, decorated veteran of the SS-Totenkopf, twice-promoted guard at a Nazi concentration camp, was again cast as the victim. A recent alumnus of the high school, whose sister worked there and was a prominent Kulle supporter, wrote in the *Oak Leaves* that the attacks on Kulle were emblematic of "man's inhumanity toward his fellow man."[2] Kulle, another Oak Parker scoffed, was a scapegoat.[3]

Jim Eitrheim published a public thank-you letter, writing that Kulle left behind "a large group of teachers and staff expressing their regret and helplessness in this whole matter. For the hundreds of small acts of kindness, for the years of dedication and concern, for the long hours of service," Eitrheim added nostalgically, "I remain his admiring friend."[4]

Students, too, criticized the board's decision. "It's not fair to judge people on their past," one junior told the *Oak Leaves*. "He didn't do anything wrong to us." Another added, "That was then, this is now." Nearly all the students interviewed disagreed with the board's decision.[5]

Delius was beside himself, writing to the *Oak Leaves* that Kulle's removal "threatens us all," and that Kulle had been "dismissed because, for reasons beyond his control, he was at a certain place at a certain time in history." He had been "slandered, blindly accused and dismissed without the slightest regard to the matter of guilt or innocence of any personal wrong doing." Delius even lambasted the board's new policy against employing former Nazis, noting that the "board had to invent a new policy on which to base its actions." It was a perversion of justice, he argued, reminiscent of the witch trials of early Salem. Delius and a few friends were even discussing a call to the American Civil Liberties Union, which had defended Frank Collin in court, hoping that the organization would do the same for Kulle.[6]

In the meantime, Kulle's friends upped the fund-raising efforts they had started in December. They estimated that Kulle's legal costs had now surpassed three hundred thousand dollars—more than an entire year's salary—and they put out calls for donations to the Kulle fund they had established at Citizens National Bank.[7] The *Wednesday Journal* reported that the fund was a response to Kulle's dismissal, and implied that it would help Kulle pay his bills. That was entirely misleading. Kulle was still receiving his salary, and was certainly not obligated to continue his expensive legal battle with the Justice Department. The Kulle Defense Fund was not intended to help the Kulle family cover its bills; it went directly to Kulle's legal defense. Eric Linden provided none of that context in his *Wednesday Journal* article, though he did include instructions for how to send donations.[8]

It was lost on no one that Kulle's most vocal opponents were Jewish, and with Kulle now situated as the victim, his supporters abandoned any subtlety as they expressed their frustrations with Oak Park's Jews. One man chastised the school board for "falling to the pressure of one group of people." He portrayed the anti-Kulle coalition as outsiders, complaining that "they bring in people from all over the Chicago area to appear at the board meeting, people who have nothing to do with this community or school," while saying nothing of Kulle's friends from Bronzeville and Forest Park who had also attended.[9] Another lambasted the board for caving after having been "harassed by village scolds," and complained that the high school taught "respect for 'the dignity and rights of each individual,' though not for janitors, apparently.... Leave it to Oak Park to give Nazi hunting a bad name."[10]

One opinion piece in the *Oak Leaves* tried to reframe the discourse. "That there is sympathy for a human being in trouble is not surprising," the unsigned piece proclaimed. "But the breadth and depth of support for Kulle is disturbing and disproportionate. It's as if a statute of limitations has expired on remembering what happened in those concentration camps. To Kulle's supporters, those millions and millions of deaths haven't the immediacy of a man losing his job."[11]

Kulle's son, Rainer, could not take any more. He wrote to the *Oak Leaves*:

Reinhold Kulle is guilty of one thing, and it is that he volunteered at the tender and impressionable age of 19 to answer his country's call to arms. If this is cause for this severe treatment and ruining his family life in his so-called upcoming golden years, then every soldier that ever answered the call to duty did so in vain.

Reinhold has paid his price to society.

1. He was wounded three times for his country.
2. He lost all his worldly possessions to the advancing Russians, including his family's large farm.
3. Again in 1957 when he came to this country, he lost everything and left it behind in West Germany.
4. And now he is again being asked to give everything up because a certain group of people will not forgive and let this matter rest.

Rainer left no confusion about who this "certain group" was: "The Jewish people act as if they are the only group of people to have ever been persecuted. If they would lead exemplary lives as a nation of people I could perhaps be a bit more sympathetic." Rainer complained about Israel, and questioned why Jews did not just "try to make the best of their situation," like "the Japanese, the blacks, and the Indians." In an explicit embrace of antisemitic tropes, he complained that other minority groups had made gains "without the benefit of repeated mass media attention and intimidation, also without the help of propaganda-type television shows.

"I think the time for the Jews has come to give the Holocaust some rest."[12]

* * *

In March, Swanson began meeting with Kulle's attorneys to coordinate the school district's separation with Kulle.[13] The simplest route was for Kulle to take an "early retirement" at the end of the 1983–84 school year and to begin receiving his pension, though there would be a penalty for collecting it early. Another option was to wait until he reached retirement age after the 1985–86 school year ended, and only then to begin receiving pension payments. If that were the case, though, it would mean two years without receiving income *or* a pension, though he then would not face a penalty.[14] A third option was for Kulle to be placed on unpaid leave for an additional year or two until he reached retirement age, potentially allowing him to maximize his benefits. After the meeting, Swanson sent a confidential memo to the business office asking for more details.

Swanson's first question asked how much additional money Kulle would receive if he waited until June 1986 to begin collecting his pension.[15] He was told that because Kulle would be making no additional payments, electing to receive the pension later would not change the amount he would receive. Swanson also asked how much Kulle had lost by virtue of the early removal. He was told that the $1,266 monthly pension for which Kulle was now eligible would have been $1,470. Swanson also asked whether Kulle's pension could be increased if he were placed on a leave of absence for the 1984–85 school year, using his unused sick leave and vacation time, and whether the school could exercise that option and also further compensate Kulle for his unused sick leave. He was told that a one-year leave of absence would increase Kulle's pension by $55 a month, but losing a year of pension payments would cost him more than $15,000; he would not break even for twenty-three years.

The next two questions dealt with two somber but realistic possibilities. If Kulle were to die, what death benefits would Gertrud receive? And what would happen if he were deported to Germany? The business office explained that upon Reinhold's death, Gertrud would receive half of Kulle's pension until her death, plus an additional $1,000 payment. If Kulle were deported, his pension would be reduced by 30 percent to account for the fact that he would no longer be paying federal tax on it.

Finally, Swanson asked whether the school district's policies allowed the school board to continue providing life, dental, and medical insurance for Kulle, even though he would no longer be an employee. And if not, "what steps could the Board take to provide such coverage?" Was there anything the board could do to make him eligible for a modified medical coverage, or life insurance coverage, after he turned sixty-five? Despite the creative thinking, there was little room for flexibility. If Kulle was considered terminated rather than retired, he could continue his health and dental insurance coverage at his own expense for two months; a private life insurance policy would be cost-prohibitive. In order to have him eligible for a modified medical coverage, the board would have to retire him.

None of the possibilities were ideal, and a delayed pension or long-term leave of absence did not seem to make much sense for Kulle. After hours of collaboration between the superintendent, the business manager, Kulle's attorneys, and representatives from the pension fund, an early retirement with some kind of arrangement between Kulle and the school board regarding his benefits seemed to be Kulle's best option.[16]

* * *

Later that month, OPRF's teachers gathered for a professional development day highlighting diversity in education. Illinois State Senator

Phillip Rock addressed a recent national report about educational access, and a prominent expert on multicultural issues gave a keynote address on academic excellence in diverse settings. At 10:30 a.m, the teachers dispersed to one of the ten breakout sessions meeting around the school. One session focused on the contributions of various ethnic groups to Chicago's history, another on gifted education, and still another on different learning styles.[17]

Michael Kotzin waited nervously to see how many teachers—and which ones—would attend his session: "Enduring Lessons of the Holocaust." The Midwest director of the Anti-Defamation League, Kotzin had followed the Kulle affair closely and had communicated with Lunin Schultz and Toperoff throughout the fall. He had given countless presentations about antisemitism and the Holocaust over the years, but there was no doubt that this setting would be unique.

Kotzin planned to discuss the importance of Holocaust education and give pointers about the difficulties teachers might encounter. He planned to show a film about an American girl whose family had lived through the Nazi rise to power, and he wanted to provide clear instructional practices that teachers could implement in their classrooms.

Some of the teachers were receptive. The world history teachers and psychology teachers, whose courses dealt with aspects of the Holocaust, appeared to be quite engaged. But some of the others present exhibited none of the curiosity of their colleagues, and had clearly come to argue, push back, and fight.

Why, one asked, couldn't the Jews of Germany have intermarried more, to save themselves? Why hadn't the Jews in the camps fought back? Kotzin warned against victim-blaming. His questioner simply left the room.

Another teacher asked Kotzin to comment on the "fanatics" who chased down former Nazis, and contrasted Jews' supposed desire for vengeance with "Christian forgiveness."

The emotionally charged atmosphere exhausted Kotzin. He had come to help, to provide an opportunity for teachers to add to their tool belts, to help them do something they should already have been doing.

There should have been nothing controversial about his presentation, but Kulle's friends seemed to perceive it as a threat. Perhaps any discussion of Nazi atrocities made it harder to defend Kulle, to cast him as the victim, to portray their support for him as just. It was hard for Kotzin to imagine a place where Holocaust education would be more difficult, or more necessary.[18]

* * *

Both OSI and Kulle's legal team submitted posttrial briefs to Judge Springer. Einhorn and Edelman worked together on OSI's submission, a summary of each witness's testimony and the evidence against Kulle. "Much of the government's evidence in this case is uncontradicted," they wrote. Kulle had produced no evidence or documents to counter the case against him. "In fact, save for respondent, all of the witnesses who testified on his behalf spoke only to his post-war life in the United States."[19]

OSI was undergoing a series of internal changes. Shortly after the Kulle hearing, Eli Rosenbaum had left the Justice Department. At lunch a few months earlier, Neal Sher explained that if Rosenbaum ever wanted to try his hand at private practice, he was running out of time; he would soon be seen as a government lawyer. Rosenbaum had taken a job as an associate at Simpson, Thatcher & Bartlett, handling securities, liabilities, and other issues for corporate clients at the white-shoe law firm in Manhattan.[20] He had had a successful run. He had worked on *Kairys* and *Kulle* and a slew of other cases. Arthur Rudolph, whose case he had built from a small footnote in a Cambridge bookstore, would soon leave for Germany, surrendering his American citizenship.[21] But the work had worn on Rosenbaum. Interviewing survivors was gut-wrenching, and the pressure he had put on himself was intense. He rarely allowed himself a day off, knowing that a relaxing Sunday for him meant an extra day of freedom for a Nazi perpetrator. After three intense years at OSI, Rosenbaum had put his Nazi-hunting days behind him.[22]

Allan Ryan had left OSI as well, and Neal Sher was promoted to director.[23] Before leaving, Ryan had been tasked with authoring an extensive report on America's postwar relationship with Klaus Barbie, the "Butcher of Lyon." Ryan's research showed that America had helped Barbie escape justice, using him for counterintelligence work and assisting his escape from France to Bolivia.[24] Ryan was also at work on a book about his time at OSI and the efforts to bring America's Nazis to justice. In an appendix that provided a short update on OSI's cases, he listed Reinhold Kulle's case as "pending."[25]

23

"REINHOLD, WE'LL NEVER FORGET YOU"

A new letter appeared in several dozen faculty mailboxes at the end of February. After hearing of Kulle's removal, several teachers had discussed hosting a retirement dinner, and the response was positive. But if they were going to host something before the end of the school year, they needed to start planning.

The letter itself was informal and friendly. "We could have a wingding of a party with just the people listed above," it joked, of the large group of teachers helping to organize the event. With so many sharing the load, the planning would be bearable, and they would be able to organize an event that Kulle would remember forever. Before they could go full steam ahead, there were certain questions they had to answer. Where should the dinner be held? Should it be at OPRF, or elsewhere? How much should they charge? Some teachers suggested raising money for Kulle, but they worried that a required donation might present a financial barrier for attendance. Could they get a party scheduled by early May? Who should be invited? How should they publicize the dinner?

Once the teachers had answered these preliminary questions, they could assign work to various committees. Their first meeting would be on Wednesday, February 29, at 4:15 p.m. The meeting would only take an hour, so everyone would still have time to "get home to our dinners and more 'romantic' pursuits on this leap year evening."[1]

Throughout March, five committees met at the school. One was placed in charge of finding a date and location for the banquet. It investigated various facilities in Oak Park and the surrounding towns, and compiled a list of potential venues. The frontrunner was the Mar-Lac House in downtown Oak Park, which had held several OPRF parties in the preceding few years. The teachers hoped to book it for either Sunday, May 6, or Sunday, May 20. Another committee worked on invitations and reservations, while a third worked on "community relations." A fourth was in charge of the program and entertainment.

Dick Rietz, the director of buildings and grounds and Kulle's direct supervisor, led the fifth group, a gift committee. On March 16 he sent out an invitation with some ideas. Gertrud had suggested a watch. Another idea was a small televsion set. Some of the custodial supply companies could donate gifts, a humorous recognition of his service. The committee discussed sending the Kulles dinners from Kentucky Fried Chicken or Wendy's. Rietz thought a gift from the school might be a nice touch. The gift committee could also coordinate a donation to help with Kulle's defense. Reitz asked everyone to think about these and other options before the meeting.

The following Monday, five members of the gift committee, including Schoepko and English teacher Norma Schultz, met in Rietz's office at the high school. They joked about keeping the meeting under cloak and dagger, and someone suggested using a password, like the comedian Joan Rivers's catchphrase, "Can we talk?" They agreed to request donations of small, funny gifts from custodial suppliers, and to obtain a history of the school to give Kulle at the banquet, along with a framed scroll of appreciation. But the major gift would be cash for Kulle's defense. The teachers settled on a donation of five dollars per person, which would be part of the ticket price. Rietz took minutes of the meeting and sent them to the other committee chairs.[2]

The venue committee met the next day, after school. For the date of the dinner, it settled on May 6 in the upstairs banquet hall at the Mar-Lac House, a former opera house that had been renovated into one of Oak Park's finest banquet halls.[3] Mixed drinks would be offered for two dollars; wine, beer, and soft drinks for one dollar. The committee would get keep twenty-five cents on each drink sold, to include as part of the gift to Kulle. The evening would start with an "Attitude Adjustment Hour" at 5 p.m., followed by a family-style dinner at 6 p.m., and a program at 7:15.[4]

The invitation came out a few weeks later. "NO MAN IS A FAILURE WHO HAS FRIENDS," it read at the top, quoting from the film *It's a Wonderful Life*. Printed on a full-size sheet of paper, the invitation explained that Kulle had been dismissed "after 25 years of distinguished service," and that "few people were able to express their regrets, or even to say goodbye to a friend." This banquet, on May 6, would provide that opportunity. "An appreciation dinner in honor of Reinhold will be held at the Mar-Lac House and we sincerely hope that you will be with us." Anyone who was not able to attend was still encouraged to contribute to a gift. RSVPs, with seventeen dollars per person for the dinner and donation, were to be sent by the end of April.[5]

In late April the committee chairs met for half an hour in the math department's workroom. With less than two weeks before the banquet, only eighty individuals were scheduled to attend, and only an additional twenty had contributed. Reservations were due in a few days, and only 15 percent of those who had received invitations had responded. The planning committees would need to talk up the event, to remind their colleagues and friends, and reach out to alumni.[6]

On May 6, throngs of Kulle's friends and supporters made their way into the Mar-Lac House to celebrate Kulle's retirement. Climbing the stairs to the Mar-Lac's refined Marina Room, Nancy Greco thought about the day a few years earlier when Reinhold Kulle had helped her in a time of great need. She had been crying in the tunnel beneath the high school's theater stages when a familiar figure approached. Kulle was not one to offer physical comforting, but he had been able to tell that something was wrong. He had found a phone and dialed Greco's house: "Are you the chubby girl's mom? Your daughter needs you." In the decade her graduation, she had gotten to know Kulle's family— Gertrud, Rainer, Ulricke, even the grandkids—and she was not going to miss the opportunity to thank him.[7]

With its twenty-four-foot ceiling and crystal chandeliers, the

"NO M███ ██ █ █████ ██ ██ AS FRIENDS"

It's a wonderful life
1946

On January 24th of this year Reinhold Kulle was dismissed
from his duties as chief custodian at Oak Park & River Forest
High School after 25 years of distinguished service. Few
people were able to express their regrets, or even to say
goodbye to a friend.

On May 6th, the chance to show Reinhold Kulle your support
and friendship, will become a unique reality. An appreciation dinner in honor of Reinhold will be held at the Mar-Lac
House and we sincerely hope that you will be with us.

In the event that you cannot attend, a contribution towards
a gift for Reinhold is an option that would be greatly appreciated.

APPRECIATION DINNER IN HONOR OF REINHOLD KULLE

SUNDAY MAY 6TH, 1984

MAR-LAC HOUSE

104 S. MARION, OAK PARK

CASH BAR 5 P.M. - DINNER 6 P.M.

$17.00 PER PERSON

Make check payable to APPRECIATION DINNER COMMITTEE

(Please fill out and return before April 27th deadline.)
- -

YES, I WILL ATTEND. NO. ATTENDING AT $17.00 per_____

NO, I CANNOT ATTEND, BUT WOULD LIKE TO CONTRIBUTE_____

(send to)

APPRECIATION COMMITTEE

1103 HOLLY CT. #305

OAK PARK, IL. 60301

(If you know of anyone else who would like to attend
please send us their name and address.)

Figure 15. Invitation to Kulle's retirement dinner, 1983.
Papers of Rima Lunin Schultz.

Mar-Lac hosted Oak Park's fanciest social and political gatherings, and Greco had dressed for the occasion.[8] The upstairs Marina Room was the larger of the Mar-Lac's two banquet halls, with space for up to five hundred guests.[9] Just a few months earlier, former Vice President Walter Mondale had held a fundraiser there during his successful campaign for the Democratic presidential nomination.[10] Greco found Kulle and went over to say hi. She was struck by his appearance. The stress must have really gotten to him, she thought. He had never been a slim man, but now he had put on a lot of weight. Perhaps even more striking was his outfit; she had never seen him in a suit before. She laughed at the sight of the custodian in an ill-fitting suit in one of the fanciest rooms in town.

Greco walked to her table, passing her former teachers as she found her seat. The room was packed. Nearly 250 guests had come to celebrate Kulle. Drinks were flowing, and soon everyone sat down for chicken and beef, served family style.

After dinner, Eitrheim took the microphone to begin the evening's entertainment. After the performers of a series of skits gently teased Kulle, a few speakers came up to honor him. Swanson fondly thanked Kulle for his dedication and service to the school. Kulle received a book signed by everyone in attendance, along with a history of the high school. Some of the gifts, including rolls of toilet paper and soap donated by the school's custodial suppliers, elicited laughs from the crowd. Kulle was then presented with a check for $1,500 from the collected donations. Dick Rietz, Kulle's former boss and the gift committee chair, gave $100 himself, a token of his appreciation. Kulle's friends hoped that for at least one night they had lifted Kulle's spirits.[11]

The highlight was a musical performance. They all knew that Kulle loved musicals, and Eitrheim had arranged for a student band to play "Edelweiss" from *The Sound of Music*, changing the lyrics to "Reinhold, we'll never forget you."[12] Everyone at the Mar-Lac House laughed and cheered, but the song was a peculiar choice. In the film, the von Trapps sing "Edelweiss" in defiance of pressure to join the Nazis.

At the end of the night, Kulle addressed the large gathering, thanking the friends who had stuck by him during the ordeal.[13] On the front page of the next week's *Wednesday Journal*, Eric Linden called the party a "royal send off."[14]

* * *

As prom and graduation neared, Kalyn Wulatin and the other student journalists put together their last issue of *Trapeze*. Wulatin went back to Swanson to ask for an update on Kulle. Swanson told her that Kulle had interviewed for two custodial positions in the private sector, but had yet to find a new job.[15] A ruling in the deportation case would come later that summer or early in the fall. It was the last update on the reporting that won Wulatin and Newbart a prestigious Gold Circle Award from Columbia University, recognizing their December story as one of the best pieces of student journalism in the country.[16]

As far as most Oak Parkers knew, the Kulle affair was over, having been resolved at the January school board meeting. The administration and the board had kept the negotiations with Kulle private, the only records of the severance pay, meetings with the IMRF, and the conversations with Korenkiewicz placed quietly in Kulle's personnel folder, tucked away in the bowels of the building. The community had moved on.

On June 28, at the end of a long school board meeting, Leah Marcus moved to go into closed session.[17] Just before 10 p.m., the board and the administration left for Swanson's office. They discussed collective bargaining issues, and reviewed the letter Kulle had sent them a week earlier, formally requesting an early retirement.[18] One of the board's attorneys suggested a formal "compromise agreement and general release," but the deal for Kulle's termination had already been hammered out.[19] The school would maintain Kulle's medical and dental insurance at school district expense until he reached the age of sixty-five, and would continue dependent coverage for Gertrud.[20] Everyone was careful to discuss the arrangement only in executive session, so that there would be no paper trail in publicly available documents. Back in open session, the school board approved the personnel recommendations that accompanied the end of the school year. One of the thirty-three items was the noncertified staff retirement of Reinhold Kulle, buildings and grounds custodian and head custodian, effective June 30, 1984. Buried deep in the minutes of the last school board notes of the year, it was sure to go unnoticed.[21]

On July 3, Swanson mailed Kulle a memo, noting that the school board had approved his request for an early retirement. The lawyers were negotiating the terms, and once it was finalized, the business office would be in touch with him regarding his benefits.

"If you have any questions," Swanson wrote to his old friend, "please give me a call."[22]

24

DEPORTATION

Leah Marcus stepped up to the lectern, placed down the seventeen typed pages she was holding, and looked up at the congregation.

Rabbi Joseph Tabachnik had made it clear that he expected her to speak that day. "You owe it to the community," he told her, and Yom Kippur seemed an appropriate time.[1] Since sundown the night before, the congregation had been asking for forgiveness and mercy. Over and over, their fists thumped their chests, reciting ancient words of confession. "We have given harmful advice; we have deceived; we have mocked." With each confession, another thump. "We are not so brazen," they chanted in Hebrew, "to say . . . that we have not sinned."[2]

But what did forgiveness mean? And who had the authority to give it?

Now, halfway through her fast, Marcus stood on the pulpit at West Suburban Temple Har Zion. She could see friends and family members, and the faces of those who had questioned the school board's handling of the Kulle affair—who had wanted them, and especially her, to act more swiftly.

"I have some personal hesitation as we begin, that I may disappoint you if you have come to hear board-member-tell-all; that I may fall short of the mark and lose the essence of the tale, in the narrative or the analysis, through a deficiency of heart or mind or words; that I may be the instrument of pain."[3]

On the wall to her right, the sun illuminated five columns of stained glass, each with eleven panels depicting biblical scenes. At the top of the second column, Cain killed Abel. It was man's first murder. Lower on the same column, a flood covered everything; the world, filled with violence and evil, seemed unsalvageable. At the bottom, a dove flew holding an olive branch. The artist, William Gropper, called it the *Window of Good and Evil.*[4] Issues of forgiveness, of good and evil, had been at the forefront of Marcus's mind for the past year, but she had kept her views closely guarded. Now, standing in front of her synagogue at an austere time typically reserved for the rabbi, she tried to speak more freely than she had since Swanson's call on a December morning almost two years earlier. The question most on her mind was not whether Kulle deserved forgiveness, but why his friends and colleagues had offered it in the first place.

"The story of Reinhold Kulle, nineteen-year-old SS volunteer, wounded on the Russian front, assigned less active duty at Gross-Rosen as an armed guard and SS trainer, fell hardest on those who know him well," Marcus said. "Twenty-three years is a long time to work in a close-knit job community, to make friends, to do good service, to be kind to coworkers' children and wives." She quoted the letters Oak Parkers had written to the local newspapers, the ones that had assumed Kulle was "not proud of his Nazi background," and that he was "tormented by his memories." She knew it was not true. She hinted as much, referring to him as "remorseless," though she kept her focus away from the man himself.

"Those who both anticipated Kulle's remorse and then suggested forgiveness for him, I believe, did so from a theological base and from great personal need." Kulle did not look like a monster, Marcus said, the visage of the middle-aged custodian standing in front of her home seared into her mind. If ordinary men could do such terrible things, Marcus noted, "might not I?"

Over the last few weeks, she had been reading proofs of Allan Ryan's forthcoming book *Quiet Neighbors*, a riveting story of brutal men who thought they had gotten away with murder, only to be tracked down by a determined group of investigators, historians, and attorneys at OSI. Endorsed by Holtzman, Wiesenthal, and the preeminent Holocaust historian Raul Hilberg, the book was a clarion call for Americans to support the nascent efforts to bring Nazis to justice.

At the pulpit, Marcus read directly from Ryan's book.

> Many people assume that those who perpetrated the Holocaust have lived for forty years with grief and contrition in their hearts. They have paid the price, or so it is believed—why hound them to their graves? My answer is that such an assumption, so far as I can tell, is simply wrong. I see no evidence whatever that any of those men have been even slightly discomforted, let alone tormented, by their actions in the past. To the contrary, when faced with overwhelming evidence of their complicity, they blandly deny they were even present at the scene, or if they admit that they were there, they minimize the significance of their actions and then rationalize even that.[5]

She looked out into the rows of congregants facing her. She knew the school board's decision-making process had been a source of acrimony for many in the room. She tried to explain that the board members had primarily been committed to fairness, that they had felt required to wait until after the election cycle and after the conclusion of the hearings before removing Kulle.

Meanwhile, Lunin Schultz and Toperoff were a few blocks north, sitting in the pews at Oak Park Temple. They had a profoundly different understanding of the school board's inaction.

The last two years had felt like a battle, and Marcus reminded the congregation that even now, the school board's decision remained "widely unpopular." She could not discuss what the board had actually done, the "compromise agreement and general release" she had signed back in July. She looked up, ready to broach perhaps the most disappointing part of the whole ordeal.

"What does one say about the antisemites?" Marcus asked. She explained how one prominent attorney had chastised Kulle's Jewish detractors for being "caught up with vengeance," And still others had told them to "let go of history." One woman had argued that abortion was worse than the Nazis' crimes. For non-Jewish neighbors, Marcus explained, the Holocaust "belongs to Jews, and not to them." Then she added, repeating Wiesenthal's words that had so captivated her at Triton: "Presenting Jewish pain would never be enough. That pain was incomprehensible to most, and beside the point to others." The sentence was underlined in the written text of her speech.

Still, she said, there was reason for optimism. She praised Lunin Schultz, the *Trapeze* reporters, and several teachers who challenged the community to be its best. And she celebrated the non-Jewish leaders in the community—especially John Lukehart of the Community Relations Commission—whose commitment to pluralism and to a "shared ownership" of the Holocaust made her remain hopeful. It had been a harrowing thirteen months, and Marcus was ready to move forward.

"I wish you a good year," she concluded, "and the vigor of youth."[6]

* * *

In November, Judge Springer issued her ruling.

Just as Einhorn had anticipated, Springer had been profoundly moved by the survivors' testimonies, calling Moldawa's account "particularly compelling."[7] "As an armed Waffen-SS guard," she wrote, Reinhold Kulle had "helped to prevent prisoners from escaping both from the camp and the camp's outside worksites; he assisted in the confinement of inmates inside the camp, by manning watchtowers overlooking the protective custody area and by serving as a perimeter guard. . . . The respondent's receipt of two promotions during his tenure at Gross-Rosen indicates that his performance was at least considered to be acceptable in the eyes of his superiors." The evidence was "clear, convincing and unequivocal," she wrote, that Reinhold Kulle had participated in persecution under the direction of the Nazi Reich.[8]

Though Springer recognized that there was no documentation that Kulle had personally committed an atrocity, she said that none was necessary. At the end of her forty-seven-page ruling, she rejected all of the various motions and applications for relief that Kulle had filed, and ordered him "deported from the United States to the Federal Republic of Germany."[9]

"We are definitely going to appeal," Korenkiewicz announced shortly after the ruling. He confidently told reporters that Kulle had an excellent appellate case and was likely to win, though he quietly admitted that he had not yet read Springer's ruling.[10] Glomming onto Springer's comment that there was no evidence Kulle had personally committed atrocities, Hans Delius told the *Oak Leaves* that he was happy to see Kulle "vindicated." Delius's wife said she was "pleased that the hearing has cleared him of any wrongdoing."

The local papers struggled to get any of Kulle's opponents to comment. Michael Fleisher declined an interview, and Toperoff replied simply that she thought the ruling was fair. John Lukehart said he was "not terribly surprised," and reminded reporters that the deportation case was completely separate from Kulle's removal from the school. "Our concern was one of what it meant to have a member of the SS at the school," he explained. "The outcome [of the hearing] wasn't really the primary concern."[11]

In the appeal they filed the following week, Korenkiewicz and Nixon argued that Gross-Rosen had not been a place of persecution, and that inmates there had been criminals or prisoners of war. They maintained that Kulle's service was involuntary and outside the camp's protective custody; and in a desperate effort, they questioned the constitutionality of the Holtzman Amendment.[12] But the walls were closing in.

On Friday night, December 21, 1984, the United States deported Feodor Fedorenko. A lawyer for the former Treblinka guard complained that Fedorenko was too ill to travel, but after holiday traffic at New York's JFK Airport briefly delayed his departure, Fedorenko left the United States and landed safely in Moscow to stand trial.[13] A week later, Judge James Moran of the US District Court for the Northern District of Illinois revoked Liudas Kairys's citizenship.[14]

Kulle's time in America, too, seemed to be winding down.

* * *

As the fortieth anniversary of the end of World War II neared in 1985, President Ronald Reagan announced plans to visit Germany, including a stop at a German military cemetery in Bitburg, where forty-nine Waffen-SS men were among the buried. During an acceptance speech for his Congressional Gold Medal in April of that year, Elie Wiesel called on Reagan to cancel the trip. The First Lady and a majority of both houses of Congress urged Reagan to cancel as well, but the president—explaining that he wanted to "focus on the future"—worried that a cancellation might offend German Chancellor Helmut Kohl.[15] Instead, there was talk of adding a trip to a concentration camp to the visit. White House communications director Patrick Buchanan, the strongest proponent of the Bitburg visit, reportedly scribbled "Succumbing to the pressure of the Jews" in his notes during meetings.[16] Reagan tried to defuse the tension, but did himself no favors when he explained that a trip to a concentration camp could make Germans feel unnecessary guilt.[17]

Rabbi Avi Weiss and other Jews camped out in Bergen-Belsen to protest, but Reagan's visit proceeded as planned. In a short speech at Bitburg, he claimed without any evidence that the average age of the buried was about eighteen, adding, "They were victims, just as surely as the victims in the concentration camps." More than one hundred Christian leaders signed a letter criticizing Reagan's "failure to distinguish between perpetrators and victims." Reagan and Kohl added a last-minute trip to Bergen-Belsen, where another Jewish group challenged the two leaders to choose between honoring the SS or honoring its victims, declaring poignantly, "They cannot do both."[18]

OSI spent much of that year fighting appeals from Laipenieks, Maikovskis, Artukovic, Linnas, and Kairys, all of whom exhausted their efforts to stay in the country. Other cases found their conclusion outside the courtroom. Bohdan Koziy fled to Costa Rica in the face of a deportation effort. A pipe bomb killed Tscherim Soobzokov,[19] and a spokesman for the Jewish Defense League, the group suspected of the attack, called it "a righteous act."[20] Another bomb exploded at the

Long Island home of Elmars Sprogis, an accused Latvian Nazi. OSI Director Neal Sher condemned the attacks, calling them detrimental to OSI's efforts.[21]

On December 10, 1985, the three-judge panel at the Board of Immigration Appeals upheld Kulle's deportation order. The judges were unimpressed by Korenkiewicz's arguments, each of which either had been disproven by the evidence or would not have affected Kulle's deportability. They summarily dismissed Korenkiewicz's constitutional arguments against the Holtzman Amendment, saying they lacked "any merit whatsoever." Little was left between Kulle and deportation.[22]

* * *

After a year in private practice, Eli Rosenbaum took a job as general counsel for the World Jewish Congress. He kept in close touch with his former OSI colleagues, but as far as he was concerned, his days of Nazi investigations were behind him. In 1986, in the lobby of the Jerusalem Hilton, he felt a hand on his shoulder. He turned around to see his boss, Israel Singer, beckoning him to a private corner of the hotel's lower lobby.

"There's something important that has to be checked out," Singer told him. "It has to do with Kurt Waldheim." Singer's tone grew serious. "It looks like our Dr. Waldheim may have been a Nazi. A *real* one."[23]

Soon, Rosenbaum was on a plane to Austria to investigate the former United Nations secretary-general, one of the world's most famous diplomats, who was now running to become president of Austria. Over the ensuing months, Rosenbaum led an investigation that uncovered Waldheim's membership in the SA and his leading role in a Nazi intelligence unit that deported the Jews of Greece to Auschwitz and committed mass murders in Yugoslavia.

Rosenbaum's investigation demanded a confrontation with the past that threatened to unmoor Austria's foundational myth as the Nazis' "first victims," and the response to the investigation followed a familiar pattern: a series of ever-changing denials, then a downplaying of Waldheim's role, and eventually, claims that he was the victim of Jewish attacks. Patrick Buchanan, who had been critical of Waldheim's tenure at the UN, suddenly came to his defense, calling the investigation "moral bullying" and "selective indignation."[24]

The defensive veneer surrounding Waldheim soon gave way to an ugly tide of explicit antisemitism. Despite, or perhaps because of, the revelations, Waldheim won the election. He spent his presidency mostly in his own country, unable to make foreign trips, as he was now persona non grata across the globe.[25] Rosenbaum's riveting and characteristically meticulous book about the Waldheim affair was poignantly entitled *Betrayal*.

***

Nixon and Korenkiewicz appealed to the 7th Circuit Court in December 1986, recycling the same arguments that had been defeated twice already. Their brief was caustic, characterizing each of the survivors as "criminals" and referring to Moldawa's book as the "pejorative and tendentious ramblings of a very bitter man. They maintained that Gross-Rosen had not been a concentration camp, and that OSI had needed to "manufacture" evidence to suggest otherwise.[26]

As Kulle waited for the Circuit Court's decision, public attention focused on Karl Linnas, who was fighting a potential deportation to the Soviet Union. Buchanan penned multiple op-eds criticizing OSI, calling it "Orwellian and Kafkaesque to deport an American citizen to the Soviet Union for collaboration with Adolf Hitler when the principal collaborator with Hitler in starting World War II was that self-same Soviet government."[27] Leaders of émigré groups joined in, saying that a deportation to the Soviet Union betrayed both anti-Communist and civil libertarian values.[28]

On April 13, 1987, in an attempt to find a solution, Attorney General Edwin Meese moved to deport Linnas to Panama, which had offered to accept him on humanitarian grounds. In a particularly galling move, Meese made the decision on the eve of Passover, when Jewish organizations would be closed and unable to respond. Catching wind of the decision, Rosenbaum and Holtzman raced to a local synagogue to wrest Menachem Rosensaft, the chairman of the International Network of Children of Holocaust Survivors, from his prayers. After the trio held a press conference on the Panamanian Embassy's steps, Panama quickly announced that it would no longer be accepting Linnas.[29]

A few hours later, Rosenbaum sat across from Buchanan on the CNN program *Crossfire* to discuss the case. Debates over the Linnas deportation and Nazi-hunting were becoming fodder for cable television. Unable to deny or even downplay Karl Linnas's guilt, Buchanan called the deportation a "lynching," and claimed that Linnas was responsible not for the thousands of deaths of which he was accused, but only for a few hundred. "How many Jewish bodies are enough to meet the quota?" Rosenbaum asked defiantly.[30]

Linnas was deported to Russia in April, and died that summer after suffering from a variety of health ailments.[31] Three weeks later, Soviet officials announced Feodor Fedorenko's execution.[32]

On August 5, 1987, Judge Robert Grant of the 7th Circuit Court of Appeals affirmed Judge Springer's deportation order. The court reprimanded Kulle's attorneys for challenging the constitutionality of the Holtzman Amendment; the same court had already rejected those same challenges in the *Schellong* case, in which Nixon was also an attorney.[33]

Kulle was taken into custody at his Brookfield home on Friday night, October 23, 1987. He spent the weekend at the Metropolitan Correctional Center in downtown Chicago, awaiting his deportation. Though it had been ten weeks since the Circuit Court's ruling, his attorneys had yet to file an appeal. Nixon was on vacation in Europe when he heard the news, and promptly returned for one final push, filing an emergency request to the Supreme Court asking for a stay of Kulle's deportation, which Justice John Paul Stevens rejected without comment. On Monday, Kulle was taken to O'Hare International Airport and placed on a plane to Germany. He landed at 12:45 a.m. on Tuesday morning, and headed to a relative's home in Lahr, the city he had left thirty years earlier. West Germany's chief Nazi crimes prosecutor,

Alfred Streim, announced that Kulle would not face charges; a preliminary investigation had turned up "no indications of a crime that can still be prosecuted."[34]

The deportation renewed dormant tensions in Oak Park. In the *Wednesday Journal*, Eric Linden referred only to Kulle's "World War II service," and stressed that Kulle had never admitted to wrongdoing.[35] Marvin Schlichting of River Forest declared Kulle innocent in a letter to the editor, writing that those who dwelled on revenge could "sometimes become worse than those they seek to punish." In a jarringly humorous juxtaposition, his note appeared next to another letter, titled "Toilet Papering Homes: It's Wrong and Wasteful," sent in by a recent victim of the teenage prank.[36]

A week later, John Frush Knox, a prominent attorney in town who had clerked at the Supreme Court, thanked the *Wednesday Journal* for printing Schlichting's letter. Three years earlier, Knox—who in a law school memoir had once called himself the greatest diarist ever—had penned a long and emotional essay chastising Kulle's prosecution. America has committed sins too, he had written, including "the horrors that our own government caused the defenseless Southern people in the 1860s." That letter had sympathized not with the newly freed slaves but with the Southern white woman, "on her knees pleading for the preservation of her plantation."[37] Now, in the wake of the deportation, he moaned in a similarly histrionic tone that "Mr. Kulle became a sacrifice to the forces of hatred. May he never be forgotten."[38]

Rabbi Joseph Tabachnik was disgusted by the "mistaken compassion," noting that Jewish businesses in Chicago's Rogers Park neighborhood had been attacked on the anniversary of Kristallnacht the previous week. "Good riddance to Reinhold Kulle," Tabachnik wrote. "We don't need more pollutants in America."[39]

Kulle was now one of several OSI defendants living freely in West Germany. Conrad Schellong was deported a year later, after nearly eight years fighting OSI in court.[40] Arthur Rudolph had flown to Germany on his American passport, and had renounced his American citizenship upon arrival.[41] He later tried unsuccessfully to return to the United States, predictably receiving support from Buchanan and LaRouche. Ohio Congressman James Traficant, a staunch John Demjanjuk supporter who tried to keep Jews off the jury when he was indicted for corruption, also advocated on Rudolph's behalf.[42]

After the Waldheim affair, Rosenbaum returned to OSI to serve as the unit's deputy director, eventually becoming director himself in 1995.[43] Under his leadership, OSI set records for prosecutions in Nazi cases, and routinely received awards and recognitions from survivor organizations and the Simon Wiesenthal Center, whose Jerusalem office was now led by Dr. Efraim Zuroff, Rosenbaum's former Justice Department colleague. OSI's mission was expanded several times, and in 2010 it merged with another unit to become the Human Rights and Special Prosecutions Section, with Rosenbaum remaining at the helm.[44]

In his role atop OSI, Rosenbaum lobbied German prosecutors to take their aging Nazis to court, but for decades those efforts fell on deaf ears. A part of him understood the hesitancy. The United States, too, struggled to grapple with its own past.[45] One of the few Nazis who did stand trial in West Germany was Hermine Braunsteiner Ryan, who was convicted of murder and a host of other horrific crimes, and sentenced to life in prison in 1981. But in 1996, facing a series of diabetes-related complications and amputations, she was released. She died in 1999.[46] Rosenbaum kept pushing, hoping that a new generation of German jurists, one still further removed from their fathers' crimes, would eventually reconsider the country's approach.[47]

Eventually, they did. John Demjanjuk, the Cleveland autoworker once accused of being Ivan the Terrible, spent decades fighting accusations that he had served the Third Reich. A winding series of trials saw Demjanjuk denaturalized, deported to Israel, convicted of being Ivan the Terrible, having the conviction overturned by the Israeli Supreme Court, and being renaturalized by the United States. OSI then reinvestigated Demjanjuk in the late 1990s, accusing him not of being Ivan the Terrible of Treblinka, but of being a guard at the Sobibor killing center. While the first trial had used eyewitness testimony, OSI—now under Rosenbaum's leadership—relied exclusively on documentary evidence. Courts stripped Demjanjuk of his US citizenship in 2002, and he was removed to Germany in 2009.[48]

By then, just as Rosenbaum had urged, German prosecutors had started to recognize service as a Nazi camp guard as inherently criminal. Demjanjuk was charged with 27,900 counts of accessory to murder, one of the first Nazis to face justice under this line of reasoning. Throughout the decades-long ordeal, he feigned illness and weakness; though he appeared immobile and nonverbal in court appearances, OSI investigators videotaped him walking independently and easily when he thought no one was watching. Demjanjuk was finally convicted in 2011, nearly forty years after his name had appeared on Michael Hanusiak's list. He died in 2012 with his conviction under appeal.[49]

A year later, German authorities arrested Hans Lipschis. In 1983 his attorney, Paul Zumbakis, had argued to anyone who would listen that Lipschis was too old and too weak to travel, but the former Auschwitz guard had lived healthily for decades in Aalen, in southern Germany. By the time the Germans finally brought charges against Lipschis, it really was too late. Deemed too weak to stand trial, Lipschis lived out his final days, dying in 2016 at the age of ninety-six.[50]

Kairys's case wove through the US court system for more than a decade before he was finally deported to Germany in 1993.[51]

After a few years in Germany, Kulle lost touch with most of his friends from Oak Park, though a reminder of his time at OPRF came in the mail each month in the form of a pension check from the Illinois Metropolitan Retirement Fund. He almost lived long enough to face charges himself, but those pension payments stopped in 2006 when he died in Germany, still a free man.[52]

EPILOGUE

INSIDE THE JANITOR'S CLOSET

In January 2012, eighth-grader Drew Johnson stood in her Oak Park kitchen, staring at the three-dimensional janitor's closet she had constructed as an installation for the Chicago Metro History Fair. She had painted the door orange and blue, and carefully written "OPRF" across its front. The exterior of the locker was covered with texts, meant to appear mundane, unremarkable. Spilling out of the mailbox affixed to the side, thirty-year-old newspaper articles, op-eds, and letters to the editor demanded that Reinhold Kulle be fired, or called for an end to the "witch hunt" against him.

Reporters and photographers from the *Wednesday Journal* had just left Drew's house. Their puzzled looks seemed to suggest surprise that a Black, Catholic girl was so interested in Kulle. She wasn't Jewish; why did he matter to her?

The previous July, as she sat aimlessly watching television, her mother had handed her David Sokol's history of Oak Park and asked, "Have you thought about your History Fair project?" Drew had flipped through the thin volume, looking for a topic that might best her older brother's project on the *Chicago Defender*. "No way!" she had exclaimed, pausing on a small paragraph. A Nazi had thrived in her little liberal bubble. How had he made this place his home? How had this place let him in? What would it have been like to keep a secret for so long?

246

Drew's research took her through the Oak Park Historical Society, the Chicago History Museum, and Freedom of Information Act requests at the high school, but there was almost no information about Kulle's life before his arrival in the States, and people who been in Oak Park during the Kulle affair seemed reluctant to talk.

But Frank Lipo, the executive director of the Oak Park Historical Society, saw promise in Drew's investigation, and encouraged her to make a research trip out east. She and her mother drove to the National Archives in College Park, Maryland, where she examined Kulle's SS files on microfilm. She did not know exactly what the German text meant, but there were enough swastikas printed on the files for her to get the idea. A young man was also doing his own research nearby in the same room, and Drew told him about Kulle. She wanted to push the village of Oak Park—not to mention the United States—to live up to its ideals and not sweep the past under the rug, she explained earnestly.

The young man had also uncovered a troubling secret. Cleaning out his late grandfather's house, he had discovered a photo of his grandfather in a Nazi uniform, shattering the stories his family had told him. "We were told we were French," he said solemnly, his voice trailing off. "We are not French. . . ."

Staff at the US Holocaust Museum and Memorial's archives provided Drew with the transcript from Kulle's deportation hearing. She had just seen Kulle's SS file, and was now reading a transcript of him lying about it. It was almost comical. Other staff members, impressed with the inquisitive fourteen-year-old, gave her rare images of Gross-Rosen from the museum's private collection.

Inside the five-foot-tall janitor's closet she had constructed, Drew placed items Kulle might have used during his shifts: a broom, a mop, buckets, various tools. The buckets were a striking red, meant to symbolize the blood shed at Gross-Rosen. The color popped against the rest of the closet, which she had spray-painted a metallic silver. She plastered the photos from the Holocaust Museum on the inner walls, buried deep behind the orange and blue doors. When a viewer opened the door, she wanted them to experience the feeling of going back in time to Gross-Rosen, as she imagined it might have appeared in the dark corners of Kulle's memory.

Drew's parents had moved to Oak Park just after she was born, wanting to raise their kids in the diverse enclave. They had bought a house about a mile north of the middle school the village had renamed after Percy Julian. Twice, though, her father had been stopped while entering their house. "What are you doing?" the police had said. "You know, they let us live here now," her father had replied.

A family friend offered to translate the documents Drew had obtained at the Holocaust Museum, but was stymied by some of the handwriting, which was in a script that had fallen out of use. Drew then asked relatives in Austria to help, and they spent countless hours translating Kulle's entire SS file so that she could piece together his story. Some of the older Oak Parkers might have been reluctant to provide assistance, but a younger generation seemed to understand the project's importance.

Drew carefully cut strips from photocopies of Kulle's SS files and placed them inside her installation. They were to represent the secrets Kulle had kept locked away. Around his broom, she wrapped parts of Kulle's handwritten CV, detailing his time in the Hitler Youth and on the Eastern Front. She positioned part of his marriage license around the mop. On the inside walls of the closet she placed grainy photos of Kulle in uniform, and the eugenic fitness forms certifying that neither his nor Gertrud's families had Jewish blood. She also installed a light, so that Kulle's secrets would be visible if anyone wanted to see them. She called her installation *Inside the Janitor's Closet*.

The *Wednesday Journal* published an article about Drew's project in late January, explaining that "in July of 1984, Reinhold Kulle was dismissed from his job at OPRF." Kulle's retirement deal was still a secret. A picture showed Drew examining documents at her dining room table, wartime photos of Gertrud next to her hand. She told the *Journal* about Kulle's years in the SS and at Gross-Rosen, and that he had admitted to lying about his Nazi past on his visa application. "Kulle denied the allegations and the feds never proved their case conclu-sively," the *Journal* falsely claimed.

The article circulated online and created a stir in the community. The initial response was overwhelmingly positive, and the precocious eighth-grader became a local celebrity.

Drew wondered about Kulle's family. They still lived in the area. They had to have seen the article. The young man she had met at the National Archives had not known about his grandfather's past, but Kulle's local relatives had known about his. What did they think now?

Within a few days, there was a backlash to the *Wednesday Journal* article: calls for Kulle to be left alone, and complaints he had been treated unfairly. "What happened to forgiveness, people?"

Drew adjusted the mailbox on her installation, which was filled with the same kinds of comments she was reading online. She peered into the closet, staring at the photograph of Kulle in his Totenkopf uni-form. It was attached to the eugenic fitness forms he had sent to Hein-rich Himmler, proving his racial purity. In the photo, taken at a slave labor camp, Kulle was wearing the uniform of an *Unterscharführer*, the result of two promotions at Gross-Rosen. He was smiling.

"Hysteria without evidence," one man had posted online. "He was a caring person," a woman had written. "I always thought he was nice," another woman had added.

Drew turned off the closet light, and closed the door.[1]

ACKNOWLEDGMENTS

This book started as a lesson plan. I wanted my students to consider how an ordinary man became a Nazi perpetrator, but our discussions kept coming back to Kulle's life in America, and to the support he had received in our community. "None of this makes sense!" one young man finally yelled in exasperation. Why had so many people of goodwill—many of whom we knew personally—supported this admitted Nazi?

We began looking through digitized editions of the local newspapers, making lists of names and hoping to find a guest speaker or two who could help us understand. I tracked down an email address for Paul Gignilliat's daughter, and she kindly connected me with her father. A few nights later, Mr. Gignilliat called, and spent an hour regaling me with stories about Kulle, Oak Park, and the Kulle affair. I reported back to my students the next day, and they assigned me a half dozen new questions to answer.

Later that week, I connected with Leah Marcus, who sent me a copy of her Yom Kippur speech and asked me to read it before we spoke. Her agony and pain was palpable over the phone forty years later; it had been a "battle zone," she told me. Next, I reached Dr. Rima Lunin Schultz, and we began a frequent correspondence over the phone and on Zoom. Then I contacted dozens of other teachers and staff members. After each call, I shared with my students what I had learned. They challenged my answers, discussed every aspect of the story, and probed for more information. Their questions drove the initial research. This book would not exist without their intense curiosity.

So many individuals from Oak Park contributed to this book coming together, including Gail Kalmerton, Amber Hooper, and Maureen Kleinman. Many details of the Kulle affair would have remained unknown if not for Sarah Spivey and the rest of the 2021 school board, who voted to uncover the executive session board meeting notes from the Kulle affair. Thank you to everyone who shared their memories in interviews, especially Paul Gignilliat, Leah Marcus, Charles Nixon, Carolyn Elliott, Dr. David and Sandra Sokol, Marjorie and Jeffrey Greenwald, Helen and Michael Fleisher, Bruce and Julie Samuels, Michael Averbach, Dr. Steven Gevinson, William "Jay Jay" Turner, Dr. John "Jack" Swanson, Richard Deptuch, Andrew Heneghan, Kalyn Wulatin, Mary-Terese Cozzola, Suzanne Perry, Richard Rietz, Nancy Greco, Gale Liebman, and the family of OSI's fifth witness. I am particularly grateful to Drew and Diane Johnson for sharing research files from Drew's project when many archives were still closed due to the covid-19 pandemic. Drew, it was cathartic to find someone who was as obsessed with this history as I was. Thank you both for allowing me to join you inside the janitor's closet.

Many individuals featured in this book have since passed away, but it has been an honor to communicate with their families. Thank you to Dan and Ron Lubash, Andrew and Peter Nussbaum, Joshua Kotzin, Erin Ryan, and Dana Rubinstein.

Though the Kulle story fascinated me, the idea of turning it into a book seemed daunting and unrealistic. One of the first people to whom I reached out for advice was Dave Revsine, whose storytelling and writing I have long admired. He walked me through the book proposal process, and encouraged me to expand the scope beyond Kulle. I am beyond grateful for his kindness.

It was hard for me not to feel like an impostor, but I found Dr. Kevin Schultz a constant source of validation. He was instrumental throughout the proposal process and gave me incisive feedback on early drafts. That he saw promise in this book and in my ability to write it was incredibly encouraging. There is no one more responsible for this book becoming a reality.

Tim Hensley, archivist extraordinaire at the Virginia Holocaust Museum, was incredibly welcoming and helpful, answering questions and making sure I knew the best places around Richmond for getting coffee and going for a run. Rachel Berlinski of the Oak Park Historical Society deserves special mention. Rachel sifted through the archives to find incredible photos of Oak Park, some of which appear in this book. Thank you also to Emily Mohney from the Illinois Holocaust Museum and Education Center, Aleksandra Kobielec and the staff at the Gross-Rosen Museum, Sean Sullivan and Margaret Kluza from Triton College, and the staff at the ADL Library for help in accessing archival documents from their respective institutions. Thanks especially to Liviu Carare and the incredible team at the United States Holocaust Museum and Memorial's David and Fela Shapell Center, who helped with a last-minute research trip.

Former members of the Office of Special Investigations were gracious with their time, and I want to especially thank Dr. Peter Black, Bruce Einhorn, Dr. Mike MacQueen, Dr. Efraim Zuroff, and of course the inimitable Eli Rosenbaum, whose enthusiasm for this project was crucial. It is a rare experience to meet your hero and find that he is even kinder and greater in real life.

Ralph Blumenthal, the esteemed journalist whose groundbreaking reporting on these cases established this historical record, was generous with his time, as was Congresswoman Elizabeth Holtzman, who took time away from campaigning to talk about her efforts to bring Nazis to justice. It was an absolute honor to speak with them.

I owe a special debt of gratitude for the scholarship of Dr. Bella Gutterman, Dr. Charles Sydnor, Eric Lichtblau, Dr. Rochelle Saidel, Lawrence Douglas, Dr. Jonna Perrillo, Stephan Talty, Christopher Simpson, Russ Bellant, Dr. Bradley Hart, Dr. Deborah Liptsadt, Andrew Nagorski, Arnie Bernstein, Dr. David Sokol, Dr. Tyrell Stewart-Harris, Dr. Richard M. Fried, and Dr. Camille Henderson.

Thank you to Dr. Malka Simkovich, David Chrisinger, Dr. Robert Johnston, Rabbi Dr. Michael Berenbaum, David Lee Preston, and Lou Carlozo for their advice, feedback, and support. I am particularly thankful for Dr. Daniel Greene, whose scholarship and teaching led me to Holocaust studies in the first place.

Rima and RaeLynne, it's hard to know where to start. This story is yours, and it was an honor to be part of telling it. Thank you for your trust.

From the start, my dream was to publish with the University of Chicago Press. Dr. Tim Mennel, Dr. Matt Briones, Dr. Andrea Blatz, Renaldo Migaldi, Kristen Raddatz, and so many others at the Press made that dream a reality. Tim, you championed this project from the beginning, and took a chance on a first-time author. I will always be grateful. Andrea, you were patient and unbelievably helpful. Renaldo, thank you so much for your keen, detailed, and perceptive manuscript editing.

My colleagues at Oak Park and River Forest High School have been incredibly supportive, listening as I droned on and on about Nazis when they really wanted to talk about work or football. Thank you to Octavius Bellamy, Andrew Brown, Lisa Faulkner, Dan Ganschow, Matt Maloney, Dan Martin, Mike Stephen, Evan Tarshish, and Bill Young. Peter Kahn has been an extraordinary colleague and mentor for years, and worked hard to help make sure this book became a reality. I also owe a special thank-you to Rich Mertz and Dr. Jessica Young, who nurtured my love of history, and to my undergraduate advisors, Dr. David Hackett Fischer and Dr. Marya Levenson. Marya, I'm nearly two decades into my career, and my main professional goal remains to make you proud.

I deeply appreciate all of our friends who provided needed breaks, support, and encouragement. I want to especially thank David and Cindy Pogrund for their critical feedback on multiple drafts. Thanks as well to Ron Balson and Neil Berkowitz.

I am lucky to be a part of a wonderful and large family that is always exceptionally gracious and giving. Thanks to my in-laws, Dr. Yechiel and Dr. Sara Berkowicz, and Dr. Alan and Kim Frankel for their endless love and help. Alan, thank you so much for your tireless work with the manuscript. Thank you to all of our siblings and grandparents for their endless love, and especially to our nieces and nephews, who bring utter joy to life.

My parents, Dr. Leonard and Robin Soffer, have always been the perfect role models. Their advice and feedback on drafts made this book possible, and I remain in awe of them both. And thank you, Dad, for your work on the index.

I regret that some of our grandparents are not here to hold this book, and I wish we could share this moment with Sid Cohen, Israel Berkowicz, Bob and Bobbe Bakal, and Arthur and Shirley Soffer. I especially regret that I was not able to talk about this book with my wife's savta, Sara Berkowicz, herself a survivor of Nazi brutality.

Ami and Talia, it was no small ask to let your dad research and write a book. Ami, you want to know and understand everything, and your inquisitive nature inspires me. Tal, you are a model of empathy and love. The two of you have the blood of a survivor pulsing through your veins. May you always remember from where you come.

And Rachelli. My goodness, Rachelli. You had the utmost confidence in this project, and knew it would be a book before I had considered writing one. You read draft after draft, talked through almost every word choice, and understood this project's importance more than anyone. I could not ask for a better or more supportive partner. If you're reading this, it means I can't edit the manuscript anymore, and that you can finally read a draft I won't immediately change. I love you.

NOTES

CHAPTER 1

1 Dan Haley, "Swansons to Devote Year to Missions," *Wednesday Journal*, April 22, 1987, p. 1; https://www.wunderground.com/history/daily/KMDW/date/1982-12-4.

2 Judy Licata, "What's in Store for 1975?" *Forest Leaves*, January 8, 1975, p. 7.

3 Richard M. Fried, *The Man Everybody Knew: Bruce Barton and the Making of Modern America*, (Chicago: Ivan R. Dee, 2005), 13; https://www.nationalcivicleague.org/america-city-award/past-winners.

4 John Swanson, interview by author, April 7, 2021; Paul Gignilliat, interview by author, December 14, 2020.

5 Maurice Possley and Don Hayer, "Deportation Bid on Suburb Man," *Chicago Sun-Times*, December 4, 1982, p. 7.

6 Marcus, "Yom Kippur Speech," 1984, provided by Leah Marcus; Leah Marcus, interview by author, December 30, 2020.

7 Marcus, "Yom Kippur Speech; Rochelle Dimaso, "Violence Delays Wiesenthel [*sic*] Talk," *Oak Park World*, November 16, 1977, p. 1.

8 Marcus, "Yom Kippur Speech."

9 Dimaso, "Violence"; Marcus, "Yom Kippur Speech."

10 Tom Segev, *Simon Wiesenthal: The Life and Legends* (New York: Schocken Books, 2010), 62.

11 Dimaso, "Violence"; Marcus, "Yom Kippur Speech."

CHAPTER 2

1 Reinhold Kulle, sworn interview, August 14, 1982, 31–32, RG-25, box 37, folder 436a, Sydnor papers, Virginia Holocaust Museum (hereafter SP-VHM), Richmond, VA; Markus Wolter, "Die SS-Garnison Radolfzell 1937–1945," in *Radolfzell am Bodensee: Die Chronik*, ed. Hildegard Bibby and Katharina Maier (Kostanz, Germany: Stadler Verlag, 2019), 273.

2 *Germany, World War I Casualty Lists, 1914–1919*, online database, Ancestry.com; list date August 26, 1918; vol. 1918_XVI, no. 2069.

3 Reinhold Kulle birth certificate from Kulle personnel file, Oak Park & River Forest High School; Kulle, sworn interview, 8–9.

4 Roger Moorhouse and Norman Davis, *Microcosm: Portrait of a Central European City* (London: Jonathan Cape, 2002), 332, 336.

5 Walter Lacquer, *Young Germany: A History of the German Youth Movement* (New York: Basic Books, 1962), 81; Moorhouse and Davis, *Microcosm*, 371–72; Abraham Ascher, *A Community under Siege: The Jews of Breslau under Nazism* (Stanford, CA: Stanford University Press, 2007), 50–51.

6 *United States v. Kulle* (1983), at 2674, 2676–77.

7 Moorhouse and Davis, *Microcosm*, 339, 367, 378; Geoffrey P. Megargee, *Encyclopedia of Camps and Ghettos, 1933–1945* (United States Holocaust Memorial Museum, 442), https://www.kz-gedenkstaette-dachau.de/en/

8 Ascher, *A Community under Siege*, 98; Lisa Pine, *Education in Nazi Germany* (Oxford, UK: Berg, 2010), 24; Erika Mann, *School for Barbarians: Education under the Nazis* (Mineola, NY: Dover, 2014), 21.

9 Gregor Ziemer, *Education for Death: The Making of the Nazi* (Oxford, UK: Oxford University Press, 1941), 16; Pine, *Education in Nazi Germany*, 48, 57; Ascher, *A Community under Siege*, 99; I. L. Kandel, "Education in Nazi Germany," *Annals of the American Academy of Political and Social Science* 182 (November 1935): 160.

10 *United States v. Kulle* (1983), at 2676–80; Kulle, sworn interview, 27; Reinhold Kulle, "Lebenslauf," SP-VHM, box 37, box 436a.

11 Bürgerliches Gesetzbuch (hereafter BGB) § 1922.

12 Michael Kater, *Hitler Youth* (Cambridge, MA: Harvard University Press, 2004), 10–11; Daniel Horn, "The Hitler Youth and Educational Decline in the Third Reich," *History of Education Quarterly* 16, no. 4 (Winter 1976): 427–28; Peter Loewenberg, "Psychohistorical Origins of the Nazi Youth Cohort," *American Historical Review*, no. 5 (December 1971): 1463.

13 Kulle, "Lebenslauf"; *United States v. Kulle* (1983), at 2681.

14 Kater, *Hitler Youth*, 24, 31; Horn, "Educational Decline," 427.

15 Kater, *Hitler Youth*, 29.

16 Megargee, *Encyclopedia*, 441–48, 289–96, 1255–63; Ascher, *A Community under Siege*, 125–33.

17 "Austrian Towns See Hitlerites Parade," *New York Times*, March 12, 1938, p. 4; Megargee, *Encyclopedia*, 559–66, 900–904; Ascher, *A Community under Siege*, 134.

18 Kater, *Hitler Youth*, 25; Moorhouse and Davis, *Microcosm*, 347.

19 "Nazi Demands Met," *New York Times*, September 30, 1938, p. 1.

20 https://sztetl.org.pl/en/towns/o/215-olesnica/99-history/137782-history-of -community.

21 Kater, *Hitler Youth*, 62; Moorhouse and Davis, *Microcosm*, 340–41.

22 Charles Sydnor, *Soldiers of Destruction: The SS Death's Head Division, 1933–1945* (Princeton, NJ: Princeton University Press, 1977), 37–42.

23 Sydnor, *Soldiers of Destruction*, 41–43; Kater, *Hitler Youth*, 210.

24 *United States v. Kulle* (1983), at 2680–81; Kater, *Hitler Youth*, 210.

25 Kulle, "Lebenslauf"; SS Race and Settlement Main Office, medical examination form, SP-VHM, box 37, folder 436a; *United States v. Kulle* (1983), at 2689.

26 Sydnor, *Soldiers of Destruction*, 117.

27 Kulle. "Lebenslauf"; Kommandatur Konzentrationslager Groß-Rosen, *Betrifft: Verleihung dor Ostmedaille*, SP-VHM, box 37, box 436a; Sydnor, *Soldiers of Destruction*, 129.

28 Sydnor, *Soldiers of Destruction*, 127–29, 143–47; *United States v. Kulle* (1983), at 2690–92.

29 Kulle, sworn interview, 32; Sydnor, *Soldiers of Destruction*, 148, 150; Geoffrey Megargee, *War of Annihilation: Combat and Genocide on the Eastern Front, 1941* (Lanham, MD: Rowman & Littlefield, 2007), 43.

30 George Stein, *The Waffen SS: Hitler's Elite Guard at War, 1939-1945* (Ithaca, NY: Cornell University Press, 1984), 102n; photo of Reinhold Kulle provided by Eli Rosenbaum, US Department of Justice.

31 Sydnor, *Soldiers of Destruction*, 153-55; Kulle, sworn interview, 40-41.

32 Megargee, *War of Annihilation*, 43; Kulle, sworn interview, 45.

33 Sydnor, *Soldiers of Destruction*, 168, 211, 217, 219; Russel H. S. Stolfi, "Chance in History: The Russian Winter of 1941-1942," *History* 65, no. 214 (1980): 215n, 221; Carolyn Elliott, interviews by author, July 18-19, 2022.

34 Sydnor, *Soldiers of Destruction*, 212; *United States v. Kulle* (1983), at 2689; Government Deposition Exhibit no. 6-A [SP-VHM, box 37, folder 436a]; Kulle, sworn interview, 45-46.

35 Stolfi, "Chance in History," 219-21; Sydnor, *Soldiers of Destruction*, 217-20; Konzentrationslager Groß-Rosen, *Verleihung der Medaille Winterschlacht im Osten, 1941/1942*, August 3, 1942, SP-VHM, box 37, folder 436a; Kulle, sworn interview, 46; *United States v. Kulle* (1983), at 2705.

36 *United States v. Kulle* (1983), 2704; government deposition exhibit no. 6-A; Kulle, sworn interview, 46-47.

37 Gignilliat, interview; *United States v. Kulle* (1983), 2704-7.

38 *United States v. Kulle* (1983), at 2705-6.

39 Dr. Neal's medical report, Kulle personnel file, OPRF.

40 *United States v. Kulle* (1983), at 2699.

41 *United States v. Kulle* (1983), at 2705-9.

42 Sydnor, *Soldiers of Destruction*, 245n, 315; *United States v. Kulle* (1983), at 2709, 2814.

43 *United States v. Kulle* (1983), at 2709-10.

CHAPTER 3

1 *United States v. Kulle* (1983), at 615-26.

2 *United States v. Kulle* (1983), at 1553-54.

3 Mieczysław Moldawa, *Gross-Rosen: A Concentration Camp in Silesia*, trans. Edwin R. Strakna (Warsaw: Ministry of National Defense, 1979), 172; *United States v. Kulle* (1983), at 620.

4 *United States v. Kulle* (1983), at 1564.

5 Moldawa, *Gross-Rosen*, 24, 171-72; *United States v. Kulle* (1983), at 622-23.

6 *United States v. Kulle* (1983), at 622-26.

7 Bella Gutterman, *A Narrow Bridge to Life: Jewish Slave Labor and Survival in the Gross-Rosen Camp System* (New York: Berghahn Books, 2008), 73, 157.

8 Gutterman, *A Narrow Bridge to Life*, 70-73, 162; Moldawa, *Gross-Rosen*, 183.

9 Gutterman, *A Narrow Bridge to Life*, 32-37, 73.

10 *United States v. Kulle* (1983), at 2710, 2722.

11 Moldawa, *Gross-Rosen*, 182.

12 *United States v. Kulle* (1983), at 660-61.

13 Moldawa, *Gross-Rosen*, 54-56.

14 *United States v. Kulle* (1983), at 661, 665–66; Isaac Engel, interview by Dr. Sidney Bolkosky, University of Michigan-Dearborn, June 16 and 25, 1992, http://holocaust .umd.umich.edu/engel/.
15 Moldawa, *Gross-Rosen*, 85, 110.
16 *United States v. Kulle* (1983), at 633; Moldawa, *Gross-Rosen*, 183–84.
17 Moldawa, *Gross-Rosen*, 17, 26.
18 Moldawa, *Gross-Rosen*, 185; Gutterman, *A Narrow Bridge to Life*, 75, 81.
19 *United States v. Kulle* (1983), at 680–81, 2716.
20 *Verleihung dor Ostmedaille*, SP-VHM, box 37, box 436a.
21 *Verleihung der Medaille, "Winterschlacht im Osten" 1941/1942*, SP-VHM, box 37, box 436a; *United States v. Kulle* (1983), at 2697–2700.
22 *Gebührnis Karte*, SP-VHM, box 37, folder 436a; Kulle, sworn interview, 49, 54–55, 79.
23 The term derives from the Yiddish word for Muslims. There are various interpretations of the term's origins, including that the prisoners were so weak that they often could not stand upright, and that to other prisoners their prone position resembled the practice of prostration common in Muslim prayer. A quick and accessible overview of various interpretations can be found at https://forward.com/culture/4149 /muselmann-in-the-camps/.
24 Moldawa, *Gross-Rosen*, 131–32, 185.
25 Moldawa, *Gross-Rosen*, 7, 11, 98, 124–36; Gutterman, *A Narrow Bridge to Life*, 104.
26 Gutterman, *A Narrow Bridge to Life*, 73–74; Moldawa, *Gross-Rosen*, 36.
27 *United States v. Kulle* (1983), at 2716; Moldawa, *Gross-Rosen*, 46, 62; Gutterman, *A Narrow Bridge to Life*, 69, 199; *United States v. Kulle* (1983), at 2752.
28 *United States v. Kulle* (1983), at 2712, 2715.
29 "Regulations of the Dachau Concentration Camp (1933)," 10–11, Office of US Chief of Council, Nuremberg Trials evidence code PS-1216, exhibit code: prosecution 85.
30 Kulle, engagement and marriage application, January 13, 1944, SP-VHM, box 37, folder 436a; Kulle, sworn interview, 97.
31 *United States v. Kulle* (1983), at 688.
32 *United States v. Kulle* (1983), at 688–89.
33 Moldawa, *Gross-Rosen*, 35.
34 Moldawa, *Gross-Rosen*, 264.
35 *United States v. Kulle* (1983), at 2733; *Gebührnis Karte*.
36 Amy Carney, *Marriage and Fatherhood in the Nazi SS* (Toronto: University of Toronto Press, 2018), 7–29.
37 Kulle, "Lebenslauf."
38 Kulle, "*Fragebogen*;" Deutsche Bundesbahn, Neumünster (list of persons employed by German railways at the Neumünster station, November 2, 1939, to October 10, 1949), Arolsen Archives, accessed at https://collections.arolsen-archives.org/en/document /70700161.
39 Kulle, Rasse-und Siedlungs-Hauptamt, SP-VHM, box 37, folder 436a; Rasse-und Siedlungs-Hauptamt: Ärztlicher Untersuchungbogen, SP-VHM, box 37, folder 436a; Carney, *Marriage and Fatherhood in the Nazi SS*, 10, 26–29.
40 Kulle, engagement and marriage application.
41 Kulle, engagement and marriage application; Standesamt zur Heiratserlaudbnis vom 7.4.1944, SP-VHM, box 37, folder 436c.

42 Moldawa, *Gross-Rosen*, 27-29; Bella Gutterman, *A Narrow Bridge to Life*, 27, 71, 191; *United States v. Kulle* (1983), at 649.

43 Moldawa, *Gross-Rosen*, 33, 168; *United States v. Kulle* (1983), at 632-33, 659.

44 Gutterman, *A Narrow Bridge to Life*, 94.

45 *United States v. Kulle* (1983), at 746; Gutterman, *A Narrow Bridge to Life*, 188, 191.

46 *United States v. Kulle* (1983), at 1291.

47 Moldawa, *Gross-Rosen*, 321-22.

48 Gutterman, *A Narrow Bridge to Life*, 195, 200-202.

49 *United States v. Kulle* (1983), at 2774.

50 Carney, *Marriage and Fatherhood in the Nazi SS*, 55.

51 Gutterman, *A Narrow Bridge to Life*, 195-97, 203.

52 *United States v. Kulle* (1983), at 2777-79; Kulle, sworn interview, 56.

53 *Moldawa, Gross-Rosen*, 265, 348; Gutterman, *A Narrow Bridge to Life*, 203.

54 *United States v. Kulle* (1983), at 710-12; Moldawa, *Gross-Rosen*, 345; Kulle, sworn interview, 56.

55 Gutterman, *A Narrow Bridge to Life*, 189, 206; Moldawa, *Gross-Rosen*, 350.

56 *United States v. Kulle* (1983), at 712-13.

57 *United States v. Kulle* (1983), at 2778-79; Kulle, sworn interview, 56.

58 Kulle, sworn interview, 56-60.

CHAPTER 4

1 *United States v. Kulle* (1983), at 2789.

2 *United States v. Kulle* (1983), at 2500, 2549-52.

3 *United States v. Kulle* (1983), at 2500, 2549-52, 2789.

4 *United States v. Kulle* (1983), at 2531.

5 Letter from Chicago Rivet & Machine Co., March 13, 1957; United States of America application for immigrant visa and alien registration, I-665353, SP-VHM, box 37, folder 436b.

6 *United States v. Kulle* (1983), at 2555.

7 Gutterman, *A Narrow Bridge to Life*, 189; Allan A. Ryan, Jr., *Quiet Neighbors* (San Diego: Harcourt Brace Jovanovich, 1984), 13-14, 20-28; Irving Engel et al., "Screening of DPs," letters to the editor, *New York Times*, January 12, 1949, p. 26.

8 Ryan, *Quiet Neighbors*, 14.

9 Kulle, visa application; Kulle, sworn interview, 17, 64-65.

10 *The Displaced Persons Act of 1948* (Pub. L. 80-774); Richard Raschke, *Useful Enemies* (New York: Delphinium Books, 2013), 14; Ryan, *Quiet Neighbors*, 18.

11 Charles Coughlin, "Address by Father C. E. Coughlin" (1938), transcribed by Dina McCarrick, 8, 9; accessed via American Catholic History Classroom, Catholic University of America, March 14, 2023.

12 Arnie Bernstein, *Swastika Nation: Fritz Kuhn and the Rise and Fall of the German-American Bund* (New York: St. Martin's Press, 2013), 77-85, 177-89.

13 Daniel Okrent, *The Guarded Gate: Bigotry, Eugenics, and the Law That Kept Two Generations of Jews, Italians, and Other European Immigrants out of America* (New York: Scribner, 2019), 362-64; Bradley Hart, *Hitler's American Friends* (New York: Thomas Dunne Books, 2018), 50-71; Leonard Dinnerstein, *Anti-Semitism in America* (Oxford, UK:

Oxford University Press, 1994), 121, 126; Arnie Bernstein, *Swastika Nation: Fritz Kuhn and the Rise and Fall of the German-American Bund* (New York: St. Martin's Press, 2013), 77-85, 177-89.

14 "Lindbergh's Anti-Jewish Speech Meets with Severe Criticism in American Press," *Jewish Telegraphic Agency*, September 15, 1941; Hart, *Hitler's American Friends*, 98-115, 160-65, 221.

15 President Harry S. Truman, "Statement by the President upon Signing the Displaced Persons Act," June 25, 1948.

16 William Harllee Bordeaux to Ugo Carusi, October 6, 1948, records of the Displaced Persons Commission, 1948-52, records of Commissioners Rosenfield and O'Connor, Rosenfield subject file, record group 278, box 44, National Archives Building, College Park, MD (hereafter NACP).

17 Rep. Noble J. Gregory to Ugo Carusi, March 8, 1949, DPC records, 1948-52, RG 278, box 49, NACP.

18 Alex E. Squadrilli to Harry N. Rosenfield, interoffice memorandum, "Subject: Berlin Document Center Reports: Your Memo of September 9, 1949," November 14, 1949, DPC records, 1948-52, RG 278, box 46, NACP.

19 Simon Wiesenthal to Mr. Bedo, October 20, 1948, DPC records, 1948-52, RG 278, box 55, NACP.

20 Squadrilli to Rosenfield.

21 Sydney Liskofsky to Harry Rosenfield, November 25, 1949; records of the Displaced Persons Commission, 1948-52, DPC records, 1948-52, RG 278, box 44, NACP.

22 Confidential memo, R. H. Hillenkoetter to Ugo Carusi, April 7, 1949, DPC records, 1948-52, RG 278, box 46, NACP.

23 Leonard Dinnerstein, *America and the Survivors of the Holocaust* (New York: Columbia University Press, 1982), 183; Raschke, *Useful Enemies*, 217; Christopher Simpson, *Blowback* (New York: Weidenfeld and Nicolson, 1988), 207, 269-70.

24 Displaced Persons Commission, volume 8; "Semi-Annual Report to the President and the Congress," 1952, 248.

25 Raschke, *Useful Enemies*, 217; Marion T. Bennett, "The Immigration and Nationality (McCarran-Walter) Act of 1952, as Amended to 1965," *Annals of the American Academy of Political and Social Science* 367 (September 1966): 129; Refugee Relief Act, & 14(a), Pub. L. no. 83-203 (1953).

26 United States Code: Immigration and Nationality, 8 U.S.C. §§ -1483 suppl. 5 1952, Refugee Relief Act; Hasia Diner, *We Remember with Reverence and Love* (New York: New York University Press, 2010), 253.

27 Ryan, *Quiet Neighbors*, 20-21, 68; George C. Browder, "Problems and Potentials of the Berlin Document Center," *Central European History*. 5, no. 4 (December 1972): 362.

28 Ryan, *Quiet Neighbors*, 20-21, 68; George C. Browder, "Problems and Potentials of the Berlin Document Center," *Central European History* 5, no. 4 (December 1972): 362.

29 Ryan, *Quiet Neighbors*, 26-27; Eric Lichtblau, *The Nazis Next Door* (Boston: Mariner Books, 2014), 24-29; Raschke, *Useful Enemies*, 217.

30 Rochelle G. Saidel, *The Outraged Conscience* (New York: New York University Press, 1984), 32-35; Ryan, *Quiet Neighbors*, 233-39.

31 *Feodor Fedorenko v. United States*, 449 U.S. 490, January 21, 1981; Ryan, *Quiet Neighbors*, 104; "Feodor Fedorenko, Accused of Wartime Atrocities at a Nazi Deathcamp," UPI, March 1, 1981.

32 *United States v. Schellong*, no. 81 C 1478 (1982).

33 Raschke, *Useful Enemies*, 57–58; Ryan, *Quiet Neighbors*, 146–50; Federal Bureau of Investigation, confidential memo, DBA-004737, Los Angeles, August 14, 1963, accessed at https://www.cia.gov/readingroom/docs/ARTUKOVIC,%20ANDREW%20%20%20VOL.%202_0042.pdf.

34 Michael Hoffman. "DP Movement to U.S. Stalls; Our Visa Policy Is Blamed," *New York Times*, August 29, 1948, p. 3.

35 Kulle, visa application.

CHAPTER 5

1 Intergovernmental Committee For European Migration, Hamburg, "Movement to the United States on the MS *Italia* ex Hamburg/Cuxhaven, Germany, October 26, 1957"; "MS *Italia*," Military Communications and Electronics Museum, http://www.c-and-e-museum.org/marville/other/maother-46.html; Micke Asklander, notation on postcard, "M/S *Kungsholm* (1928)," http://www.faktaomfartyg.se/kungsholm_1928.htm; Kulle, visa application.

2 Thomas O'Toole, "Citizen Accused as Death Camp Guard," *Washington Post*, August 14, 1980, p. A25; John McCarron and James Coates, "Chicago Man Denies He Was a Nazi Guard," *Chicago Tribune*, October 1, 1978, p. 1; Andrew Gottesman, "U.S. Still Pressing Fight on War Criminals," *Chicago Tribune*, February 8, 1993, p. D1; *United States v. Kairys*, 782 F.2d 1374 (7th Cir. 1986); "Aplink mus," *Draugas*, April 21, 1971, p. 8; "Mokslas Menas, Literatūra," *Draugas*, August 31, 1974, p. 5.

3 *United States v. Kairys* (1980), transcript, US Department of Justice, Office of Special Investigations (USDOJ-OSI), denaturalization cases transcripts and decisions, record group-06.029, US Holocaust Memorial Museum Archives, Washington, 1164.

4 Wolfgang Buescher, "Hans Lipschis: 'I Was Only a Cook in Auschwitz,'" *Die Welt*, April 21, 2013; William B. Crawford Jr. and Marianne Taylor, "'Sweet Man' Is Tied to Nazis." *Chicago Tribune*, June 9, 1982, pp. 1, 11.

5 Conrad Schellong file, records of the Central Intelligence Agency, second release of name files under the Nazi War Crimes and Japanese Imperial Government Disclosure Acts, record group 263, NAID 139391949, box 112, folder 5.

6 Jay Branegan, "Chicagoan Hid Nazi Role: US." *Chicago Tribune*, March 18. 1981, p. E1.

7 Ron Grossman and *Tribune* reporter, "Area Was Haven for Nazi-Era Figures," *Chicago Tribune*, March 8, 2009, p. 2.1; "Former SS Guard at Sachsenhausen Agrees to Leave the United States," Jewish Telegraphic Agency, June 2, 1992; Matt O'Connor, "Chemist Accused of Lying on Nazi Links," *Chicago Tribune*, January 22, 1993, p. S3; Mike Mac-Queen, interview by author, 2021; Eli Rosenbaum, interview by author, 2021.

8 Justin G. Riskus, *Images of America: Lithuanian Chicago* (Charleston, SC: Arcadia Publishing, 2013), 61, 77.

9 "World Lithuanian Charter," Supreme Committee for the Liberation of Lithuania, 1949; "Rally for Captive Nations," *New York Times*, May 23, 1956, p. 22.

10 Camille Henderson Zorich, "Black vs. White? Reexamining Residential Transition in the Chicago Metropolitan Area: Oak Park, 1960–1979" (PhD diss., University of Chicago, 2005), 31–32; Matthew Frye Jacobson, *Whiteness of a Different Color: European Immigrants and the Alchemy of Race* (Cambridge, MA: Harvard University Press, 1999), 272–77; Maria Kalefas, *Working-Class Heroes: Protecting Home, Community, and* *a Nation in a Chicago Neighborhood* (Berkeley: University of California Press, 2003), 33–36.

11 Kulle, visa application.

12 "The Story of Forest Park's History," Forest Park Historical Society, https://www .forestpark.net/dfp/wp-content/uploads/2020/03/FPHistory.pdf, pp. 2, 6; "Throwback to Otto's Restaurant," *Forest Park Review*, May 1, 2019.

13 "Reset Stones in Waldheim; 2 More Tipped," *Chicago Tribune*, January 20, 1960, p. 16; "Forest Park Police Probe New Swastika," *Chicago Tribune*, February 23, 1960, p. 10.

14 Reinhold Kulle, job application to Oak Park & River Forest High School, January 30, 1959, Kulle personnel file, OPRF; Suburban Cut Stone advertisement, *Forest Leaves*, April 29, 1992, p. 96; Richard Deptuch, interview by author, July 25, 2022.

15 Jonna Perrillo, *Educating the Enemy: Teaching Nazis and Mexicans in the Cold War Borderlands* (Chicago: University of Chicago Press, 2022), 14, 85.

16 Perrillo, *Educating the Enemy*, 33, 63–64.

17 Proviso East High School yearbook, 1965, pp. 87, 143; Proviso East High School yearbook, 1966, p. 141.

18 Kulle, job application.

19 Kulle, job application.

20 David Sokol, *Oak Park: The Evolution of a Village* (Charleston, SC: History Press), 33, 70, 86, 94–95, 101–2, 139.

21 Joseph Ruzich, "Oak Park & River Forest H.S. Celebrates Football Stadium's 90th Year," *Chicago Tribune*, October 17, 2014; Maynard Brichford, *Bob Zuppke: The Life and Football Legacy of the Illinois Coach* (Jefferson, NC: McFarlands, 2008), 4; Harvey Woodruff, "Meet the Bob Zuppke of 1913: Illinois' New Football Coach," *Chicago Tribune*, October 29, 1937, p. 29.

22 "Illinois Football Chicago Spring Game Set for April 11: Illini Head to Oak Park–River Forest, home of Robert Zuppke," *Daily Illini*, March 31, 2009; Steven A. Riess, *Sports in America from Colonial Times to the Twenty-First Century: An Encyclopedia* (London: Routledge, 2011), 437.

23 Thacher Howland Guild, "The Illinois Loyalty Song" (1907), https://www.loc.gov /item/2017570121/; Brichford, *Bob Zuppke*, 40.

24 Fried, *The Man Everybody Knew*, 10–13.

25 "Annexation," *Encyclopedia of Chicago*, http://www.encyclopedia.chicagohistory.org /pages/53.html; Sokol, *Evolution*, 65, 74–76.

26 Carole Goodwin, *The Oak Park Strategy: Community Control of Racial Change* (Chicago: University of Chicago Press, 1978), 34–35.

27 Henderson Zorich, "Black vs. White?" 44–45.

28 Sokol, *Evolution*, 81, 119–20; "Temple Har Zion's History," wsthz.org.

29 "Illinois: The New Neighbor," *Time*, December 4, 1950; Henderson Zorich, "Black vs. White?" 1–3, 39.

30 Henderson Zorich, "Black vs. White?" 1–3, 39; Evan McKenzie and J. Ruby, "Reconsidering the Oak Park Strategy: The Conundrums of Integration," *Midwest Political Science Association*, 2002. 10–11.

31 Kenneth T. Jackson, *Crabgrass Frontier: The Suburbanization of the United States* (New York: Oxford University Press, 1985), 244.

32 William H. Whyte, *The Organization Man* (New York: Simon & Schuster, 1956), 300.

33 "Ilinois: The New Neighbor"; Henderson Zorich, "Black vs. White?" 1–3, 39.

34 Isabel Wilkerson, *The Warmth of Other Suns: The Epic Story of America's Great Migration* (New York: Random House, 2010), 388; "Arrest 20 during S. Side March," *Chicago Tribune*, August 22, 1966, p. 1.

35 Henderson Zorich, "Black vs. White?" 41, 54–58; Tyrell Stewart-Harris, "Oak Park: Discourses of Suburban Diversity," PhD diss., University of Illinois at Chicago, 2015, p. 89.

36 Village of Oak Park, "Diversity Statement," 1973.

37 Goodwin, *The Oak Park Strategy*, 160, 36.

38 Richard Rietz, interview by author, April 14, 2021; various documents in Kulle personnel file, OPRF; memos of August 1 and September 26, 1963, Kulle personnel file, OPRF.

39 Carolyn Elliott, interview by author, 2022.

40 Oak Park telephone directory, June 6, 1959, p. 198; Forest Park Historical Society, "Throwback."

41 Oak Park telephone directory, June 1, 1961, p. 49; Proviso East High School yearbook, 1965, pp. 87, 143; Proviso East High School yearbook, 1966, p. 141.

42 Ryan, *Quiet Neighbors*, 151–55.

43 Rep. James Utt, speaking on "The Persecution of Andrija Artukovic," on July 29, 1955, 84th Congress, First Session, *Congressional Record* Volume 101, Part 1, 12152.

44 Ryan, *Quiet Neighbors*, 158, 171, 174.

45 See, for example, Isser Harel, *The House on Garibaldi Street*; Zvi Aharoni and Wilhelm Dietl, *Operation Eichmann: The Truth about the Pursuit, Capture and Trial*; Peter Malkin, *Eichmann in My Hands*; Neal Bascomb, *Hunting Eichmann*.

46 United Nations Security Council resolution 138.

47 Raanan Rein, "The Eichmann Kidnapping: Its Effects on Argentine-Israeli Relations and the Local Jewish Community," *Jewish Social Studies* (new series) 7, no. 3 (spring/summer 2001): 109; Deborah Lipstadt, *The Eichmann Trial* (New York: Schocken Books, 2011), 20–36 (broadcast of trial made available online by Israel's State Archives and Yad Vashem at https://www.youtube.com/user/EichmannTrialEN); Deborah Lipstadt, "America and the Memory of the Holocaust, 1950–1965," *Modern Judaism* 16, no. 3 (October 1996): 207.

48 George Salomon, "The End of Eichmann: America's Response," *American Jewish Year Book* 64 (1963): 247–50.

49 Jerome S. Legge Jr., "The Karl Linnas Deportation Case, the Office of Special Investigations, and American Ethnic Politics," *Holocaust and Genocide Studies* 24, no. 1 (Spring 2010): 30–33.

50 "Searches: The Nazi of Damascus," *Time*, November 11, 1985.

51 Saidel, *The Outraged Conscience*, 28.

52 Saidel, *The Outraged Conscience*, 55–63.

53 Saidel, *The Outraged Conscience*, 62.

54 Saidel, *The Outraged Conscience*, 48, 56–63; "See How They Run: Ten Mice Scatter 500," *Chicago Tribune*, May 20, 1963, p. 14; "Chicago Woman Arrested for Using Mice to Harass Anti-Nazi Meeting," Jewish Telegraphic Agency, May 31, 1963.

55 Michael J. Neufeld, *Von Braun: Dreamer of Space, Engineer of War* (New York: Alfred A. Knopf, 2007), 404–7; Tom Lehrer, "Wernher von Braun," 1965.

CHAPTER 6

1 Joseph Lelyveld, *Omaha Blues: A Memory Loop* (New York: Farrar, Straus, and Giroux, 2005), 175-76; Joseph Lelyveld, "Former Nazi Camp Guard Is Now a Housewife in Queens," *New York Times*, July 14, 1964, p. 10; Joseph Lelyveld, "Breaking Away," *New York Times Magazine*, March 6, 2005, p. 57.

2 Douglas Martin, "A Nazi Past, a Queens Home Life, an Overlooked Death," *New York Times*, December 2, 2005, p. A25; Lelyveld, "Breaking Away," 57; Dorothy Rabinowitz, *New Lives: Survivors of the Holocaust Living in America* (New York: Knopf, 1976), 22.

3 Lelyveld, "Breaking Away," 57.

4 Charles Wyzanski, "Nuremberg: A Fair Trial? A Dangerous Precedent," *Atlantic*, April 1946; Lawrence Douglas, *The Right Wrong Man* (Princeton, NJ: Princeton University Press, 2016), 144, 174.

5 Douglas, *The Right Wrong Man*, 167, 174, 184.

6 See Tomaz Jardim, *Ilse Koch on Trial: Making the "Bitch of Buchenwald"* (Cambridge, MA: Harvard University Press, 2023). Neither Koch's American trial nor her West German trial found sufficient evidence of the lampshade accusation.

7 Douglas, *The Right Wrong Man*, 144; Caroline Sharples, "In Pursuit of Justice: Debating the Statute of Limitations for Nazi War Crimes in Britain and West Germany during the 1960s," *Holocaust Studies* 20, no. 3 (Winter 2014): 81-108.

8 Stephan Talty, *The Good Assassin* (Boston: Mariner Books, 2020), 189.

9 Mary Fullbrook, *Reckonings: Legacies of Nazi Persecution and the Quest for Justice* (Oxford, UK: Oxford University Press, 2018), 356; Tom Segev, *Soldiers of Evil* (New York: McGraw Hill, 1988), 181-82.

10 Ronen Steinke, *Fritz Bauer: The Jewish Prosecutor Who Brought Eichmann and Auschwitz to Trial*, trans. Sinéad Crowe (Bloomington: Indiana University Press, 2020), 3-4.

11 Talty, *The Good Assassin*, 135-38.

12 Victoria Fareld, "History, Justice, and the Time of the Imprescriptible," in *The Ethos of History: Time and Repsonsibility*, ed. Jayne Svenungsson and Stefan Helgesson (New York: Berghan Books, 2018), 65n.

13 Talty, *The Good Assassin*, 206, 214, 225-27; Douglas, *The Right Wrong Man*, 146; Robert A Monson, "The West German Statute of Limitations on Murder: A Political, Legal, and Historical Exposition," *American Journal of Comparative Law* 30, no. 4 (Autumn 1982): 611-17; "Nazi Involved in Killing Jews in Riga Found Dead in Uruguay," *Jewish Telegraphic Agency*, March 8, 1965.

14 "U.S. Studies Entry of Ex-Nazi Guard," *New York Times*, July 15, 1964, p. 38; Raschke, *Useful Enemies*, 32; Morris Kaplan, "Citizenship Lost By Queens Woman," *New York Times*, September 29, 1971, p. 30.

15 Raschke, *Useful Enemies*, 33; Howard Blum, *Wanted!* (New York: Quadrangle / New York Times, 1977), 27-31.

16 Saidel, *The Outraged Conscience*, 13-15.

17 "Coming Attractions," *New York Times*, February 11, 1973, p. 417; Blum, *Wanted!* 30-31.

18 "'Nazi Hunter' Accuses 2 Funds of Aiding Accused War Criminals." *New York Times*, May 15, 1977, p. 29; Final Report of the Select Committee on Assassinations, US House of Representatives, Ninety-Fifth Congress, Second Session, (House report no. 95-1828), January 2, 1979, pp. 381–82.

19 Select Committee on Assassinations, 381–82; Melissa Fay Greene, *The Temple Bombing* (New York: Fawcett Columbine, 1996), 227–31, 408–9.

20 Carol Mason, *Reading Appalachia from Left to Right: Conservatives and the 1974 Kanawha County Textbook Controversy* (Ithaca, NY: Cornell University Press, 2009), 75.

21 Murray Schumach, "Neighbors Defend Ex-Nazi Guard," *New York Times*, June 26, 1972, p. 20; Edward Hudson, "Queens Woman Explains Lies in Deportation Case," *New York Times*, May 10, 1972, p. 4; Rabinowitz, *New Lives*, 26–29.

22 Schumach, "Neighbors."

23 Rabinowitz, *New Lives*, 33–34.

24 Raschke, *Useful Enemies*, 32; Blum, *Wanted!* 31–35.

25 Raschke, *Useful Enemies*, 44–45, 50.

26 Morris Kaplan, "U.S. to Extradite Ex-Guard in Camp," *New York Times*, May 2, 1973, p. 1; Ralph Blumenthal, "Ex-Chief Immigration Trial Attorney Quits Abruptly," *New York Times*, December 8, 1973, p. 72; Raschke, *Useful Enemies*, 53.

CHAPTER 7

1 Andrew Heneghan, interview by author, December 22, 2021.

2 Deptuch, interview.

3 Various memos, Kulle personnel file, OPRF.

4 Rietz, interview; various memos, Kulle personnel file, OPRF.

5 Employer's first report of injury or illness, June 7, 1973, and August 31, 1973, Kulle personnel file, OPRF.

6 Grievance form, December 19, 1969, Kulle personnel file, OPRF.

7 Heneghan, interview; Marjorie Greenwald, interview by author, February 10, 2021; Nancy Greco, interview by author, April 27, 2021.

8 Heneghan, interview.

9 Heneghan, interview.

10 Memo, October 30, 1970, Kulle personnel file, OPRF; Rima Lunin Schultz, interviews by author, 2020–22; Swanson, interview.

11 Deptuch, interview.

12 Deptuch, interview.

13 Memo, March 31, 1981, Kulle personnel file, OPRF.

14 Jerry Idoux, "At Night, He's Boss at High School," *Oak Leaves*, August 24, 1977, p. 75.

CHAPTER 8

1 Elizabeth Holtzman and Cynthia Cooper, *Who Said It Would Be Easy?* (New York: Arcade, 1996), 90; Elizabeth Holtzman, interview by author, 2022.

2 David E. Rosenbaum, "Ford Defends Pardon before House Panel and Says There Was 'No Deal' with Nixon," *New York Times*, October 18, 1974, p. 85; "Liz the Lion Killer," *Time*, July 3, 1972, p. 14.

3 Holtzman and Cooper, *Who Said It Would Be Easy?* 90; Holtzman, interview.

4 Holtzman and Cooper, *Who Said It Would Be Easy?* 90; Holtzman, interview.

5 Holtzman, interview; Holtzman and Cooper, *Who Said It Would Be Easy?* 90-91.

6 Ralph Blumenthal, interview by author, January 31, 2022; Ralph Blumenthal, "Panoply of Investigations," *New York Times*, December 5, 1973, p. 50.

7 Thomas J. Fallace, *The Emergence of Holocaust Education in American Schools*, (New York: Palgrave MacMillan, 2008), 27-28.

8 Fallace, *Emergence*, 29.

9 Ralph Blumenthal, "Bishop Makes Plea in Nazi Executions," *New York Times*, July 15, 1969, p. 1; Blumenthal, interview.

10 Blumenthal, interview.

11 Ralph Blumenthal, "Bishop nder Inquiry on Atrocity Link," *New York Times*, December 26, 1973, p. 45.

12 Ralph Blumenthal, "U.S. Opens New Drive on Former Nazis," *New York Times*, December 30, 1973, pp. 1, 23; Holtzman and Cooper, *Who Said It Would Be Easy?* 91.

13 Holtzman and Cooper, *Who Said It Would Be Easy?* 91; Holtzman, interview.

14 US Congress, House, Immigration and Naturalization Service Oversight, Hearings before the Subcommittee on Immigration, Citizenship, and International Law, 93rd Cong., 2nd sess., April 3 and June 25, 1974, 22-25.

15 Saidel, *The Outraged Conscience*, 106.

16 Ralph Blumenthal, "Bishop Is Facing Expanded Inquiry," *New York Times*, April 5, 1974, p. 12.

17 Holtzman, interview.

18 Ralph Blumenthal, "Rep. Holtzman Calls U.S. Lax on Nazi Inquiries," *New York Times*, May 21, 1974, p. 8; Saidel, *The Outraged Conscience*, 108.

19 "U.S. Immigration Agency Lists 37 in Inquiry on Nazi War Crimes," *New York Times*, June 6, 1974, p. 30; Raschke, *Useful Enemies*, 107.

20 Raschke, *Useful Enemies*, 107-10.

21 Zachary Groz, "When Yale Harbored a Nazi," *New Journal*, September 23, 2021.

22 John Harris, "Nazi Ties Revealed; Samarin Quits Faculty," *Yale Daily News*, September 20, 1976, p. 1.

23 Harris, "Nazi Ties Revealed," 1.

24 Groz, "When Yale"; Harris, "Nazi Ties Revealed."

25 Thomas C. Lourie, "Samarin," *Yale Daily News*, September 20, 1976, p. 2.

26 Harris, "Nazi Ties Revealed."

27 "Rally against Former Nazi," Jewish Telegraphic Agency, May 14, 1974; "Protest Nazis in U.S.," Jewish Telegraphic Agency, May 7, 1976; US Department of Justice, "Andrija Artukovic OSS File," declassified and released by Central Intelligence Agency, Nazi War Crimes Disclosure Act, Nazi War Crimes and Japanese Imperial Government Records Interagency Working Group, accessed at archive.org; "ADL to Investigate War Criminals," Daily News Bulletin, Jewish Telegraphic Agency, July 31, 1978.

28 Ralph Blumenthal, "Some Suspected of Nazi War Crimes Are Known as Model Citizens," *New York Times*, October 18, 1976, p. 16.

29 Saidel, *The Outraged Conscience*, 15; "Deportation Hearing against Former Nazi from Latvia Postponed Till Feb.," Jewish Telegraphic Agency, November 16, 1976; Blumenthal, "Model Citizens."

30 "War Criminal Faces Deportation," Jewish Telegraphic Agency, February 16, 1977,

p. 2; Frederic U. Dicker, "Nazi Probe's Shadow Reaches Capitaland: Washington Co. Resident Linked to Latvian Crimes," *Sunday Times Union*, November 28. 1976.
31 Blumenthal, "Model Citizens."
32 Robert Jay Lifton, "Hiding Out in America," *New York Times*, January 16, 1977, p. 236.
33 Ralph Blumenthal, "Nazi War Crimes Suspect Asserts C.I.A. Used Him as Anti-Soviet Spy," *New York Times*, October 15, 1976, p. 12.
34 Ralph Blumenthal, "The Mixed Reasons for News, U.S. Nazi-Hunt," *New York Times*, November 28, 1976, p. 185.
35 Saidel, "The Outraged Conscience," 97.
36 Joshua Eilberg to Elmer B. Staats, January 13, 1977, in "Widespread Conspiracy to Obstruct Probes of Alleged Nazi War Criminals Not Supported by Available Evidence Controversy May Continue," Government Accountability Office, report by the comptroller of the United States, released May 16, 1978, appendix 1.
37 *United States v. Walus*, 453 F. Supp. 699 (N.D. Ill. 1978).
38 "Urge Probe of Radio Liberty for Using Scripts by Ex-War Criminal," Jewish Telegraphic Agency, February 18, 1977; "Radio Liberty Drops Nazi Suspect," Jewish Telegraphic Agency, February 23, 1977.
39 "U.S. Sues to Revoke the Citizenship of Man Accused of Executing Jews," *New York Times*, August 16, 1977, p. 12; "Ohioan Is Called Nazi War Criminal," *New York Times*, August 26, 1977, p. 14.
40 "War Criminal Faces Deportation," Jewish Telegraphic Agency; Ryan, *Quiet Neighbors*, 60–61.
41 Jim Casey, "Man Hurls Mace at Suspected Nazi, Seized," *Chicago Sun-Times*, February 2, 1977; Roy R. Silver, "Man Accused of Nazi War Crimes Is Wounded by Shots at L.I. Home," *New York Times*, August 5, 1978, p. 20.
42 Fallace, *Emergence*, 35–36.
43 "N.Y.C. School Board Officials Refuse to Bow to Demands for Dropping Experimental Curriculum on Holocaust," Jewish Telegraphic Agency, October 11, 1977.
44 Douglas E. Kneeland, "German Americans Grow Uneasy," *New York Times*, June 24, 1978, p. 6.
45 Neufeld, *Von Braun*, 474.
46 Volume I: Alleged Nazi War Criminals. Hearing before the Subcommittee on Immigration, Citizenship, and International Law of the Committee on the Judiciary, House of Representatives, 95th Congress, First Session on Alleged Nazi War Criminals, August 3, 1977, serial no. 95-39; "Hearing against Accused Nazi War Criminal Is Entering Third Week," Jewish Telegraphic Agency, November 8, 1977.
47 "Hearing against Accused Nazi War Criminal Is Entering Third Week," Jewish Telegraphic Agency, November 8, 1977.
48 GAO report, i, iii, 16–17.
49 Saidel, *The Outraged Conscience*, 118–19.
50 "NBC-TV Says 'Holocaust' Drew 120 Million," *New York Times*, April 21, 1978, p. B4; Edward Tabor Linenthal, *Preserving Memory: The Struggle to Create America's Holocaust Museum* (New York: Columbia University Press, 1995), 12–13; Fallace, *Emergence*, 40–41.
51 Ryan, *Quiet Neighbors*, 212–13.
52 Saidel, *The Outraged Conscience*, 206.

53 Silver, "Wounded by Shots."

54 Lichtblau, *The Nazis Next Door*, 106–13; Patrick J. Buchanan, letter to the editor, "Dr. Hammer's Role in 'Ivan the Terrible' Trial; Get It Out in the Open," *New York Times*, April 7, 1987, p. A34.

55 Public Law 95-549: "An Act to Amend the Immigration and Nationality Act to Exclude from Admission into, and to Deport from, the United States All Aliens Who Persecuted Any Person on the Basis of Race, Religion, National Origin, or Political Opinion, under the Direction of the Nazi Government of Germany, and for Other Purposes," 92 Stat. 2065, October 30, 1978.

56 "Holtzman Bill Authorizing Deportation of Nazi War Criminals Becomes Law," press release from Rep. Holtzman's office, March 15, 1979, as quoted in Saidel, *The Outraged Conscience*, 119.

57 Martin Mendelsohn, "Oral History Interview with Martin Mendelsohn," by Linda Hunt, United States Holocaust Museum and Memorial, oral history accession number: 2003.44.2.26, RG number RG-50.702.0026; Judy Feigin, "The Office of Special Investigations: Striving for Accountability in the Aftermath of the Holocaust," leaked internal Justice Department report (2010), 4–6.

58 *United States v. Fedorenko*, 455 F. Supp. 893 (S.D. Fla. 1978).

59 Douglas, *The Right Wrong Man*, 45.

60 Prepared statement of Associate Attorney General Michael J. Egan before the Subcommittee on Immigration, Refugee and International Law, House Committee on the Judiciary, concerning INS authorization, March 28, 1979.

61 A. O. Sulzberger, "Agency Studying Nazis Is Upgraded," *New York Times*, March 29, 1979, p. 19.

CHAPTER 9

1 "Statement Regarding Employment Status of Reinhold Kulle," OPRF school board, January 24, 1984; "Annual Report of the Township Treasurer," *Oak Leaves*, November 11, 1970, p. 73.

2 Suzanne Perry, interview by author, April 13, 2021; Greco, interview.

3 *United States v. Kulle* (1983), at 2597–98, 2606.

4 Entry for Paul Sierra, Cook County (Illinois) deaths 1871–1998, accessed March 18, 2018, through FamilySearch database, https://familysearch.org/ark:/61903/1:1: Q2MN-KP8B.

5 Memo, December 29–30, 1975, Kulle personnel file, OPRF; *United States v. Kulle* (1983), at 2611.

6 Possley and Hayer, "Deportation Bid;; *United States v. Kulle* (1983), at 2597–2605.

7 Jerry Crimmins, "Neighborhood Surprised, Shocked by Accusation." *Chicago Tribune*, December 19, 1981, p. 4.

8 "Oak Park Is Named an All-American City," *Chicago Tribune*, April 15, 1976, p. 3.

9 David Axelrod, "Oak Park Acts to Defuse Tensions of Integration," *Chicago Tribune*, July 1, 1976, p. N10.

10 "Dates and Deadlines," *Forest Leaves*, April 7, 1976, p. 100; "School Vote Suit Called 'Possible,'" *Oak Leaves*, May 8. 1976, p. 8; "Vivian Halliburton: She's an Achiever," *Forest Leaves*, February 1, 1978, p. 21.

11 Paul Sassone, "Racist Mail Returns Aren't for Real," *Oak Leaves*, December 3, 1975, p. 10; "Police Reports," *Forest Leaves*, October 6, 1976, p. 62A.

12 Axelrod, "Oak Park."

13 Philippa Strum, *When the Nazis Came to Skokie: Freedom for Speech We Hate* (Lawrence: University of Kansas Press, 1999), 5, 15; National Socialist Party of America, "We Are Coming" flyer, October 1976, Skokie History Digital Collections, accessed January 4, 2023.

14 Jeffrey Kaplan, ed., *Encyclopedia of White Power: A Sourcebook on the Radical Racist Right* (Walnut Creek, CA: AltaMira Press, 2000), 3; Strum, *Skokie*, 5–6; Jesse Dukes, "The Nazis' Neighborhood," *Curious City*, WBEZ radio, April 23, 2017.

15 Maggie Daly, "Nazi 'Hot Line' Cooled by Unpaid Bill." *Chicago Tribune*, June 15, 1978, p. B18.

16 Strum, *Skokie*, 15.

17 Strum, *Skokie*, 16; "Skokie Passes Three Ordinances," Skokie History Digital Collections, accessed January 4, 2023, at https://skokiehistory.omeka.net/exhibits/show/attempted-nazi-march/timeline/may-2-board-meeting; *Village of Skokie v. National Socialist Party of America, et al.*, docket no. 77-2702, Circuit Court of Cook County, IL, Chancery Division.

18 Arthur Butz, *The Hoax of the Twentieth Century* (Torrance, CA: Institute for Historical Review, 1976).

19 Dimaso, "Violence"; Marcus, interview.

20 Dimaso, "Violence"; Triton College police report, complaint no. 77-7286, November 15, 1977, FOIA request 033121; "Collin and Nazi Aide Are Fined," *Chicago Tribune*, March 15, 1978, p. B5.

21 Kaplan. *Encyclopedia of White Power*, 62; Jeffrey Kaplan, *Radical Religion in America: Millenarian Movements from the Far Right to the Children of Noah* (Syracuse, NY: Syracuse University Press, 1999), 36; Elizabeth Wheaton, *Code Name GREENKIL: The 1979 Greensboro Killings* (Athens: University of Georgia Press, 1979), 190–91.

22 Kathy Catrambone, "Nazis Plan to Rally Here," *Oak Leaves*, August 27, 1980, p. 5; *Wednesday Journal*, September 3, 1980, p. 1.

23 "Local Groups Plan Anti-Nazi Activities," *Oak Leaves*, June 21, 1978, p. 8; Bob Miodonski, "Decision Due on Nazi Rally," *Oak Leaves*, September 10, 1980, p. 5.

24 Minutes of an adjourned regular meeting of the president and board of trustees of the Village of Oak Park, Wednesday, September 3, 1980, FOIA request #21-00452, Village of Oak Park.

25 David Sokol, interview by author, April 18, 2021.

26 Sokol, interview.

27 Minutes of an adjourned regular meeting of the president and board of trustees of the Village of Oak Park, Monday, September 15, 1980, FOIA request #21-00452, Village of Oak Park; Sokol, interview; "Nazi Rally Sept. 27," *Oak Leaves*, September 17, 1980, p. 5.

28 Park Board of Commissioners, "Participate by Not Participating," *Wednesday Journal*, September 24, 1980, p. 6; "Let 'Em March" (op-ed), *Oak Leaves*, September 3, 1980, p. 20; Bob Miodonski, "Decision Due on Nazi Rally," *Oak Leaves*, September 10, 1980, p. 5; Sokol, interview.

29 Kim Pierce, "Article on Nazis' Rally Was the Pits," *Oak Leaves*, September 3, 1980,

p. 21; Cy Jaffe, "Truth about Nazis Must Be Told, Retold." *Oak Leaves*, September 10, 1980, p. 20; Mike Proko, "Why Roll Over and Play Dead for Nazis?" *Oak Leaves*, September 17, 1980, p. 18.

30 Mark McAdams, "While Nazis Rallied, 45 Told of 'Outrage,'" *Forest Leaves*, October 1, 1980, p. 9; Sandra Sokol, interview by author, April 18, 2021; Bob Miodonski, "Nazi Rally Set for Saturday," *Forest Leaves*, September 24, 1980, p. 6.

31 "Ignoring Nazis Not the Solution" (op-ed), *Oak Leaves*, October 1, 1980, p. 20; editorial, "Cheap Theater at Nazi Rally," *Wednesday Journal*, p. 6; Bob Miodonski, "Protestors Drown Out Nazi Rhetoric," *Oak Leaves*, October 1, 1980, p. 5; *Wednesday Journal*, October 1, 1980, p. 1; Eric Linden and Anne Duggan, "Small Crowd, Loud Voices Dominate Nazi Rally," *Wednesday Journal*, October 1, 1980, p. 5.

32 Harriet Vrba, "Hate Dirtied a Patch of Green Saturday," *Oak Leaves*, October 1, 1980, p. 20.

33 H. Vivian Halliburton, "Are Nazis Hated for Wrong Reason?" *Oak Leaves*, October 8, 1980, p. 22.

34 Idoux, "At Night."

CHAPTER 10

1 Mary-Terese Cozzola, interview by author, May 5, 2021.

2 "Justice Dept Names a Chief for Nazi War Criminal Unit," *New York Times*, May 7, 1979, p. 12; Feigin, "Striving For Accountability," 8.

3 Maurice A. Butler, *Out of the Shadow: The Story of Charles L. Gittens Who Broke the Color Barrier in the United States Secret Service* (Bloomington, IN: Xlibris, 2012), 182–84.

4 Rosenbaum, interview.

5 Ralph Blumenthal, "War Crimes Alleged in Suit on Citizenship of L.I. Man," *New York Times*, November 22, 1979, p. 25; Feigin, "Striving For Accountability," 570–609.

6 "Special to the JTA Spotlight on Accused War Criminals," Jewish Telegraphic Agency, January 7. 1980.

7 *Escape from Justice: Nazi War Criminals among Us*, ABC News, 1980; "'Escape from Justice' Pursues Nazi War Criminals," *New York Times*, January 13, 1980, p. D27.

8 Feigin, "Striving For Accountability," leaked internal Justice Department Report (2010), 9. Saidel, *The Outraged Conscience*, 129–32.

9 Ryan, *Quiet Neighbors*, 66, 66n.

10 *United States v. Fedorenko*, 597 F. 2d 946 (1979).

11 Ryan, *Quiet Neighbors*, 66–67.

12 *Fedorenko v. United States*, 449 U.S. 490 (1981).

13 Holtzman, interview.

14 Raschke, *Useful Enemies*, 277.

15 Ryan, *Quiet Neighbors*, 214–17.

16 Feigin, "Striving for Accountability," 21–22; Debbie Cenziper, *Citizen 865* (New York: Hachette Books, 2019), 35–38, 41.

17 McCarron and Coates, "Chicago Man"; Gottesman, "U.S. Still Pressing."

18 "Skriauda Turi Būti Atlyginta," *Draugas* 72 (October 11, 1978): 3.

19 Janet Cawley, "Alleged Nazi Aide's Citizenship on Line," *Chicago Tribune*, August 14, 1980, p. 3.

20 Jay Branegan, "Chicago Man's Prints Match Nazi's, Court Told." *Chicago Tribune*, April 3, 1981, p. B8; Robert Enstad, "Immigrant Denies Role in Nazi Camp," *Chicago Tribune*, June 15, 1982, p. 13.

21 *Cleveland Jewish News*, February 13, 1981, p. 15; Vivian Witt, "Ukrainians Fill Courtroom in Demjanjuk Trial Here," *Cleveland Jewish News*, February 13, 1981, p. 21.

22 Stephen G. Esrati, "Demjanjuk Attorneys Play on Jewish Issue." *Chicago Jewish Post & Opinion* 47, no. 25 (March 6, 1981).

23 "Man Accused by Justice Department of Nazi Activities Killed by Train," Jewish Telegraphic Agency, December 21, 1981.

24 Jerry Crimmins and William B. Crawford Jr., "Alleged Ex-Nazi Killed by Train in Cicero," *Chicago Tribune*, December 19, 1981, p. A1.

25 Crimmins, "Neighborhood Surprised"; Jerry Crimmins, "Son Defends Father Alleged to Have Been Nazi: 'He Cared,'" *Chicago Tribune*, December 27, 1981, p. 16.

26 Feigin, "Striving For Accountability," 10; see, for example, Juri Raus, "East European Groups Confer with Justice Department Reps," *Ukrainian Weekly*, February 14, 1982, pp. 1, 14.

27 Ieva Zake, "'The Secret Nazi Network': Post–World War II Latvian Immigrants and the Hunt for Nazis in the United States," *Journal of Baltic Studies* 41, no. 1 (March 2010): 106–7.

28 See Sylvia Foti, *The Nazi's Granddaughter* (Washington: Regnery History, 2021).

29 Simpson, *Blowback*, 269–70.

30 Jerome Bakst, Elliot Welles, and Eli Rosenbaum, "The Campaign against the Justice Department's Prosecution of Suspected Nazi War Criminals," Anti-Defamation League of B'nai B'rith, ADL special report, 1985, p. 2; Mary Thornton, "East European Emigres Are Accused of Impeding Hunt for Nazis in US," *Washington Post*, April 6, 1985.

31 Feigin, "Striving For Accountability," 534.

32 "Soviet Harvest: KGB Propaganda Bears Fruit at Long Last," latvianlegion.org.

33 *United States v. Liudas Kairys*, no. 80 C 4302, N.D. IL, June 14, 1982, at 157 (USHMM RG 06.029.01x17 2008.205).

34 Rosenbaum, interview.

35 *United States v. Kairys* (1980), at 282.

36 *United States v. Kairys* (1980), at 1266.

37 *United States v. Kairys* (1980), at 1081.

38 Deborah Lipstadt, *Denying the Holocaust* (New York: Free Press, 1993), 105, 144–46.

39 Drew Pearson, "Judge Rules against Liberty Lobby," *Free Lance-Star*, November 2, 1966, p. 4.

40 *Fedorenko v. United States*, 449 U.S. 490 (1981).

41 Gregory S. Gordon, "Taking the Paper Trail Instead of Memory Lane: OSI's Use of Ancient Foreign Documents in the Nazi Cases," *U.S. Attorneys' Bulletin* 54, no. 01 (Office of Special Investigations, January 2006): 18; "Berlin Document Center," https://www.bundesarchiv.de/fachinformationen/01001/index.html.de.

42 Peter Black, interview by author, October 5, 2021.

43 Charles Gittens, memo to Donna Cooper, September 3, 1981 (Record Group 59: general records of the Department of State, select documents released under the Nazi War Crimes and Japanese Imperial Government Disclosure Acts relating to Nazi War Crimes, 593953, box 11, folder 1).

CHAPTER 11

1 Neal Sher to Reinhold Kulle, July 28, 1982, SP-VHM, box 37, folder 436a.
2 *Wednesday Journal*, June 9, 1982, p. 23.
3 Bruce Einhorn to Reinhold Kulle, August 4, 1982 SP-VHM, box 37, folder 436a.
4 Bruce Einhorn, interview by author, June 28. 2021.
5 Einhorn, interview.
6 Kulle files, SP-VHM; Einhorn, interview.
7 *Matter of Laipenieks*, in deportation proceedings, A-11937435.
8 Einhorn, interview.
9 Black, interview.
10 Rosenbaum, interview; Black, interview.
11 Einhorn, interview; Kulle, sworn interview.
12 Unless otherwise noted, all dialogue in this chapter is quoted from sworn interview of Reinhold Kulle, August 14, 1982, SP-VHM, box 37, folder 436a.
13 Black, interview.
14 Black, interview.
15 Einhorn, interview.
16 Einhorn, interview.
17 Einhorn, interview.
18 Einhorn, interview.
19 "On the Case; Ronnie L. Edelman '75, Government Crime-Fighter," *UB Law Forum*, 13, no. 2 (fall 2000): 38–39.
20 Julia Klein, "In Pursuit of Justice," *Pennsylvania Gazette*, February 22, 2017.
21 David Ian Klein, "75 Years after Nuremberg, America's Top Nazi Hunter Looks Back," *The Forward*, June 3, 2021; Andrew Nagorski, *The Nazi Hunters* (New York: Simon & Schuster, 2016), 243; Rosenbaum, interview.
22 Rosenbaum, interview.
23 Rosenbaum, interview; Lichtblau, *The Nazis Next Door*, 154–59.
24 "Neal Sher, Nazi Hunter & Former AIPAC Official," *Talkline with Zev Brenner* (podcast), July 18, 2021.
25 Lichtblau, *The Nazis Next Door*, 159–63.
26 Neufeld, *Von Braun*, 474–76.
27 Rosenbaum, interview.
28 *United States v. Kairys*, defendant's posttrial reply brief, November 18, 1982, p. 4, Reagan Library, John G. Roberts files, JGR/Nazi prosecutions folder 5 of 9, box 33.
29 *United States v. Kulle*, order to show cause.

CHAPTER 12

1 Possley and Hayer, "Deportation Bid"; Andy Knott, "U.S. Seeking to Deport Suburb Man as Ex-Nazi," *Chicago Tribune*, December 4, 1982, p. N5.
2 Eric Linden, "High School Maintenance Man Accused of Being Nazi SS Guard." *Wednesday Journal*, December 8, 1982, p. 3.
3 Heneghan, interview.
4 Swanson, interview.

5 *Wednesday Journal*, December 8, 1982, p. 1.
6 Linden, "Maintenance Man Accused."
7 Linden, "Maintenance Man Accused."
8 Marcus, interview.
9 Marcus, interview.
10 "Sisterhood," *Oak Leaves*, May 2, 1973, p. 18; "Mrs. Philip Marcus Takes Top Honors as Bond Salesman," *Forest Leaves*, August 28, 1974, p. 17.
11 Marcus, interview.
12 Leah Marcus, "World of River Forest," *Oak Park World*, March 1, 1978, p. 14.
13 Leah Marcus, "World of River Forest," *Oak Park World*, November 29, 1978, p. 25.
14 Marcus, interview.
15 "OP-RFHS Graduation Is Thursday," *Forest Leaves*, June 11, 1980, p. 66; *Wednesday Journal*, January 21, 1981, p. 14; Marcus, interview.
16 Swanson, interview.
17 William "Jay Jay" Turner, interview by author, June 17, 2021.
18 Gignilliat, interview.
19 Swanson, interview.
20 Turner, interview.

CHAPTER 13

1 Rosenbaum, interview; Saidel, *The Outraged Conscience*, 6; Leslie Maitland, "A German Citizen Ordered Deported," *New York Times*, December 24, 1982, p. 30.
2 Deptuch, interview.
3 Charles W. Nixon, interview by author, June 3, 2021.
4 Jeff Ferenc, "Case against Accused Nazi to Continue," *Oak Leaves*, January 19, 1983, p. 5.
5 Einhorn, interview.
6 *Kulle v. Springer*, 566 F. Supp. 279 (N.D. Ill. 1983).
7 *Kulle v. Springer*, 566 F. Supp. 279 (N.D. Ill. 1983); Einhorn, interview.
8 Rosenbaum, interview.
9 Rosenbaum, interview.
10 Einhorn, interview.
11 Efraim Zuroff, cable to George Garand, March 8, 1983, submitted March 10, 1983. Provided by Dr. Efraim Zuroff.
12 Efraim Zuroff, cable to George Garand, March 12, 1983, submitted March 15, 1983. Provided by Dr. Efraim Zuroff.
13 Bruce Einhorn, cable to Dr. Efraim Zuroff, March 23, 1983. Provided by Dr. Efraim Zuroff.
14 Einhorn, cable to Zuroff.
15 Rosenbaum, interview.
16 Ralph Blumenthal, "U.S. Unsure of Whereabouts of Deported Ex-Nazi Guard," *New York Times*, April 23, 1983, p. 8.
17 "Nazi Who Lived Here Is 'Free' in W. Germany," *Chicago Tribune*, April 29, 1983, p. 14.
18 Samuel G. Freedman, "U.S. Judge Orders Guard at Death Camp Deported," *New York Times*, February 25, 1983, p. 15; John T. McQuiston, "L.I. Man Is Ordered Deported for Concentration Camp Role," *New York Times*, May 22, 1983, p. 43.

19 *United States v. Kulle* (1983), at 225.

20 Moldawa, *Gross-Rosen*, 3.

21 Einhorn, interview.

22 "Front Page News," Holocaust Memorial Foundation of Illinois, 1983. Provided by Illinois Holocaust Museum and Education Center.

23 Bruce Einhorn memorandum: Preliminary interview of Mr. Marion Wojciechowski, May 23, 1983. SP-VHM, box 34, folder 431a.

24 Einhorn, interview; Rosenbaum, interview.

25 *United States v. Kulle* (1983), at 1513–15, 2489–90.

26 Oak Park & River Forest High School board meeting notes, 1982–83.

27 Memo to Board of Education from John C. Swanson, Jonathan L. Smith, and Larry Walker, re: "OTHER" SALARY ADJUSTMENTS FOR 1983–1984 REVISED, in Oak Park & River Forest High School board meeting notes, June 16, 1983.

CHAPTER 14

1 Einhorn, interview.

2 Unless otherwise noted, courtroom dialogue in this chapter comes from the transcript of *United States v. Kulle* (1983) A10 857 195, from August 10–11, 1983.

3 Sylvia Kucenas, "Current Events: OSI Collaborates with KGB," *Lituanus* 30, no. 1 (spring 1984).

4 Flora Johnson, "The Nazi Who Never Was," *Washington Post*, May 10, 1981.

5 Einhorn, interview.

6 Einhorn, interview.

7 Cenziper, *Citizen 865*, 44; Black, interview.

8 Samuel L. Adams, "U.S. Says Ex-Nazi 'Lied His Way' into Country," *Chicago Tribune*, August 11, 1983, p. A12.

9 RaeLynne Toperoff, interview by author, February 4, 2021; Lunin Schultz, interview.

10 Einhorn, interview.

11 Lunin Schultz, interview; Toperoff, interview.

12 Lunin Schultz, interview.

13 Rosenbaum, interview.

14 Lunin Schultz, interview.

15 Toperoff, interview.

CHAPTER 15

1 Unless otherwise noted, courtroom dialogue in this chapter comes from the transcript of *United States v. Kulle* (1983) A10 857 195, from August 12–22, 1983.

2 Nixon, interview.

3 Einhorn, interview.

4 Einhorn, interview.

5 An abbreviation of *Geheime Staatspolizei*—the German secret police.

6 Moldawa, *Gross-Rosen*, 55.

7 Gutterman, *A Narrow Bridge to Life*, 134.

8 Moldawa, *Gross-Rosen*, 33.

9 Moldawa, *Gross-Rosen*, 99.

10 Moldawa, *Gross-Rosen*, 110.

11 Einhorn, interview.

12 Lunin Schultz, interview.

13 Einhorn, interview.

14 Rosenbaum, interview.

15 Einhorn, interview.

16 The family requested that their mother's name remain anonymous.

17 Rosenbaum, interview; the witness's daughter, interview by author, February 8, 2022.

18 Rosenbaum, interview.

19 Eric Linden, "Nazi Deportation Trial Opens for High School Employee." *Wednesday Journal*, August 17, 1983, p. 7.

20 "Nazi Deportation Case Recessed for Now," *Wednesday Journal*, August 31, 1983, p. 10.

21 Toperoff, interview.

CHAPTER 16

1 Toperoff, interview; Lunin Schultz, interview.

2 OPRF custodial staff, "Articles Not Fair to Reinhold Kulle," *Oak Leaves*, August 31, 1983, p. 16.

3 Toperoff, interview.

4 Eric Linden, "Kulle's Life Goes On despite Deportation Trial," *Wednesday Journal*, September 7, 1983, p. 7.

5 Jeff Ferenc, "Suspend Accused Nazi, School Asked," *Oak Leaves*, October 12, 1983.

6 Lunin Schultz, interview.

7 Norman Roth, Tadeusz Lampert, and Harry Gaynor, letter to the editor, *Wednesday Journal*, September 14, 1983, p. 10.

8 Lunin Schultz, interview.

9 Stefan Fenichel, letter to the editor, *Wednesday Journal*, September 14, 1983, p. 10.

10 Toperoff, interview.

11 Unless otherwise noted, courtroom dialogue in this chapter comes from the transcript of *United States v. Kulle* (1983) A10 857 195, from August 23, 1983, and September 19–22, 1983.

12 Einhorn, interview.

13 Lunin Schultz, interview.

14 Einhorn, interview.

15 Rosenbaum, interview.

16 Einhorn, interview; Rosenbaum, interview.

17 Bruce Einhorn, interview.

18 Einhorn, interview.

19 Einhorn, interview.

20 Toperoff, interview; Lunin Schultz, interview.

21 Lunin Schultz and Toperoff, letter to the members of the Community Relations Commission and the staff, September 21, 1983. Papers of Rima Lunin Schultz.

22 Harris Dicker et al., letter to Paul Gignilliat from Oak Park Temple board of directors, October 1983. Papers of Rima Lunin Schultz.

23 OPRF school board meeting notes, October 4, 1983, p. 3.

24 OPRF school board meeting notes from executive session, October 4, 1983.

25 Deptuch, interview.

26 Marcus, interview.

27 OPRF executive session notes, October 4, 1983.

CHAPTER 17

1 "A Decision Not Reached," *Wednesday Journal*, October 4, 1983, p. 10.

2 "Statement to OPRF Human Relations Committee," October 5, 1983. Papers of Rima Lunin Schultz.

3 Lunin Schultz, interview.

4 Mary and Stef Krieger, letter to the editor, *Wednesday Journal*, October 19, 1983, p. 10.

5 Jeff Ferenc, "Suspend Accused Nazi, School Asked." *Oak Leaves*, October 12, 1983, p. 7.

6 Deptuch, interview.

7 OPRF school board notes, September 13, 1983, p. 5.

8 Lunin Schultz, interview; Bruce and Julie Samuels, interview by author, March 29, 2021.

9 Frank Lynn, "LaRouche Slate Is Fought in Races for School Board," *New York Times*, April 22, 1983, p. B3; Leon Winter, "School Board Election Battle," *Washington Post*, March 1, 1984; Jean Latz Griffin and Michael Arndt, "3 School Boards Full of New Faces, Hopes," *Chicago Tribune*, November 7, 1985; Louise Saul, "School Vote: Local Issues in Spotlight," *New York Times*, April 1, 1984, section 11NJ, p. 1.

10 Howard Blum and Paul L Montgomery, "U.S. Labor Party: Cult Surrounded by Controversy," *New York Times*, October 7, 1979, pp. 1, 16.

11 Stephen E. Atkins, *Encyclopedia of Right-Wing Extremism in Modern American History* (Santa Barbara, CA: ABC-CLIO, 2011), 108–10.

12 Jeff Ferenc, "Right-Wing Group Recruits Candidates," *Forest Leaves*, September 21, 1983, p. 7.

13 Lunin Schultz, interview; Samuels, interview.

14 CIRC summary statement, October 21, 1983. Papers of Rima Lunin Schultz; Samuels, interview.

15 Samuels, interview; Lunin Schultz, interview.

16 Marcus, "Yom Kippur Speech."

17 Lunin Schultz, interview.

18 Letter to members of the OPRF school board, October 19, 1983. Papers of Rima Lunin Schultz.

19 Lunin Schultz, interview.

20 Kari Juel, "Kulle One Reason to Be Proud of School," *Oak Leaves*, October 19, 1983, p. 21.

21 Toperoff, interview.

22 Juel, "One Reason."

23 Juel, "One Reason"; Lunin Schultz, interview.

24 Lunin Schultz, interview; Community Relations Commission of Oak Park, letter to OPRF school board, October 20, 1983. Papers of Rima Lunin Schultz.

25 Toperoff, interview.

26 OPRF school board meeting notes, October 20, 1983.

27 CIRC summary, October 21, 1983.
28 School board notes, October 20, 1983.
29 School board notes, October 20, 1983.
30 Marcus, interview.
31 OPRF school board notes from executive session, October 20, 1983; school board notes, October 20, 1983.
32 CIRC summary, October 21, 1983.
33 Jeff Ferenc, "Kulle Had a Chance for Early Retirement." *Oak Leaves*, February 15, 1984, p. 5.
34 "Past Award Recipients," OPRF website, https://www.oprfhs.org/alumni/past-award-recipients-toe#1983.
35 Fried, *The Man Everybody Knew*, 13.
36 See Marcia Charletain, *Franchise: The Golden Arches in Black America* (New York: Liveright, 2020).
37 Fried, *The Man Everybody Knew*, 139.
38 Kalyn Wulatin, interview by author, 2021.
39 Wulatin, interview.
40 Wulatin, interview; Currie, interview.
41 Wulatin, interview.
42 Jeff Ferenc, "PTO-Backed Candidates Seek Dist. 200 Seats," *Oak Leaves*, October 26, 1983, p. 9.
43 Anne Downs, "We're All Human and Make Mistakes," *Oak Leaves*, November 2, 1983, p. 20.
44 Gary Neudahl, "We Should Leave Vengeance to God," *Oak Leaves*, November 2, 1983, p. 20.
45 Corinne Barron, "Don't Destroy a Life Because of Emotion," *Oak Leaves*, November 2, 1983, p. 20.
46 Ronald Napier, "Kulle Being Hounded on a Technicality," *Oak Leaves*, November 2, 1983, p. 20.
47 Barron, "Don't Destroy;" Neudahl, "Vengeance."
48 Downs, "Mistakes."
49 Hans Delius, "Treat People on Merit, Not Background," *Oak Leaves*, November 2, 1983, pp. 20, 23, 24.

CHAPTER 18

1 Holtzman, interview.
2 ADL special report, 10.
3 Russ Bellant, *Old Nazis, the New Right, and the Republican Party* (Boston: South End Press, 1988), 2, 20, 23.
4 Rasa Razgaitis, "Deporting Nazi Collaborators," *Washington Post*, April 18, 1983, p. A10.
5 ADL special report, 10.
6 Kucenas, "OSI Collaborates."
7 Edward M. O'Connor, "Our Open Society under Attack by the Despotic State," *Ukrainian Quarterly* 40 (spring 1984): 17–49.
8 ADL special report, 32.

9 "Press and Plumbers," *Executive Intelligence Review*, August 14–20, 1979, 3; "How Abscam and Brilab 'Sting,'" *Executive Intelligence Review*, June 3, 1980, p. 22; "'Fedgate' May Ensnare Ohio Solon," *Executive Intelligence Review*, August 14–20, 1979, p. 33.

10 ADL special report, 15.

11 Patrick Buchanan, "A Lesson in Tyranny Too Soon Forgotten," *Chicago Tribune*, August 25, 1977, section 3, p. 3.

12 Patrick Buchanan, "'Ivan the Terrible': More Doubts," *New York Post*, March 17, 1990; See also Patrick J. Buchanan, *Churchill, Hitler, and the "Unnecessary War"* (New York: Three Rivers Press, 2008); and Patrick J. Buchanan, "Did Hitler Really Want War?" Creators Syndicate, September 2, 2009.

13 Howard Kurtz, Pat Buchanan, "The Jewish Question," *Washington Post*, September 20, 1990.

14 ADL special report, 15.

15 Foti, *The Nazi's Granddaughter*.

16 Enstad, "Immigrant Denies;" Grossman and reporter, "Area Was Haven"; *United States v. Schellong*, 547 F. Supp. 569 (1982).

17 "Ex-Soviet Spy at Nazi trial," *Chicago Tribune*, June 24, 1982, p. 1.

18 Mike Casey, "A Defense Attorney for John Demjanjuk," UPI archives, October 27, 1983.

19 Deptuch, interview.

20 Deptuch, interview.

21 Richard Deptuch, "Petition to School Board," November 7, 1983. Papers of Rima Lunin Schultz.

22 Deptuch, interview.

23 Michael Averbach, interview by author, December 22, 2020; Steven Gevinson, interview by author, December 22, 2020; Deptuch, interview.

CHAPTER 19

1 Wulatin, interview; Lunin Schultz, interview.

2 Wulatin, interview.

3 Unless otherwise noted, courtroom dialogue in this chapter comes from the transcript of *United States v. Kulle* (1983) A10 857 195, from November 15–16, 1983.

4 Notebook. Papers of Rima Lunin Schultz.

5 https://jwcdaily.com/hinsdalelivingmagazine/2015/05/24/european-luxury-within-reach/.

6 Einhorn, interview.

7 Notebook, papers of Rima Lunin Schultz.

8 Julie Deardorff and *Tribune* staff writer, "Robert Wehli, 82, Longtime Coach, Teacher," *Chicago Tribune*, August 28, 2000.

9 Lunin Schultz, notebook.

10 Wulatin, interview.

11 Lunin Schultz, interview; Lunin Schultz, notebook.

12 Wulatin, interview.

13 Sworn affadavit of Don Offerman, 1983. Kulle personnel file, OPRF.

14 Toperoff, interview.

15 Lunin Schultz, interview.

16 Wulatin, interview.

17 Lunin Schultz, notebook.

18 Lunin Schultz, notebook; Lunin Schultz, interview.

19 Consolidated election results, November 8, 1983, in OPRF school board meeting notes, November 15, 1983.

20 OPRF school board notes, November 15, 1983, pp. 2–3.

21 OPRF school board notes, November 15, 1983, p. 5.

22 Deptuch, interview.

23 OPRF school board notes, November 15, 1983, pp. 5–7.

CHAPTER 20

1 Eric Linden and Susy Schultz, "Nazi Trial Ends; School Action Demanded," *Wednesday Journal*, November 23, p. 1.

2 Lunin Schultz, interview.

3 Jeff Ferenc, "Kulle Says He Did Not Abuse Prisoners," *Oak Leaves*, November 23, 1983, p. 7.

4 Dorothy Samachson, "Innocent until Proven Guilty? Not for Kulle," *Wednesday Journal*, November 23, 1983, p. 21.

5 Hans Delius, letter to the editor, *Wednesday Journal*, November 23, 1983, p. 50.

6 Raymond Kinzie, "Torementing Memories Punishment Enough," *Oak Leaves*, November 30, 1983, p. 21.

7 Dorothy Samachson, "Pro-Kulle Sentiment Is Disgraceful," *Oak Leaves*, November 30, 1983, p. 21.

8 Raymond Kinzie, "Kulle Defender Sets Record Straight," *Oak Leaves*, December 21, 1983, pp. 19–20.

9 Lunin Schultz, interview.

10 Fundraising note, December 5, 1983. Papers of Rima Lunin Schultz. Lunin Schultz, interview.

11 Rosenbaum, interview.

12 OPRF school board statement, published in *Oak Leaves*, "School Board Explains Its Positions on Kulle Matter," *Oak Leaves*, December 7, 1983, p. 23.

13 Turner, interview.

14 Lunin Schultz, interview.

15 Wulatin, interview.

16 Gevinson, interview.

17 Kalyn Wulatin and Dave Newbart, "Echoes of the Past Engulf the Present," *Trapeze*, December 9, 1983, pp. 1, 5.

18 Gignilliat, interview; Lunin Schultz, interview; Toperoff, interview; Gail Liebman, interview by author, 2023.

19 OPRF school board meeting notes, December 13, 1983, pp. 1–3.

20 Toperoff, interview.

21 Lunin Schultz, interview.

22 Michael Fleisher, statement to OPRF school board, December 13, 1983.

23 OPRF school board notes, December 13, 1983, p. 4.

24 Lunin Schultz, interview; Toperoff, interview.

25 OPRF school board Notes, December 13, 1983, pp. 4–7.

26 Turner, interview.
27 OPRF school board notes from executive session, December 13, 1983.
28 Charlotte Cooper, "Holocaust Lessons Missing the Mark?" *Oak Leaves*, December 14, 1983, p. 9; Lunin Schultz, interview.
29 Fallace, *Emergence*, 61–63.
30 Fallace, *Emergence*, 97–101; 37–38.
31 Fallace, *Emergence*, 79–80.
32 Jeff Ferenc, "Candidates Urge 'Return to Basics,'" *Oak Leaves*, October 9, 1983, p. 9; Jeff Ferenc, "PTO-Backed Candidates Seek Dist. 200 Seats," *Oak Leaves*, October 9, 1983, p. 9.
33 Lunin Schultz, interview.
34 Cooper, "Holocaust Lessons."
35 Lunin Schultz, interview.
36 "December 1983: Arctic Cold Invades Chicago," WGNTV.com, https://wgntv.com/weather/weather-blog/december-1983-arctic-cold-invades-chicago/.
37 OPRF school board meeting notes from executive session, December 21, 1983.
38 About 125 South Wacker, Hines.com, https://www.hines.com/properties/125-south-wacker-chicago.
39 "Arctic Cold."
40 OPRF school board notes from executive session, December 21, 1983.
41 Executive Committee, Oak Park–River Forest Community of Churches, "Open Letter of the Churches and to the Oak Park and River Forest Communities," *Wednesday Journal*, December 21, 1983, p. 11.
42 OPRF school board notes from executive session, December 21, 1983.
43 Andrew Nussbam, eulogy for Bernard "Bud" Nussbaum, law.uchicago.edu/news/bernard-nussbaum-551931-2019.
44 OPRF school board notes from executive session, December 21, 1983.
45 "Arctic Cold."
46 Cam Richardson, "Case of Ex-SS Guard Splits Oak Pk.," *Chicago Sun-Times*, January 1, 1984, pp. 4, 22.
47 Tadeusz Lampert, "Holocaust Illiteracy," unpublished essay sent to Rima Lunin Schultz on April 9, 1984, papers of Rima Lunin Schultz.
48 Triton College police report, complaint no. 77-7286, November 15, 1977. FOIA request 033121.
49 Lunin Schultz, interview.
50 Meyer Rubinstein, "How Death Camp Worked," *Chicago Sun-Times*, January 9, 1984.
51 Gignilliat, interview.
52 OPRF school board notes from executive session, January 14, 1984.
53 Turner, interview.
54 Gignilliat, interview.
55 Gignilliat, interview.
56 Gignilliat, interview.

CHAPTER 21

1 Estimate of IMRF retirement pension, Illinois Municipal Retirement Fund, January 18. 1984, Kulle personnel file, OPRF.

2 Gignilliat, interview.
3 Letter from Rima Lunin Schultz, January 15, 1984, papers of Rima Lunin Schultz.
4 OPRF school board, public statement published in *Oak Leaves*, January 18, 1984, pp. 17-18.
5 Lunin Schultz, interview.
6 Gignilliat, interview.
7 IMRF estimate.
8 John Swanson, memo to faculty, February 1, 1984, Kulle personnel file, OPRF; Swanson, interview; George Papajohn, "Former SS Guard Loses School Post," *Chicago Tribune*, January 25, 1984, p. A1.
9 Jeffrey Greenwald, interview by author, 2021; Marjorie Greenwald, interview by author.
10 Toperoff, interview.
11 "Statement Regarding Employment Status of Reinhold Kulle," OPRF school board, January 24, 1984.
12 Toperoff, interview.
13 Liebman, interview.
14 Jeffrey Greenwald, interview by author; Marjorie Greenwald, interview by author.
15 The notes from these board meetings were unsealed in 2021.
16 Eric Linden, "Ex-Nazi Dismissed by High School Board," *Wednesday Journal*, February 1, 1984, p. 1; Memo "Re: MEETING WITH BOARD PRESIDENT," January 25, 1984 (misdated 1983), OPRF.
17 Marcus, interview; Marcus, "Yom Kippur Speech."
18 Linden, "Ex-Nazi Dismissed;" Jeff Ferenc, "Kulle on Paid Leave; Won't Return to Job," *Oak Leaves*, February 1, 1984, p. 1.
19 Linden, "Ex-Nazi Dismissed."
20 Ferenc, "Kulle on Paid Leave."
21 Unnamed handwritten notes, Kulle personnel file, OPRF.
22 Memo to OPRF business office, "Reinhold Kulle, Head Custodian," January 27, 1984. Kulle personnel file, OPRF.
23 Notice of employee separation, January 30, 1984, Kulle personnel file, OPRF.
24 Swanson, memo to faculty.
25 Lunin Schultz, interview; Toperoff, interview.
26 Menu from Nielsen's Restaurant, papers of Rima Lunin Schultz; Toperoff, interview.

CHAPTER 22

1 "A Hollow 'Victory,'" *Wednesday Journal*, February 1, 1984, p. 10.
2 Matt Brennock, "Oak Park Speaks Out," *Oak Leaves*, February 1, 1984, p. 19.
3 Jim Bowman, "Nazi Hunting Gets Bad Name Here," *Oak Leaves*, February 15, 2022, p. 15.
4 Jim Eitrheim, "Teacher Always Will Remember Kulle," *Oak Leaves*, February 15, 1984, p. 22.
5 Jeff Ferenc, "Reaction to Kulle Decision," *Oak Leaves*, February 8, 1984, p. 6.
6 Hans Delius, "Dismissal of Kulle Threatens Us All," *Oak Leaves*, February 29, 1984, p. 18.
7 "Friends Start Legal Defense Fund for Kulle," *Oak Leaves*, February 1, 1984, p. 9.

8 Eric Linden, "Reactions Vary to Kulle Dismissal: A Fund Started," *Wednesday Journal*, February 1, 1984, p. 1.
9 Thomas Murphy, "School Board Gave in to Pressure from Few," *Oak Leaves*, February 15, 1984, p. 22.
10 Bowman, "Nazi-Hunting."
11 "Kulle Supporters Forget Past Too Easily," *Oak Leaves*, February 15, 1984, p. 22.
12 Rainer Kulle, "Kulle Only Guilty of Serving His Country," *Oak Leaves*, March 14, 1984, p. 21.
13 Confidential memo, March 8, 1984. Reinhold Kulle personnel file, OPRF.
14 Memo, March 13, 1984. Reinhold Kulle personnel file, OPRF.
15 Confidential memo, March 8, 1984.
16 Memo, March 13, 1984.
17 "Teachers to Explore Cultural Diversity," *Forest Leaves*, March 14, 1984, p. 96.
18 Michael Kotzin, "Spotlight on a Case," *Community*, June, 1984, pp. 1–2.
19 US Department of Justice, post-trial brief for petitioner, *United States v. Kulle*, A10 857, 64.
20 Rosenbaum, interview.
21 Ralph Blumenthal, "German-Born NASA Expert Quits U.S. to Avoid a War Crimes Suit," *New York Times*, October 18, 1984.
22 Rosenbaum, interview; Eli M. Rosenbaum with William Hoffer, *Betrayal: The Untold Story of the Kurt Walheim Investigation and Cover-Up* (New York: St. Martin's Press, 1993), 1–3.
23 Feigin, "Striving For Accountability," 11.
24 Allan A. Ryan, Jr., *Klaus Barbie and the United States Government: A Report to the Attorney General of the United States, August 1983* (Washington: United States Department of Justice, 1983).
25 Ryan, *Quiet Neighbors*, 357.

CHAPTER 23

1 Memo, "Re: Reinhold's Party," February 27, 1984. Reinhold Kulle personnel file, OPRF.
2 Kulle party committee memos, various dates. Kulle personnel file, OPRF.
3 Cheri Bentrup, "Fabbri Close to Buying New Facility," *Forest Leaves*, January 9, 2002, p. 9.
4 Kulle party committee memos.
5 Invitation to Kulle appreciation dinner. Papers of Rima Lunin Schultz.
6 Kulle party committee memos.
7 Greco, interview.
8 Bentrup, "Mar Lac."
9 Toni Coleman, "One Oak Park Area Eases Wedding Planning," *Forest Leaves*, November 5, 1997, p. 115.
10 *Oak Leaves*, March 28, 1984, p. 3.
11 Greco, interview; Rietz, interview; Eric Linden, "High School Staff, Other Friends Toast Reinhold Kulle's 25 Years," *Wednesday Journal*, May 16, 1984, p. 1.
12 Linden, "High School Staff."

13 Swanson, interview.

14 Linden, "High School Staff."

15 Kalyn Wulatin, "Legal Decision Due in Summer," *Trapeze*, May 25, 1984, p. 4.

16 "1984: Awards for Student Work Gold Circle Awards—Scholastic Recipients"; https://cspa.columbia.edu/recipient-lists/1984-awards-student-work-gold-circle-awards-scholastic-recipients.

17 OPRF school board notes, June 28, 1984, 7.

18 Letter to OPRF school board from Reinhold Kulle, "Notice of Election to Take Early Retirement," received June 19, 1984. Kulle personnel file, OPRF.

19 OPRF school board notes from executive session, June 28, 1984.

20 OPRF, "Compromise Agreement and General Release," July 1984.

21 OPRF school board notes, June 28, 1984.

22 Letter from John Swanson to Reinhold Kulle, July 3, 1984. Kulle personnel file, OPRF.

CHAPTER 24

1 Marcus, interview.

2 Vidui prayer.

3 Marcus, "Yom Kippur Speech."

4 "The Gropper Windows: Genesis in Glass," wsthz.org/gropper-windows.

5 Ryan, *Quiet Neighbors*, quoted in Marcus, "Yom Kippur Speech."

6 Marcus, "Yom Kippur Speech."

7 *In the matter of Reinhold Kulle*, A10 857 195 (November 20, 1984), 28.

8 *In the matter of Reinhold Kulle*, 42, 4.

9 *In the matter of Reinhold Kulle*, 47.

10 Jeff Ferenc, "Kulle to Fight Court Deportation Order," *Forest Leaves*, December 5, 1984, p. 5.

11 Ferenc, "Kulle to Fight."

12 *Matter of Kulle: In Deportation Proceedings*, 318, 322, 334.

13 United Press International, "US Deports Fedorenko to Moscow," *Washington Post*, December 23, 1984, p. A10.

14 600 F. Supp. 1254 (N.D. Ill. 1984).

15 Deborah Lipstadt, "The Bitburg Controversy," *American Jewish Year Book* 87, 23, 25, 29; Grzegorz Nycz, "The Bitburg Controversy from the New Cold War Perspective: Reagan's Vies on WWII Nazi Germany's Soldiers' Victimhood," *Ad Americam: Journal of American Studies* 22 (2021): 38.

16 Eleanor Randolph, "Buchanan's Jottings Cited 'Pressure' of Jews, NBC Says," *Washington Post*, May 3, 1985.

17 Lipstadt, "Bitburg," 23.

18 Lipstadt, "Bitburg," 26–36.

19 Feigin, "Striving For Accountability," 510; "Man Cleared of Nazi Charges Dies of Bomb Injuries," AP News, September 6, 1985.

20 Ralph Blumenthal, "Man Accused on Nazi Past Injured by Bomb in Jersey." *New York Times*, August 16, 1985, p. B2.

21 "Bombing of Homes of Alleged Nazi War Criminals Condemned as Detrimental to Ongoing OSI Efforts," *Jewish Telegraphic Agency*, September 11, 1985.

22 *Matter of Kulle In Deportation Proceedings.*

23 Rosenbaum, *Betrayal*, 1–3.

24 Patrick J. Buchanan, "We Condemn Waldheim—but Embrace the Real Bad Guys," *Chicago Sun-Times*, March 3, 1988, p. 40.

25 Leslie Maitland Werner, "Waldheim Barred from Entering U.S. over Role in War," *New York Times*, April 28, 1987.

26 *Kulle v. INS*, brief of petitioner.

27 "Nazi Case Stirs Up Protests," *Washington Post*, July 13, 1986.

28 Jay Mathews, "U.S. Nazi Hunters Brace for Criticism: Doubts about Soviet Evidence Surround Move to Deport Linnas," *Washington Post*, July 13, 1986, p. A5.

29 Lichtblau, *The Nazis Next Door*, 181–88; Raschke, *Useful Enemies*, 252–72.

30 Raschke, *Useful Enemies*, 256–57.

31 Bill Keller, "Estonian Sent to Face Death in Soviet Dies in a Hospital," *New York Times*, July 2, 1987, p. 2.

32 Mark J. Porubcansky, "Fedorenko Executed for War Crimes, Soviets Say," Associated Press, July 28. 1987.

33 *Reinhold Kulle, Petitioner, v. Immigration & Naturalization Service, Respondent*, 825 F.2d 1188 (7th Cir. 1987).

34 "Germans Won't Charge Ex-SS Guard, Officials Say," *Chicago Tribune*, October 28. 1987, p. A8; Dan Obermaier, "Deportation Stay Fails, Former Janitor Deported," *Oak Leaves*, October 28, 1987, p. 6; "Prosecutor: No Trial Planned for Deported Nazi," *Associated Press*, October 27, 1987.

35 Eric Linden, "After Final Appeal, Ex-Nazi Deported to West Germany," *Wednesday Journal*, November 4, 1987, p. 10.

36 Marvin Schlichting, "What Proof of Kulle's Crime?" *Wednesday Journal*, November 11, 1987, p. 15; "Toilet Papering Homes: It's Wrong and Wasteful," *Wednesday Journal*, November 11, 1987, p. 15.

37 John Knox. "One View." *Wednesday Journal*, July 4, 1984, p. 11; John Knox, *The Forgotten Memoir of John Knox: A Year in the Life of a Supreme Court Clerk in FDR's Washington*, ed. Dennis J. Hutchinson and David J. Garrow (Chicago: University of Chicago Press, 2002), xiv.

38 John Knox, letter to the editor, *Wednesday Journal*, November 18, 1987, p. 22.

39 Rabbi Joseph Tabbachnik, "Letter on Deported Kulle Is Mistaken Compassion," *Wednesday Journal*, November 18, 1987, p. 22.

40 "Former Nazi Guard Deported," *New York Times*, September 24, 1988, p. 6.

41 Blumenthal, "German-Born NASA Expert."

42 Patrick Buchanan, "Pat Buchanan's Response to Norman Podhoretz's Op-Ed," *Wall Street Journal*, November 5, 1999; editorial, "The KGB Runs the Justice Department," *Executive Intelligence Review* 15, no. 6 (February 5, 1988): 72; "Congressman Defending Scientist Who Is Suspected in War Crimes," *New York Times*, May 15, 1990, p. A10; Marilyn Karfeld, "Traficant Fears Bias; Wants to Keep Jews off Jury Trial," *Cleveland Jewish News*, January 24, 2002.

43 Jerome S. Legge Jr., "Prosecuting Nazi Collaborators and Terrorists: Eli Rosenbaum and Managing the Office of Special Investigations," *Public Administration Review* 71, no. 2 (March-April 2011): 279.

44 "Ensuring Accountability for Human Rights Violations and Extraterritorial Violent Crime," justice.gov.

45 Rosenbaum, interview.

46 Bradley Graham, "Eight Are Sentenced for Nazi Crimes," *Washington Post*, July 1, 1981; Martin, "A Nazi Past."

47 Douglas, *The Right Wrong Man*, 154; Rosenbaum, interview.

48 Douglas, *The Right Wrong Man*, 109–37; *U.S. v. Demjanjuk*, CASE NO. 1:99 CV 1193, N.D. Ohio, February 21, 2002; "Former Nazi Death Camp Guard John Demjanjuk Deported to Germany," ICE press release, May 11, 2009.

49 Douglas, *The Right Wrong Man*, 22–25, 216, 220.

50 *Gemeinschaftsblättle: Informationen für den Bezirk Aalen* 44 (January–April 2017), https://web.archive.org/web/20180630214350/https://www.die-apis.de/fileadmin/BEZIRKE/Aalen/Medien/Gemeinschaftsbl%C3%A4ttle_Jan.-Apr._2017.pdf; Felix Bohr, "Auschwitz Trial: Late Case Raises Questions about Justice System," *Der Spiegel*, September 30, 2013.

51 "Alleged Ex-Guard at Treblinka Deported from U.S. to Germany," Jewish Telegraphic Agency, April 12, 1993.

52 Illinois Metropolitan Retirement Fund, Reinhold Kulle pension payments, FOIA request.

EPILOGUE

1 Deb Quantock McCarey, "8th Grader Picks Up Trail of Oak Park Nazi," *Wednesday Journal*, January 24, 2012; Drew Johnson, personal interviews by author.

SOURCES

ARCHIVES AND PRIMARY SOURCES

Arolsen Archives
Illinois Holocaust Museum and Education Center
National Archives at College Park, Maryland
Oak Park Historical Society
Oak Park and River Forest High School
Papers of Leah Marcus
Papers of Dr. Rima Lunin Schultz
Papers of Dr. Efraim Zuroff
Ronald Reagan Presidential Library
Skokie History Digital Collections
Syndor papers, Virginia Holocaust Museum
David and Fela Shapell Family Collections, Conservation and Research Center, US Holocaust Museum and Memorial

INTERVIEWS

Michael Averbach, interview by author, December 22, 2020
Dr. Peter Black, interview by author, October 5, 2021
Ralph Blumenthal, interview by author, January 31, 2022
Mary-Terese Cozzola, interview by author, May 5, 2021
Richard Deptuch, interview by author, 2022
Bruce Einhorn, interview by author, June 28, 2021
Carolyn Elliott, interviews by author, July 18-19, 2022
Isaac Engel, interview by Dr. Sidney Bolkosky, University of Michigan-Dearborn, June 16 and 25, 1992 (http://holocaust.umd.umich.edu/engel/)
Dr. Steven Gevinson, interview by author, December 22, 2020
Paul Gignilliat, interview by author, December 14, 2020
Jeffrey Greenwald, interview by author, 2021
Marjorie Greenwald, interview by author, February 10, 2021
Nancy Greco, interview by author, April 27, 2021
Andrew Heneghan, interview by author, December 22, 2021
Elizabeth Holtzman, interview by author, 2022

Drew Johnson, interviews by author
Gail Liebman, interview by author, 2023
Rima Lunin Schultz, interviews by author, 2020–22
Leah Marcus, interview by author, December 30, 2020
Dr. Mike MacQueen, interview by author, 2021
Charles W. Nixon, interview by author, June 3, 2021
Suzanne Perry, interview by author, April 13, 2021
Richard Rietz, interview by author, April 14, 2021
Eli Rosenbaum, interview by author, August 16, 2021
Bruce and Julie Samuels, interview by author, March 29, 2021
Neal Sher, "Neal Sher, Nazi Hunter and Former AIPAC Official," *Talkline with Zev Brenner* (podcast), July 18, 2021
Dr. David Sokol, interview by author, April 18, 2021
Sandra Sokol, interview by author, April 18, 2021
Dr. John Swanson, interview by author, April 7, 2021
RaeLynne Toperoff, interviews by author, 2021–22
William "Jay Jay" Turner, interview by author, June 17, 2021
Witness's daughter, interview by author, February 8, 2022
Kalyn Wulatin, interview by author, 2021

GOVERNMENT DOCUMENTS

Documents obtained through the Freedom of Information Act
Displaced Persons Commission
Federal Bureau of Investigation
Government Accountability Office
Oak Park and River Forest High School
Oak Park Village Board
Triton College Police Department
UN Security Council
US Department of Justice
US Congressional Record
US House Select Committee Reports

TRIAL TRANSCRIPTS, RULINGS, AND COURT DOCUMENTS

Kulle case

Sworn interview of Reinhold Kulle, August 14, 1982. Courtesy of Dr. Charles W. Sydnor Jr., Virginia Holocaust Museum
Kulle v. Springer, 566 F. Supp. 279 (N.D. Ill. 1983)
United States v. Kulle, Immigration Court, A10 857 195 (1983–84)
Matter of Kulle: In Deportation Proceedings, Board of Immigration Appeals, interim decision #3002, A10 857 195 (1985)
Reinhold Kulle, Petitioner, v. Immigration & Naturalization Service, Respondent, 825 F.2d 1188 (7th Cir. 1987)

Fedorenko case

United States v. Fedorenko, 455 F. Supp. 893 (S.D. Fla. 1978)
United States v. Fedorenko, 597 F. 2d 946 (1979)
Fedorenko v. United States, 449 U.S. 490 (1981)

Kairys case

United States v. Kairys, 1982
United States v. Kairys, 600 F. Supp. 1254 (N.D. Ill. 1984)
United States v. Kairys, 782 F.2d 1374 (7th Cir. 1986)

Schellong case

United States v. Schellong, no. 81 C 1478 (1982)
United States v. Schellong, 547 F. Supp. 569 (1982)

Skokie case

Village of Skokie v. National Socialist Party of America, et al., docket no. 77–2702, Circuit Court of Cook County, Illinois, Chancery Division

Other cases

Matter of Laipenieks, in deportation proceedings, A-11937435
U.S. v. Demjanjuk, CASE NO. 1:99 CV 1193, N.D. Ohio, February 21, 2002

SELECTED NEWSPAPERS, NEWSLETTERS, AND PERIODICALS

Associated Press
Chicago Jewish Post & Opinion
Chicago Sun-Times
Chicago Tribune
Cleveland Jewish News
Creators Syndicate
Daily Illini
Draugas
Executive Intelligence Review
Forest Leaves
Jewish Telegraphic Agency
Lituanus
New York Post
New York Times
Oak Leaves
Oak Park World
Spotlight

Sunday Times Union
The Atlantic
The Free Lance-Star
Time
Trapeze
UPI
Washington Post
Wednesday Journal

INDEX

Holocaust Memorial Foundation of Illinois, 128

Holocaust Museum and Memorial, US, 247–48

Holocaust Research Center at Bar-Ilan University, 126

Holtzman, Elizabeth: antisemitic attacks against, 176; death threats against, 174; hearings on Nazis in America and, 78, 81; investigations into INS and, 68–72, 75–76; Linnas deportation proceedings and, 241–42; OSI leadership, relationships with, 94; *Quiet Neighbors*, endorsement of, 236. *See also* Holtzman Amendment; House Subcommittee on Immigration, Citizenship and International Law

Holtzman Amendment: clarification of Immigration and Nationality Act, 124; constitutionality of, 238, 240, 242; Kulle, applicability to, 114, 124, 181; passage of, 78–80

House Subcommittee on Immigration, Citizenship and International Law, 69, 71, 81

Human Rights and Special Prosecutions Section, 244

Hungarian Arrow Cross, 174

I Aim at the Stars, 53

Illinois Board of Elections, 83

Illinois Municipal Retirement Fund, 210–11, 232

Immigration and Nationality Act: Kulle, applicability to, 114; prioritization of immigrants from Northern and Western Europe and, 32–33. *See also* Holtzman Amendment

Immigration and Naturalization Service: Artukovic case and, 49–50, 76; Braunsteiner case and, 55, 58–59; investigative delays and mismanagement at, 61, 69–72, 74–76, 80, 95; Kulle documents and, 104; Special Litigations Unit, 78, 80–81, 95; unresolved cases at, 93–94, 100, 102; Walus, erroneous prosecution of, 76, 78, 95, 131

immigration subcommittee. *See* House

Subcommittee on Immigration, Citizenship and International Law

IMRF. *See* Illinois Municipal Retirement Fund

INS. *See* Immigration and Naturalization Service

International Military Tribunal at Nuremberg, 49, 52, 87, 93

International Network of Children of Holocaust Survivors, 242

International Refugee Organization, 31–33

Investigation, The (Weiss), 111

IRO (International Refugee Organization), 31–33

Iron Guard, 34, 70

It's a Wonderful Life, 229

Ivan the Terrible, 104, 244

Izhak, Flora, 126

Jackson, Robert H., 86–87

Janowska, 145

Javits, Jacob, 72

JDL. *See* Jewish Defense League

Jerusalem Hilton, 240

Jewish Currents, 51–52

Jewish Daily Forward, 55

Jewish Defense League, 74, 77, 79, 239

Jewish Exponent, 112

Jews of Greece, deportation of, 240

Johnson, Drew, 246–49

"Judeo-Bolshevism," 11, 175

"Judeo-Bolshevist" conspiracy, 11, 175

Judiciary Committee, House of Representatives, 68

Juel, Kari, 166

Julian, Anna, 45–46

Julian, Percy, 45–46, 248

Juodis, Jurgis, 175

Justice, Department of: Criminal Division of, 94; Honors Program, 112; Office of Special Investigations, oversight of, 94, 99, 111, 175. *See also* Office of Special Investigations

Kairys, Liudas: Chicago, life in, 37–39, 49, 53, 95, 178; denaturalization proceedings

Wiesenthal, Simon (*continued*)
  endorsement of, 235–36; SS members
  who escaped justice, feelings about, 50–
  51; Trifa, tip on whereabouts of, 69–70;
  Triton College speech, 3–4, 78, 85, 237;
  United Nations' International Refugee
  Organization, letter to, 31. *See also* Simon
  Wiesenthal Center
Window of Good and Evil (Gropper), 235
Wojciechowski, Marion, 128–29, 155–57
Wojciechowski, Wadyslawa, 128
Wolf, Michael, 96
Women's Society of the German Old
  People's Home, 39
World Jewish Congress, 31, 240
Wright, Frank Lloyd, 1, 42, 152

Wulatin, Kalyn, 169–71, 180, 184–86, 197–
  98, 206, 232
Wyspiański, Stanislaw, *The Wedding*, 24

Yad Vashem, 126, 145–46
Yale Daily News, 73–74
Yale University, 73
YIVO Institute for Jewish Research, 70
Yom Kippur, 84, 154, 159, 234
Yugoslavia, 49–50, 102, 240

Zumbakis, Paul, 123–24, 127, 175, 245
Zuppke, Robert, 42
Zuroff, Efraim, 125–26, 145, 244
Zutty, Sam, 72